Worship God with Love
for
Your Neighbor

Worship God with Love for Your Neighbor

A BIBLICAL VIEW OF THE HORIZONTAL DIMENSION OF WORSHIP

Dr. Don W. Robertson

This book represents work from a Doctoral Project submitted to the Faculty of Reformed Theological Seminary, Orlando in Partial Fulfillment for the Degree of Doctor of Ministry on May 24, 2019.

New Creation Publications
Pearland, TX 77581

Worship God with Love for Your Neighbor
© 2020 by Don W. Robertson

Published by New Creation Publications
1010 North Sunset, Pearland, Texas 77581

All rights reserved. No part of this publication may be reproduced, stored in a retrieval system, or transmitted in any form by any means, electronic, mechanical, photocopy, recording, or otherwise---except for brief quotations for the purpose of review or comment, without the prior permission of the publisher, New Creation Publications, 1010 North Sunset, Pearland, TX 77581.

First printing 2020
Printed in the United States of America

Scripture quotations are from The Holy Bible, English Standard Version, copyright © 2001 by Crossway Bibles, a division of Good News Publishers. Used by permission. All rights reserved.

ISBN: 978-0-9709072-1-9

Cover design by Cathy and Micah Robertson

DEDICATION

I would like to dedicate this book to the precious people who belong to Reformed and Evangelical churches all over the world. They are the bride of Christ which is dear to my heart and more importantly deeply loved by the Lord. It is my hope that this study will enrich the worship of the church and contribute to bringing more souls into her ranks through faith in Jesus for the glory and praise of God.

CONTENTS

ACKNOWLEDGMENTS xi
ABSTRACT xii
INTRODUCTION 1
   Thesis 1
   Statement of the Problem 1
   Definition of Key Terms 8
   Assumptions 11
   Significance 12
   Research Questions 12
   Research Strategy 14
   Proposed Outcome 15

Part 1: BIBLICAL AND THEOLOGICAL FOUNDATIONS FOR THE HORIZONTAL DIMENSION 17
   1. Trinitarian Foundation 19
   2. Covenantal Connection 23
   3. Worship with Love for Your Neighbor 31
       Exodus 20:1-17 and Deuteronomy 5:6-21 31
       1 Samuel 15:22-23 36
       Hosea 6:6-8 39
       Matthew 9:13 43
       Matthew 22:36-40 48
       John 13:31-35; John 15:12-17; 1 John 4:7-21 51
       1 Corinthians 10:31-11:1 57

1 Corinthians 13.. 61
4. Worship with Justice for Your Neighbor................................. 65
　　Psalm 82.. 65
　　Proverbs 18:5 68
　　Isaiah 1:10-20 70
　　Amos 5:10-15, 21-24; 2:6-7; 8:5-6 73
　　Micah 6:6-8 75
5. Worship with Your Neighbor.. 81
　　Psalm 40.. 81
　　Isaiah 29:13-14 83
　　John 4:21-24 86
　　1 Corinthians 10:14-17; 11:22-33 91
　　1 Corinthians 12... 96
　　1 Corinthians 14... 99
　　Ephesians 5:19 102
　　Colossians 3:16... 105
　　James 2:1-13; 3:9 108
　　Summary 114

Part 2: HISTORICAL CONSIDERATIONS 117
6. Martin Luther 121
　　General Issues 121
　　Music 125
7. John Calvin 131
8. Reformed Creeds & Catechisms... 147
　　Belgic Confession 147
　　Heidelberg Catechism 149
　　Westminster Confession... 154

9. Westminster Directory of Worship 167
10. Summary 177
Part 3: CONTEMPORARY LITERATURE REVIEW 179
11. Robert G. Rayburn 181
12. David Peterson 189
13. Marva Dawn 195
14. Bob Kauflin 205
15. John Frame 211
16. R.C. Sproul 221
17. Conclusion 225
Part 4: MINISTRY MODEL 227
18. The Vertical/Horizontal Dimension Dynamic 229
19. Worship Samples that Incorporate the Horizontal 231
    Worship Sample 1 (Liturgy of the Word): 231
    Worship Sample 2 (Liturgy of the Word): 239
    Worship Sample 3 (Liturgy of the Lord's Supper): 246
20. Sunday School Lesson Outlines 251
    Lesson 1 Outline: 251
    Lesson 2 Outline: 257
    Lesson 3 Outline: 265
    Lesson 4 Outline: 269
    Lesson 5 Outline: 273
    Lesson 6 Outline: 276
21. Sermon Series Outlines 281
    Sermon 1 Outline: 281
    Sermon 2 Outline: 285
    Sermon 3 Outline: 289

    Sermon 4 Outline: 294
  22. CONCLUSION 301
APPENDIX A 305
    Luther's German Mass (Annotated) 305
APPENDIX B 307
    Checklist for Developing the Horizontal Dimension 307

BIBLIOGRAPHY 315
SCRIPTURE INDEX 333
VITA 339

ACKNOWLEDGMENTS

I would like to thank my wife, Cathy Lee, for her gracious attitude, care, editorial input, and general support during the research and writing of this project. Her prayers and love for worship have been a constant blessing in seeing this work to the end.

It is important for me to also express special thanks to professor Mike Glodo of Reformed Theological Seminary in Orlando, Florida. Professor Glodo served as my advisor while working on my doctoral project which I have converted into this book. His years of experience in teaching on the subject of worship were immensely helpful in developing my thoughts for this thesis. He offered many insights that helped me to sharpen my thoughts and maintain a balance between the vertical and horizontal dimensions of worship. I will always be grateful for his encouragement and wisdom.

I also wish to express appreciation for the loving and kind support of my congregation, Faith Community Church, a people who truly love God and desire to follow his Word. The prayers and support of my brothers and sisters in Christ in the pursuit of completing this project have encouraged me to grow in my understanding of how to please God in worship. They inspired me to pursue this topic to better equip them to faithfully praise the Lord and love their neighbors.

ABSTRACT

Many churches today are accused of being cold and stiff in their worship. Visitors often remark that they were not welcomed or acknowledged. This frequently happens in churches that misunderstand the horizontal dimension of worship or dismiss the importance of the horizontal in relation to the vertical. Some churches that emphasize the horizontal can appear disingenuous or mechanical in the way they treat their guests. Leaders in vertically-oriented congregations often defend their inhospitable service by arguing that their approach to worship is God-centered rather than man-centered. Consequently, advocates of vertically-oriented worship criticize the horizontal dimension by claiming it encourages a sinful inclination to prioritize man over God. As a result, those who stress the vertical minimize the horizontal dimension and overemphasize the vertical in their worship services. They fail, however, to appreciate the importance of the horizontal dimension in relation to the vertical direction of worship. These two aspects of worship should not be in competition but should complement one another.

This project addresses whether the principle of the horizontal dimension in worship is biblical and supported by the Reformed tradition as well as contemporary writings. This project's focus upon the horizontal dimension does not advocate the seeker-driven movement or promote a particular worship style represented in traditional versus contemporary worship debates. Rather, this project seeks an approach to worship that incorporates both biblical love for one's neighbor and worship that is pleasing to God. The Reformed view of the horizontal dimension encourages the evangelical church to balance the vertical with the horizontal. It supports the connection of the horizontal dimension of worship to the vertical. Worship that truly honors God practices the biblical balance between the vertical and horizontal. The conclusions provide practical ways to implement the horizontal dimension of worship in every Christian worship service.

INTRODUCTION

Thesis

How can church leaders encourage their congregation to pursue a biblically faithful and theologically Reformed understanding of the horizontal dimension of worship in their worship services both in theory and in practice? In other words, how can church leaders encourage their congregation to express biblical love to their neighbors through the application of the horizontal dimension in their corporate worship?

Statement of the Problem

The catalyst that led me to pursue this topic involved a serious disagreement with one of our church leaders. He began spreading the idea that Reformed worship is focused solely on God to the exclusion of any consideration of our neighbor in the worship service. He noted that worship is a vertical experience which has nothing to do with the horizontal dimension. He could not connect the idea of the vertical to the horizontal. His view of the vertical excluded the horizontal concerns that believers should have for their neighbor in the pew. The vertical direction or dimension refers to us directing our worship to God and God's ministering to us as we worship him. Therefore, the vertical involves a bi-directional engagement between God and us. The horizontal dimension points to those thoughts, things, and actions carried out in the worship service that affect the people attending corporate worship. Some have defined the horizontal as those "person-to-person" aspects in worship in distinction to the vertical which involves the "person-to-God" aspects such as prayers and praise.[1] This perspective, however, misses the importance of God's horizontal concern for people as his children express his concern for one another in their worship. The horizontal involves biblical consideration of other people by both God and his servants. We simply cannot disconnect the vertical from the horizontal in our worship. This leader pointed out that the number one thing that the church should do is worship God in a vertical fashion by focusing on God alone. He tried to convince others in the church of his perspective which created disunity and confusion, especially among various church leaders. His sentiment is expressed by Frame's comments on worship:

> Some may think that a focus on the humanness of worship detracts from its God-centeredness. Some may think that the very idea of talking about the human side of worship is inappropriate. People have sometimes taught that in worship we should be so focused on God, so passionately obsessed with him, that we never even think of ourselves or of our fellow worshippers. Worship, they say, should be "vertical," and not at all "horizontal."[2]

This leader's view of vertical worship led several people to disagree with my understanding of Reformed worship and cultivated dissension among some members who eventually left our fellowship. If I had available, during this controversy, a study which addressed the legitimacy of the horizontal dimension, I may have been able to articulate its importance and perhaps settle the question for many of those who left. I hope that this project will encourage future pastors and church leaders who may encounter similar opposition regarding this worship issue and enable them to head off potential dissension in their congregations.

Having convinced some of the church leaders, this opponent argued that his viewpoint was taught by R. C. Sproul, a Reformed

---

1. Bryan Chapell, *Christ-Centered Worship: Letting the Gospel Shape Our Practice* (Grand Rapids, MI: Baker Academic, 2009), 121.
2. John M. Frame, "Worship and the Reformation Gospel," *Frame-Poythress.org*, last modified May 30, 2012, accessed February 16, 2017, http://frame-poythress.org/worship-and-the-reformation-gospel/.

theologian. He referred to sermons that Sproul had preached, and the elder shared them with various elders to bolster his viewpoint. Although I believe he took Sproul's views against seeker-driven worship out of context to further his position, he nevertheless was able to highlight certain remarks about vertically-oriented worship to further attack the concept of the horizontal dimension of worship. By holding to a vertical-only mentality, this attack eventually affected some elders to the point that they sought to exclude anything that was horizontal in the service. Our leaders' concern and love for their neighbors in the pew during our services was diminished. This attitude also spilled over into the way a number of these leaders dealt with people outside our worship times. One elder was so influenced that he exclaimed, "I don't believe in fellowship," meaning he did not see a need for the consideration of others in the service or any fellowship at all. This vertical-only perspective further led several of the elders to dismiss any concern for unbelievers in our services. The spirit of evangelism outside of our corporate worship was also discouraged, and the importance of the Great Commission was downplayed.

This crisis in the church caused me to engage in biblical research on the matter to determine whether such an understanding of worship conformed to Scripture and the Reformed faith. I concluded that if our church decided to pursue a vertical-only philosophy of worship to the exclusion of the horizontal dimension, it would create an inhospitable and impersonal worship service. People would not experience the biblical love and care of God working through his people when they attended our services. Their view of God would be limited in that they would not witness God's grace, love, and truth demonstrated in the way we treated others in our corporate worship. I believed that this vertical-only perspective would consequently bring about a decline in the growth and health of our church. More importantly, I was convinced that such worship would not be pleasing to God.

As I continued to study the matter, it became apparent that most Reformed discussions on worship focused on the vertical rather than the horizontal dimension. This research uncovered a serious gap in this subject in worship studies. The absence of a careful discussion of the topic likely contributes to a misunderstanding about whether we should consider others in our corporate worship. Marva Dawn comments briefly about some possible contributing factors that may undermine attention to the horizontal dimension of worship. She addresses the tendency toward individualism in our society as a possible reason people may distort the vertical in their worship services. Dawn remarks, "In our fragmented and alienated, individualistic and competitive society, many people wonder if the Christian Church is any different. Congregations and denominations seem constantly to be fighting within or against each other; strangers who visit a worship service often are not welcomed or even acknowledged by anyone."[3]

The leader in our church who advocated vertical-only worship continued to try to bolster his viewpoint by stating that his idea of worship was the right understanding and application of the answer to the first question of the Westminster Shorter Catechism: "What is the chief end of man?" The catechism states, "Man's chief end is to glorify God and to enjoy him forever." This leader pointed out that the catechism answer confirmed his view that worship should be done solely from a vertical perspective void of the horizontal. He would remark that his view was the Reformed perspective on worship. Disturbingly, I found in reading literature from various writers who claim to be Reformed that they gave little to no attention to the horizontal dimension when discussing the first catechism question, especially in relation to worship. Although silence on the subject did not validate a vertical-only view, it encouraged the elder to persist in his argument.

People often become confused as they think about our vertical calling to worship God. They mistakenly conclude that the vertical is divorced from the horizontal. John Frame comments on how some people might draw similar false conclusions in the way they understand the vertical direction of worship when he states, "Christian worship is 'vertical,' directed to our triune God for his pleasure. The focus of our effort in worship should be on pleasing him. From this principle, some

---

3. Marva J. Dawn, *A Royal Waste of Time: The Splendor of Worshiping God and Being Church for the World* (Grand Rapids, MI: W.B. Eerdmans, 1999), 178.

might conclude that we should not pay any attention to human needs in worship."[4]

The leader presumed that the catechism's focus on glorifying God (i.e., a vertical focus) excluded consideration of others in corporate worship. After carefully considering what it means to glorify God, I came to realize that such a view of the catechism was not in line with Scripture. Pondering the meaning and application of the concept of glorifying God, it became clear that the Catechism answer does not exclude the horizontal dimension of worship but rather demands it. If Christians properly glorify God, they should seek to honor and emulate God's affections not only in daily life but especially when they worship him (Eph.5:1). When believers carefully ponder the Lord's affections toward those who worship, they must deduce from Scripture that he cares deeply about the people who are worshiping him. So, if we wish to honor and respect our God who cares, we likewise should care deeply about people before, during, and after our worship services. As we strive to glorify God, there is no cease and desist button regarding our calling to love others when we begin our time of corporate worship. A vertical-only perspective of glorifying God easily leads people to disconnect worship from the worshipper's responsibility and calling to love his neighbor at all times, especially when he is worshiping the God of love (1 John 4:8).

If we are going to be faithful to Scripture in our understanding of the horizontal dimension, we also must accept the importance of our covenantal community in our worship. It demands that we rightly think about God and how we should properly glorify him as we worship together in community. We cannot focus on God to the exclusion of the community worshiping with us and expect God to be pleased. Marva Dawn wisely makes this point when she speaks about the necessity of community in corporate worship. She states, "Before we consider some practical ways to build community, we must note this obvious, but often overlooked, truth: the Triune God wants our churches to be genuine communities."[5] If we embrace a view of

---

4. John M. Frame, *Worship in Spirit and Truth* (Phillipsburg, NJ: P & R Publishing, 1996), 7-8.

5. Marva J. Dawn, "Body Building: Worship That Develops Strong Community," *Reformed Worship* 45 (September 1997): 26–29, accessed March 21, 2019,

glorifying God in our worship which excludes others in the service, this can lead to a dismissal of the importance of community (a horizontal reality). It can also undermine fellowship, one of the important means of grace and essential biblical expressions of the horizontal dimension. Such distortions which dismiss the importance of community will ultimately move God's people away from properly glorifying the Lord in their personal and corporate worship. To fall prey to such distortions is fundamentally idolatrous worship because it involves creating a false god who cares nothing about the horizontal. To put it bluntly, vertical-only worship is not acceptable to God and will displease him since the true God of the Bible expects the community of believers to love and care about one another as they worship. If this is the case, all Christians should take note and give careful thought to the topic of the horizontal dimension in their understanding and practice of worship.

I hope that by addressing this vital topic, Reformed and evangelical churches will be encouraged to appreciate the horizontal in their worship. In addition, it is my prayer that this study will inspire Christians to see worship in its rightful place regarding the church's call to glorify God in a manner that expresses God's calling to love our neighbor as we praise and honor his name. In my study of various authors who espouse the Reformed faith, I have frequently discovered a neglect of the horizontal dimension of worship. I believe such neglect is detrimental to the practice of worship in many churches. I will argue in this project that worship that ignores or neglects the horizontal dimension cannot be rightly called Christian worship. It will be demonstrated that worship devoid of the horizontal is not pleasing to God. In other words, God will not find such worship to be acceptable if his people focus solely upon him without consideration of others in the service. If this premise is true, and there are professing Christians engaging in such vertical-only worship in the church today, this study will be a great help to them.

Those with horizontal concerns are often accused of having seeker-driven motives. This argument against the horizontal

---

http://search.ebscohost.com.rts.idm.oclc.org/login.aspx?direct=true&db=rfh&AN=ATLA0001029668&site=ehost-live.

dimension is a straw man argument because it sets up the false idea that being supportive of the horizontal dimension is the same as being in support of the seeker-sensitive movement. This project, however, rejects the seeker-sensitive movement that strives to cater to the sinful inclinations of unbelievers. The Bible teaches that no one seeks God in their depraved state (Rom. 3:11). The seeker-sensitive movement improperly attempts to conduct worship in a way that is man-centered and compromises the Word to please sinful hearts. If the horizontal dimension of worship is practiced biblically, it cannot be done in isolation from the goal of honoring God according to his Word. In addition to distinguishing this study from the seeker-sensitive movement, there will be no attempt to tailor corporate worship to the whimsical feelings and passions of people. Many churches easily fall prey to emphasizing the horizontal to the point that their services focus solely upon an emotional experience versus praising, pleasing, and honoring God. Such worship is nothing more than idolatry since it substitutes the direction of our worship for God with humans or something else. Although we acknowledge various abuses in worship services that emphasize emotions or social connections, we must, however, be very careful not to throw out our biblical responsibilities to be sensitive to people who attend our services. Efforts to be sensitive to others in our worship services in this way should lead to a responsible understanding of the horizontal dimension. If we are biblically sensitive, we will seek to both edify God's people and bring the unsaved to Christ.

This project attempts to show the biblical concerns we should have for everyone who attends corporate worship and what practical things we can do or say that properly express the horizontal dimension in our services. Emotional responses will not be our litmus test for discerning whether we have met the mark of pleasing God in our worship. Since emotions are unpredictable, it is possible that if we properly worship God and do our duty regarding the horizontal dimension some people will not respond biblically. The prophet Jeremiah warns us that the human heart is deceptive and desperately sick and often tramples upon the things of God (Jer. 17:9-10). But if we intentionally carry out biblical applications of the horizontal dimension, we will have done our duty to God and our neighbor (Mark

12:30-31). We will be faithful in exercising a more thoroughly biblical faith in our worship. It is hoped that we will worship God in "spirit and in truth" as he desires (John 4:23-24).[6] In short, we will please God. For all the true children of God, this is their desire. They wish to please and honor their Lord in their worship and in every area of life. So, let us embark upon this important study of the horizontal dimension of worship to honor and please the Lord. As a result of this project, we will discover that we should seek to worship with love for our neighbor as we express love for our God.

Definition of Key Terms

The following terms will be used in this study:

1. *Gospel*: The gospel refers to the good news about the saving person and work of Christ. This includes the fact that Jesus Christ came into this world and lived the perfect life that sinful human beings cannot live. He obeyed the law of God perfectly, never committing any sin thus fulfilling the covenant of works. Jesus then died as a substitutionary atonement upon a cross outside Jerusalem for the sins of his people (the elect, Matt. 1:21). He was the perfect sacrifice. On the cross, Jesus also bore the punishment due to sinners by enduring the very wrath of God the Father (Rom. 3:25). He then died and lay in a tomb for three days (1 Cor. 15:3-4). On the third day, Jesus rose from the dead with a new resurrected body proving that he had conquered sin, death, and the Devil. Jesus demonstrated that he alone has the power to forgive sinners, grant eternal life, and transform lives. He now offers to humanity forgiveness of sins, eternal life, and an abundant life if people will humble themselves, repent of their sins, believe in Jesus alone as their Savior, and follow Him as their Lord (Acts 2:38; John 3:16, 10:10; Acts 16:31; Rom. 3:22, 24, 26, 28-30; Eph. 2:8-9). The gospel is also the good news of the kingdom of God. By embracing the gospel, Christians submit to Christ as their king and

---

6. Unless otherwise noted, all references to the Bible will be from the English Standard Version.

seek to obey the commands of his kingdom in all areas of life (Matt. 28:18-20). This kingdom includes both the spiritual and material realms of the universe. Jesus is the "King of kings and Lord of lords" (Rev. 19:16), and the rules of his kingdom are contained within the Old and New Testaments. By submitting to Christ as Lord, believers commit themselves to serve their king by bringing all aspects of creation into submission to his rule (2 Cor. 10:5). Presenting the inaugural address at the dedication of the Free University, Abraham Kuyper spoke about Christ and the extent of his rule. He said, "There is not a square inch in the whole domain of our human existence over which Christ, who is Sovereign over all, does not cry: 'Mine!'"

2. *Horizontal Dimension*: The horizontal dimension of worship refers to that aspect of worshiping God which includes considering one's neighbor in the worship service. While the horizontal primarily includes the thoughts, actions, and words of people toward one another, it should be noted that it also does not include those human aspects in which God is speaking to his people or vice versa.

3. *Vertical Dimension*: The vertical dimension of worship is bidirectional. It includes both an upward and downward focus. The upward direction of worship involves the worshipper in giving adoration, praise, glory, and honor to God (1 Cor. 10:31). To worship anything or anyone else other than God as he is revealed in the Bible is idolatry. It is also idolatrous to worship God in a manner he does not prescribe. The downward direction in the vertical dimension also involves God's ministry to and through man as he worships God. The Lord's ministry to man may include conviction of sin, encouragement, strengthening, inspiring, compelling, soothing, healing, correcting, admonishing, empowering, enlightening, etc. God's work in and through people is mysterious but well planned in his sovereign will for his own glory (Rom. 11:36; Eph. 1:11).[7]

---

7. For a visual explanation of how the horizontal and vertical dimensions work together, see the Vertical/Horizontal Dimension Dynamic diagram in chapter eighteen.

4. *Glorify*: To glorify means to give honor and weight to the one who is being glorified. From a Christian perspective, there is no one greater than the God of the Bible who is due glory. The Old Testament often uses the Hebrew word *kabōd* which is translated as "glory." Holladay defines the term as, "I. non-theological:—weight, splendor, magnificence, distinction, respect, mark of honor . . . II. theological:—give honor to Yahweh . . .; power, authority, honor of God, but also connected with manifestations of light."[8] This idiomatic expression points to the superiority of God's person and worth. Since God has the greatest weight metaphorically imaginable in his person and work, the term is appropriately used to refer to him since there is no one greater. It behooves us to give him our fullest attention, devotion, and honor in our worship (Matt. 4:10).

5. *Worship*: Smith comments that "The word 'worship' in English is derived from the Anglo-Saxon 'woerthscipe' meaning 'worth' 'shape.' It denotes worthiness of an individual to receive special honor in accord with that worth."[9] Worship that is pleasing to God is grounded in his Word of truth and should be done with a biblical attitude. Worship should not be based upon the vain imaginations of men. Its elements are prescribed in the Bible and should be done in an orderly manner (John 4:23-24; 1 Cor. 14:26-40). Two primary Greek words convey the fundamental meaning of worship. The more commonly used word is *proskuneo* meaning "to express in attitude or gesture one's complete dependence on or submission to a high authority figure, *(fall down and) worship, do obeisance to, prostrate oneself before, do reverence to, welcome respectfully.*"[10] This word emphasizes the humility and dependence demanded in worshiping God (e.g., Matt. 4:10; Luke 4:8; John 4:22-24; Judg. 7:15 [LXX]; Rev. 4:10, 5:14, 22:9). It highlights a submissive posture acknowledging the greatness and superiority of the Lord. The second lesser-used Greek word is *latreia* which is translated as

---

8. *A Concise Hebrew and Aramaic Lexicon of the Old Testament* (Leiden: Brill, 2000), s.v. "כָּבוֹד."

9. Morton Smith, *The Regulative Principle of Worship: Is It Biblical?* (Greenville, SC: Greenville Presbyterian Theological Seminary, 1995), 1.

10. *A Greek-English Lexicon of the New Testament and Other Early Christian Literature*, 3rd ed. (Chicago: University of Chicago Press, 2000), s.v. "προσκυνέω."

"*service/worship (of God)*."[11] This word is used in Hebrews 9:1, 4 and 12:28 and Romans 12:1. It includes the attitude of joy and reverence (Heb. 12:22, 28). The emphasis of worship using the word *latreia* is upon the act of service as one engages in the worship of God. Therefore, worship is about serving God and ministering to others in worship versus serving oneself. This means that when people approach God, they should come with attitudes of service to God and others rather than a self-serving mentality or posture. Worship that honors God must be done in the context of God's redemptive plan fulfilled in Jesus Christ alone (Gen. 3:15; Matt. 28:18-20; 1 Cor. 15). In this sense, it must be evangelical because the gospel (*evangel*) of Christ is central to God's plan to redeem mankind and the universe (Rom. 8:18-25; Gal. 3:13). In redeeming humanity, God saves people and creates new worshippers through the proclamation of his gospel of grace by the power of the Holy Spirit. For this reason, biblical worship always includes the gospel as integral to God's purposes, character, and glory (1 Cor. 10:31-11:1).

Assumptions

The following assumptions have been made before beginning the research:

1. The importance of corporate worship. This study assumes a view that corporate worship is commanded by God and essential to the health, growth, and expansion of the church and therefore how it is done is vital to Christ's Great Commission.

2. God's call to love. This study assumes that God's call to love others does not stop at the doors of the sanctuary before the church meets for worship. Worship, in fact, ought to be one of the most visible places where Christian love and concern is expressed.

---

11. *A Greek-English Lexicon of the New Testament*, s.v. "λατρεία."

3. Biblical worship does not present us with a mutually exclusive choice between the vertical and horizontal dimensions of worship.

4. When we pursue all that the Scriptures say about the vertical and the horizontal aspects of worship, both dimensions will be present.

Significance

This study is significant in that it will enable church leaders to rightly understand the place of the horizontal dimension of worship in the church's call to glorify God. It will also contribute to a Reformed understanding of the importance of the horizontal dimension in relation to the vertical direction of worshiping the Lord. Christians will discover the biblical balance needed for worship to be pleasing to God. Churches will be encouraged to express biblical love in their corporate worship services in such a way that people will truly experience the love and presence of God through the love and concern of his people for those attending corporate worship. Lord willing, those churches that embrace the position and recommended practices of this project will reach more people for Christ and further enrich the worship of believers so that God will be honored and praised. Churches that imbibe the values and practices of this project will experience the reality of God's love, the work of the Holy Spirit, and the truth of God's Word applied in corporate worship through a biblical administration of the horizontal dimension of worship.

Research Questions

1. What is the horizontal dimension of worship?

2. Why is the horizontal dimension of worship important?

3. In what way is the vertical view of worship enhanced and more greatly achieved by a healthy incorporation of horizontal worship?

4. How does the horizontal dimension relate to the vertical direction of worship?

5. What major Old Testament passages in the Bible support the horizontal dimension?

6. Are there key New Testament texts that contribute to the discussion of the horizontal dimension of worship?

7. What Scripture texts may have been used against the horizontal dimension of worship?

8. Are there any theological constructs that contribute to the necessity and/or application of the horizontal dimension (e.g., covenant theology, the doctrine of the Trinity, etc.)?

9. Do the reformers and major doctrinal statements of the Reformation support the theological idea of the horizontal dimension of worship?

10. Do modern Reformed and evangelical writers provide any insights about the horizontal dimension of worship?

11. How might the church today apply any scriptural, historical, and theological support for the horizontal dimension of worship in the way it conducts its corporate worship services?

12. What problems are solved by the research on this topic regarding worship in the church today? In other words, why does the study of the horizontal dimension matter?

13. In what way might the application of the horizontal dimension of worship in the church contribute to both the edification and

expansion of the church in obedience to the Great Commission of Christ given in Matthew 28:18-20?

14. How might this project's research be provided and promoted for the benefit of the church both locally and abroad?

Research Strategy

Research for this project will include the use of biblical commentaries, original language exegesis, systematic theologies, the writings of major Reformers, doctrinal statements by the Reformed church, modern Reformed writers and pertinent books on worship, especially from contemporary Reformed authors.

Regarding the biblical and theological resources, key Scriptures related to the topic of the horizontal dimension will be addressed using Greek and Hebrew language tools. The meaning of said passages will be explored and considered regarding their relevance to the horizontal dimension in worship. Reformed writers will be given special consideration in their interpretation of relevant passages. Views of Reformed systematic theologies will also be consulted for their understanding of the passages in question.

Primary literary resources from major Reformed theologians, creeds, and directories of worship will be used to understand whether the Reformed tradition includes the horizontal dimension of worship in its liturgy and understanding of worship explicitly or indirectly. Attention will be given to writers such as Calvin and Luther. This research is meant to provide an understanding of whether the Reformed tradition gives a basis for the promotion of the horizontal dimension. An attempt will be made to answer the question, "Did the Reformers and their early predecessors promote the horizontal dimension in some form?" Consequently, can we say that the idea of a horizontal dimension of worship is Reformed? Research may bear out some weaknesses regarding this project's thesis, or it may provide evidence that there is an overemphasis upon the vertical dimension of worship within the Reformed tradition.

Regarding the literature review, books and articles primarily in the last twenty years will be explored concerning the authors' perspective on the horizontal dimension of worship. If the literature bears out the support of this project's thesis, special attention to the practical application of the horizontal dimension will be researched to provide a sense of how modern writers are putting into practice their acceptance of the horizontal dimension. An application of this material will be provided.

Research for the project will be done through obtaining materials through interlibrary loans, reading purchased books, using internet resources, reading online periodicals, exploring the Puritan hard drive, visiting libraries, reading dissertations on the subject of worship, and considering the worship practices of Reformed and evangelical churches.

Proposed Outcome

The first desired outcome is that our church will mature in its understanding of the horizontal dimension of worship and that this research will contribute to the numeric and spiritual growth of our church. I desire that our congregation will especially grow in its horizontal concern for those attending our worship services so that more people will declare that God is truly among us. This goal could also be achieved through a seminar that develops from the findings of this study and the integration of this research and its conclusions into our church's membership class, Sunday school ministry, and leadership training. Practical examples of how to promote the horizontal dimension of worship as a complement to the vertical direction of worship will be provided. Secondly, it is the hope of the writer that the proposed outcome will include the eventual publishing of a book on the horizontal dimension for the benefit of the Reformed and the evangelical community. I would like to develop a seminar to aide other churches in strengthening their worship services in applying the horizontal dimension. The desire is that this material would help churches, that either undermine or dismiss the horizontal dimension of worship, see the horizontal dimension as a vital aspect of biblical and Reformed worship. I plan to create instruction on the internet through such media as YouTube to encourage a biblical understanding and implementation of the findings from this project. This material could also be shared through social media sites such as Facebook for the benefit of a wider audience.

Part 1

BIBLICAL AND THEOLOGICAL FOUNDATIONS FOR THE HORIZONTAL DIMENSION

The practices of worship must be grounded upon a solid biblical foundation. One of the hallmarks of the Reformation was that all worship should be regulated by Scripture. As we consider the horizontal dimension of worship, we must ask ourselves whether the horizontal dimension fits within the guidelines of the Bible. Otherwise, we are basing our practices and thoughts upon the ideologies and philosophies of men. Worship is a gift from God to his people that allows them to express their love, thanks, praise, reverence, and adoration. The biblical terms used in Scripture for worship express obeisance towards God and include an orientation of service to the Lord. Unlike man-centered entertainment, Christian worship makes God the primary audience. In this sense, all worship must and should be solely directed toward God (i.e., the vertical dimension). Although the focus of Christian worship is on God who alone is worthy of worship, it also includes a horizontal dimension in which the people who are worshiping should consider how the message and practice of their worship affect their fellow worshippers. This means that worship should include both the vertical and horizontal dimensions since they are often found together throughout the Bible. The horizontal is not limited to the concern that people should show for one another but also should reflect the attitude that God has for those who worship him. The horizontal is fundamentally relational and exhibits the concerns within the Godhead and God's desire to be in a relationship with mankind. Since much has been written about the vertical dimension of worship, we will give special attention to some theological concepts and consider key biblical texts that provide support for the horizontal dimension in worship. As we reflect upon the Scriptures, we will discover that the theme of the horizontal is represented in various texts which focus upon God's calling to love our neighbor, show justice, and demonstrate concern for others in our worship. One helpful place to begin our discussion is with the doctrine of the Trinity

1

Trinitarian Foundation

A key theological underpinning of the horizontal dimension can be found in some of the relational dynamics we see within the Trinity. God is inherently relational within himself. The relational dynamic that exists within the Trinity lays the groundwork for the relational obligations and concerns that Christians should have for one another in their worship since they are made in the image of God as relational creatures. As we ponder the three persons of the Godhead, we are faced with the reality of the plurality of God as well as his unity. The principle of one but many is exemplified in our theology of God. There is community within the Godhead. God is one God but three persons: the Father, the Son, and the Holy Spirit. There is a relationship within the Trinity in which the three persons interact and inter-relate with one another. At the heart of the relationship between the members of the Trinity is the relational dynamic of love and mutual respect. In commenting about the love of God within the Trinity, Berkhof remarks that this love "may be defined as that perfection of God by which He is eternally moved to self-communication."[1] As each person of the Trinity expresses love for the other such interaction reflects the perfect goodness of God. The Father loves the Son. John states, "The Father loves the Son and has given all things into his hand" (John 3:35). The Father said, "This is my beloved Son, with whom I am well pleased" (Matt. 3:17). The Son loves the Father. Jesus said, "but I do as the Father has commanded me, so that the world may know that I love the Father. Rise, let us go from here" (John 14:31). Although the Scriptures do not explicitly say that the Spirit loves the Son or Father, we can deduce by the work of the Spirit that he loves both the Father

---

1. Louis Berkhof, *Systematic Theology*, 4th ed. (Grand Rapids, MI: Eerdmans, 1949), 71.

and the Son since he produces *agape* love in the lives of believers (e.g., Gal. 5:22-23). The Spirit demonstrates his love for the Father by promoting the will of the Father (2 Tim. 3:16) and shows love for the Son in glorifying him (John 16:4). The Holy Spirit exhibits the love he possesses within the Trinity by taking the love of God and translating it to the children of God. Augustine reminds us of the Spirit's love when he teaches, "Love, therefore, which is of God and is God, is specially the Holy Spirit, by whom the love of God is shed abroad in our hearts, by which love the whole Trinity dwells in us. And therefore, most rightly is the Holy Spirit, although He is God, called also the gift of God (Acts 8:20)."[2] Lest we forget that love is central to the relational dynamic within the Trinity, the apostle John exclaims, "Anyone who does not love does not know God, because God is love" (1 John 4:8). As they relate to one another, the members of the Trinity express the deepest level and purest expression of love imaginable because they are love. Their loving essence and practice of love provide believers with a pattern of perfect love which they are called to imitate (Eph. 5:1) among themselves in all areas of life including worship.

Christian tradition also teaches us that the Father, the Son, and the Holy Spirit share the same essence (see the Nicene Creed [AD 325], The Definition of the Council of Chalcedon [AD 351], and The Westminster Confession of Faith Ch. 2, par. 3). This doctrine of sharing the same essence is the basis for the unity and relationships within the Trinity. Not only do the members of the Trinity share the same essence but they also communicate with each other, a fundamental reality of true relationships. McGrath reminds us that "There is a continuity of relationships between Father, Son, and the Spirit, thus establishing an unbreakable link between encounter with or experience of the Spirit, the Son and the Father."[3] We see this dynamic throughout the Bible. For example, Genesis records, "Then God said, 'Let us make man in our image, after our likeness'" (Gen.

---

2. Augustine of Hippo, *St. Augustine: On the Holy Trinity, Doctrinal Treatises, Moral Treatises*, vol. 3, *On the Trinity*, ed. Philip Schaff, trans. Arthur West Haddan, A Select Library of the Nicene and Post-Nicene Fathers of the Christian Church, First Series (Buffalo, NY: Christian Literature Company, 1887), 217.

3. Alister E. McGrath, *Understanding the Trinity* (Grand Rapids, MI: Academie Books, 1988), 129.

1:26). The word for God is the plural title *'ĕlōhîm*. Although there is not a total consensus among all scholars, many theologians believe the phrase "Let us make," a phrase in the verbal plural form, points to the interpersonal Trinitarian decision within the Godhead to create man. It appears that this was a mutual and contemplated decision. The apostle Paul also reveals that each member of the Trinity works in perfect harmony with the others for our salvation and sanctification. Ephesians 1 reminds us that the Father predestines (Eph. 1:4-5), the Son redeems (Eph. 1:7), and the Spirit seals us guaranteeing our salvation (Eph. 1:13-14). Theologians also speak of the covenant of redemption which points to the unified decision-making that happens within the Godhead. This covenant between the persons of the Trinity occurred outside of time. God planned to redeem a people for himself and to predestine the elect to be redeemed. Erickson defines this covenant as the "agreement made between God the Father and God the Son whereby the latter would give his life for the salvation of the human race."[4] Shedd says, "The covenant of redemption is made between the Father and the Son. The contracting parties here are the first and second persons of the Trinity; the first of whom promises a kingdom, a glory, and a reward, upon condition that the second performs a work of atonement and redemption."[5] Dabney remarks, "The original parties to the Covenant of Redemption are the Father and the Son."[6] The Scripture reveals that the Spirit brings about the reality of the covenant of redemption in his work of regeneration thus unifying his actions with the redemptive will of both the Father and the Son (John 3:3-8; Titus 3:5). These redemptive decisions made within the Trinity were relational interactions. They exemplify the horizontal dimension present between the persons of the Godhead. The covenant of redemption points to the ongoing fellowship within the Trinity and provides a basis for believers to express horizontal concerns for their fellow worshippers who are made in the image of God and called to imitate him (Eph. 5:1). Human beings derive their

---

4. Millard J. Erickson, *The Concise Dictionary of Christian Theology* (Wheaton, IL: Crossway Books, 2001), 43.
5. William Greenough Thayer Shedd, *Dogmatic Theology*, ed. Alan W. Gomes, 3rd ed. (Phillipsburg, NJ: P & R Publishing, 2003), 679.
6. R. L. Dabney, *Systematic Theology*, 2nd ed. (Houston: Banner of Truth, 1985), 516.

relational nature from their relational God who communicates his relational communicable attributes to man. Christians are called to pursue relationships with one another due to the grace they have received in Christ (John 13:34-45). They are inherently relational since their God is relational. God's relational nature provides the basis for responsible horizontal considerations in worship. This reality establishes a foundation for the horizontal dimension between people within every Christian worship service.

Communication that happens in the Trinity models relational patterns and concerns that may occur between God's people in worship. The Father talks to the Son (Matt. 3:17), Jesus talks to the Father about believers (John 17:20-23), and the Holy Spirit speaks to the Father in his intercession on behalf of the saints (Rom. 8:26-27). Trinitarian communication by its very nature involves relational dynamics that encourage believers to express care and concern for one another in worship as they seek to imitate the mutual care they observe within the Godhead.

In this section, we have covered just a few of the inter-relational dynamics within the Trinity that provide a foundation for supporting the principle of the horizontal dimension within our services. Of course, the theological considerations not only apply to interactions within corporate worship but also apply to the day-to-day relationships of God's people with their neighbors outside of corporate worship. The relational interactions within the Godhead lead us to consider another basis for the horizontal dimension—the Lord as a covenant-making and covenant-keeping God.

2

Covenantal Connection

One cannot give proper consideration to the horizontal dimension without also thinking about covenant theology. The Bible reveals that the Lord is a covenant-making and -keeping God. As we have noted above, God made a covenant within himself to redeem humankind. This relational commitment within the Godhead naturally extends to God's covenant with humans. The Lord is not some distant deity who wishes to sit aloof on Mount Olympus far removed from humanity, the pinnacle of his creation. God desires to be in a relationship with people in a way distinctly different than with any of his other creatures. We see the importance of relationships to the Lord when he makes Adam, places him in the Garden of Eden, and communes with him (Gen. 1-2). God assigns him duties but also sets boundaries within that relationship (Gen. 2:28-30). He tells Adam that he can enjoy everything within the garden but cannot eat the fruit from the tree of knowledge of good and evil (Gen. 2:15-17). This arrangement is called the covenant of works. The Westminster Confession states, "The first covenant made with man was a covenant of works, wherein life was promised to Adam; and in him to his posterity, upon condition of perfect and personal obedience."[1] The Lord warned Adam that if he ate of the forbidden fruit, he would "surely die" (Gen. 3:17). This was a warning that not only would humans physically and spiritually die, but that sin would break their covenantal relationship with God. A covenant is fundamentally a relational agreement. It is the Lord's relational agreement with humankind with promises and stipulations. The Hebrew word for covenants in the Old Testament is *bĕrît*, which

---

1. *The Westminster Confession of Faith and Catechisms As Adopted By the Presbyterian Church in America with Proofs Texts* (Lawrenceville, GA: Christian Education & Publications, 2007), WCF 7.2.

means "agreement, alliance, covenant."[2] The verb often associated with initiating a covenant is "to cut" which referred to the practice of cutting animals into two halves, between which the parties would take their oaths to keep the covenant. These ritual elements involved in a covenant ceremony represented the sacred commitment between the parties involved. The parties of the covenant were obligated to keep the stipulations of the covenant which can be summed up as loyalty to the other party. If they violated the covenant, there would be grave consequences. The two sides would demonstrate the solemnity and covenantal obligations by walking between the "cut" animal parts to seal the covenantal agreement between them. This visual ritual demonstrated to all those involved, including heavenly witnesses, that the stipulations of the covenant were binding and that each participant in the covenant should be treated as the severed animals if they did not keep the stipulations. Such an agreement was very serious and sacred indeed. It was fundamentally a matter of life and death sealed in blood. Covenants in the ancient world often involved a superior king (suzerain) making a pact with a lesser king (vassal). Such covenants were known as suzerainty-vassal treaties. The result of breaking the covenant by the lesser king would typically bring judgment upon the vassal by the suzerain.[3] This ancient context in which covenants were often made provides a rich background to the covenants we see between God and man in the Old Testament. Robertson describes divine-human covenants as "a bond in blood sovereignly administered. When God enters into a covenantal relationship with men, he sovereignly institutes a life-and-death bond. A covenant is a bond in blood or a bond of life and death, sovereignly administered."[4]

Using some of the elements of Robertson's definition, we could view God's covenants with humankind throughout the Scriptures as a life-love-bond unilaterally initiated and sustained by God with humans with promises and expectations. God's blessings are promised to those who are obedient, and his curses are promised to those who are

---

2. *A Concise Hebrew and Aramaic Lexicon of the Old Testament* (Leiden: Brill, 2000), s.v. "ברית."

3. Meredith G Kline, "Dynastic Covenant," *The Westminster Theological Journal* 23, no. 1 (November 1960): 1–15.

4. O Palmer Robertson, *The Christ of the Covenants* (Grand Rapids, MI: Baker, 1980), 4.

disobedient (Deut. 28). Notice in this definition that God is motivated to covenant with man out of his love (Deut. 7:6-13). This fits well with the reason he predestines his people as Paul explains, ". . . he chose us in him before the foundation of the world, that we should be holy and blameless before him. In love he predestined us for adoption to himself as sons through Jesus Christ, according to the purpose of his will" (Eph. 1:4-5). God enters into covenant with human beings because he loves them. His love is unconditional when he unilaterally initiates a covenantal relationship with humanity. A clear example of unconditional love is shown when God initiates a covenantal relationship with Abraham when the patriarch was a pagan who was not interested in the Lord, but nevertheless, God calls him to be his own (Gen. 12). The Scriptures teach that God loves his people by calling them to himself when they are rebellious sinners unworthy of his love (Rom. 5:8, 9:11, 16; Titus 3:4-5; 1 John 4:10). Such love is at the heart of God's covenantal love for his children. As perfect love exists between the persons of the Trinity, God chooses to express that love to redeem and relate to mankind. We see the Creator's intention to continue a relationship with fallen humans shortly after the fall of Adam in the Garden of Eden. The Lord could have easily chosen to discard human beings or create another race of creatures to relate to, but he does not. He decides to make a promise to save humanity through the seed of the woman (Gen. 3:15). This promise demonstrates the ongoing covenantal disposition of God toward mankind. He simply will not allow this relationship, which he values greatly, to end. Genesis 3:15, otherwise known as the *proto-evangelium* (first reference in the Bible to the gospel), foretells the coming of Christ who would be born of the Virgin Mary to redeem mankind through the cross and to crush the power of the Devil. God says, "I will put enmity between you and the woman, and between your offspring and her offspring; he shall bruise your head, and you shall bruise his heel" (Gen. 3:15). Most Reformed theologians see this passage as the beginning of the covenant of grace and view this covenant as, "the great and all-comprehensive good which God in infinite mercy grants unto sinners, a good including all the blessings of salvation, and therefore also regeneration."[5] The covenant of grace was unilaterally initiated by God with mankind man due to the fact that Adam fell into sin and became rebellious in his nature against fellowship with God. Without God initiating this covenant of grace with Adam, humanity was doomed. God's initiating this covenant demonstrates his commitment to bridge the relational gulf between himself and the human race through his promised Son Jesus. God holds this relational covenant in high esteem. How does this covenant take root in the heart of people? God brings it into reality when he sends the Holy Spirit to regenerate the fallen heart of a person to enable their will to respond to God's unilateral offer of the gospel of grace (John 3:3; Eph. 2:1-5; Titus 3:5). When people respond positively, they exercise human responsibility by choosing to repent of their sins and then trusting in Christ alone for their salvation. The result is not just a decision, but a converted person who is given a new relationship with the living God. Human beings are brought back into fellowship with their Creator. Paradise is restored through Christ in the life of the believer who can now commune with God and seek a harmonious communion with other people. This is the consequence and reality of the covenant of grace realized through faith in Jesus. It is relational at its core. It establishes peace between God and the converted person (Rom. 5:1; Col. 1:20). This relational covenant of grace progressively unfolds throughout the Old Testament until its fulfillment in the new covenant in Christ, demonstrating God's commitment to have a relationship with the humankind through his Son (cf. Jer. 31:31; 1 Cor. 11:25; Matt. 26:28; Mark 14:24; Luke 22:20). Each major covenant God initiates builds upon the previous ones, thus providing a rich tapestry of God's unfolding plan of redemption. Every covenant illustrates his desire to create a people to be in a relationship with himself, providing the roots for holy relationships to exist among God's covenant children. The relational theme that runs throughout the Bible that presents God's desire to have a relationship with humanity is shown in the repeated phrase, "I shall be your God and you shall be my people" (Gen. 17:7; Exod. 6:6-7; 19:4-5; Lev. 11:45; Deut. 4:20; 2 Kings 11:17; Ezek. 34:23; 2 Cor. 6:16; Heb. 8:10;

---

5. Berkhof, *Systematic Theology*, 455-456.

Rev. 21:3). God's plan to build a relationship with redeemed humanity is based primarily upon his relationship with Abraham and his descendants, Israel, his covenant people. In the Old Testament, those outside of Israel are called the Gentiles, but they were also invited into the covenantal community of the Jews if they trusted in Israel's God and received the sign of the covenant, circumcision, along with making a commitment to follow the law of God. God later promises a New covenant which eventually creates a new people including both redeemed Jews and Gentiles (Eph. 2:11-22). This new family of people is the Jewish-Gentile church of God and is not grounded in an acceptance of circumcision and commitment to the ceremonial laws of the Old Testament (see Galatians; Rom. 4). This new people of God is not bound together by biology or the traditions of Israel. They are joined together by a common faith in Christ (Gal. 3:7).

The Lord's desire to be in a relationship with his elect brings about a new relationship between redeemed people. They become one new man brought together through God's special work of grace through the power of the Holy Spirit (Eph. 2:15; 1 Cor. 12). This is the reality of the New covenant brought about through the blood of Christ. It was applied to the elect and was realized through a common faith in Christ alone through the promised work of the Holy Spirit (Ezek. 36:25-28; Jer. 31:31-34; Luke 22:20; 1 Cor. 11:25; Heb. 8:6-8). In Christ, the walls of division between races, classes, and genders are abolished (Gal. 3:23-29). As a consequence of God's covenant of grace fulfilled in the new covenant in Christ, one new people is established. Paul rightly declares, "So then you are no longer strangers and aliens, but you are fellow citizens with the saints and members of the household of God" (Eph. 2:19). This new group of people is bound together in a covenantal relationship with one another through their covenant with God. Their horizontal relationships flow through their common vertical relationship with their relational God. The horizontal dimension is inherently covenantal because the Christian family's vertical tie to God is grounded in its relational covenant with God the Father. This occurs through a relationship with Christ brought about by the work of the Holy Spirit (Eph. 4:4). This relational dynamic, which is tied to God's covenant with man, provides a basis for a proper balance between the horizontal and vertical, especially as the people of

God worship together. To resist, dismiss, or diminish the horizontal dimension in worship would be to deny the very real and essential relational aspects of covenant theology which are foundational to a Reformed understanding of the Bible.

Another important reality that should inform our appreciation of our covenantal bond with God is the doctrine of double union. The covenantal bond is grounded in our spiritual union with Christ through faith, and this union creates a spiritual union between believers who are united to Christ. It is a union based not simply on obedience and obligation. Symbolized by baptism (Rom. 6; Col. 2.6-14), this union also involves a mysterious spiritual vertical union with the Savior who mysteriously unites all Christians horizontally as one people of God. This one new people the New Testament calls the body of Christ (1 Cor. 12). The experience of double union means that believers who are in covenant with God will seek to worship Christ vertically due to their union with Christ but will also pursue the horizontal dimension because of their spiritual union with the people of Christ. This double union stands in the center of the covenant between God and the people of the covenant. The Holy Spirit, as mentioned earlier, is instrumental in cementing and fostering not only the covenant but the spiritual union between God and his children who live in covenant with one another (Eph. 4:3-6). This covenantal union is exemplified visibly when Christians partake of the Lord's Supper. The Supper is a communion of God's people with Christ and one another. The doctrine of double union provides a rich theological and spiritual foundation for Christians as they spiritually feed upon Christ. Not only do they experience union with the Savior, but they enjoy a spiritual union with one another as one body through the Spirit and their common faith in Christ. The covenantal bond with God and between the people of God should also elicit appreciation of the horizontal dimension in worship and should encourage Christians to seek to love their neighbor in the pew as they express their covenantal love for God with praise, attentiveness, adoration, and communion.

As a by-product of the love we experience in our relationship with God, there should always exist a special love between those united to Christ (John 14:34-35; 1 John 4:19-21). The covenantal call to love and praise God raises the question, "How should we treat our neighbor as we seek to glorify God in worship?" The covenant between Christians and God calls for a careful consideration of the relational dynamics involved between the people of God and others. Covenantal theology demands that that the church not only understand its obligation to worship God with a clear grasp of its vertical relationship with Him but also calls the church to seek to discover its horizontal responsibilities to others in worship. This quest should encourage Christians to diligently study what God's Word says about loving our neighbor in worship.

3

Worship with Love for Your Neighbor

God calls his children to show biblical love not only to himself but to other human beings. In showing love to both God and man we not only honor God but express our respect for the people he has created. Loving our neighbor must also occur in the context of worship. Without loving others in our corporate worship we have not truly loved God as we should. He expects his people to love one another as they worship. This theme of love for one's neighbor is essential if we wish to develop a scriptural view of worship. Loving one's neighbor is inherently horizontal, and many texts convey the importance of such love. The principles of neighbor love should always be considered in the way we construct our worship services and personally engage in worship that pleases God. Let us consider some of the key passages that present the biblical principle of loving our neighbor as we worship the Lord and consequently support the horizontal dimension of worship. A good place to begin this discussion is with the giving of the Law on Mount Sinai, a setting of worship and honor to God.

Exodus 20:1-17 and Deuteronomy 5:6-21

God's moral law lays down a blueprint for the vertical and horizontal dimensions to take place in corporate worship. Moses was given the Decalogue to teach Israel how they should approach God and treat one another in response to God's grace. In short, the Ten Commandments reinforce the mutual concepts of loving God and loving our neighbor. This dual structure within the Ten Commandments encourages the church to engage in the pursuit of the vertical and horizontal. We cannot only focus upon the section of the Law that primarily deals with the vertical and leave out the horizontal in our daily lives, especially in our worship.

God's grace should motivate every believer to honor the Law both in life and worship. Enns states, "The law . . . is based on God's gracious act of saving his people; it is not a condition of becoming God's people, for that has already happened in the Exodus."[1] Prior to Sinai, the Lord had decided to deliver Israel based upon his covenant promises to Abraham, Isaac, and Jacob (Exod. 2:24). God precedes the giving of the commandments by referencing his miraculous deliverance of Israel from her slavery in Egypt (Exod. 19:1-6). Thus, the Law of God and motivation to keep it is undergirded by the grace and redemption of the Lord. When we closely examine the structure of the Ten Commandments, we find that they are bi-directional in that they deal with two foci—our relationship to God and our relationship to man. Hamilton draws attention to the two-fold intent of the Ten Commandments stating, "It is quite obvious that the intent of the first four commandments is different from that of the last six. The first four are vertical in their orientation and have to do with one's relationship to God. The last six are horizontal and deal with man's relationship to his fellow human beings."[2] Although this line of demarcation is revealed as we ponder the moral law, the vertical commandments should not be understood in contradistinction to the horizontal commandments. These Laws are derived from the nature of God. Childs reminds us of this fact when he states, "The expression of God's will in the Decalogue was commensurate to his nature. The Old Testament never recognized a hiatus between his revealed and actual nature. The commands were best understood when kept in closest relation to the God of the covenant who laid claim upon a people and pointed them to a new life as the people of God."[3]

The first four commandments primarily convey a vertical focus upon God (Exod. 20:1-11; Deut. 5:7-15). They establish the Law in God's person, name, and provision of the Sabbath. Without these essential commands, we have no basis for our responsibilities to our fellow man. The first four commandments forbid the sins of idolatry,

---

1. Peter Enns, *Exodus* (Grand Rapids, MI: Zondervan, 2000), 412.
2. Victor P. Hamilton, *Handbook On the Pentateuch: Genesis, Exodus, Leviticus, Numbers, Deuteronomy* (Grand Rapids, MI: Baker, 1982), 200.
3. Brevard S. Childs, *The Book of Exodus: A Critical, Theological Commentary* (Philadelphia: Westminster Press, 1974), 400-1.

blasphemy, and disrespect for authority. They call us to give our wholehearted devotion to the Lord. Our respect for these commands must be present if we wish to treat others with the honor and love that their image-bearing positions deserve. Without love and devotion to God, there is no ultimate reason why we should show any kindness and mercy toward other people. Without the vertical, life is void of purpose and meaning. When there is no respect for God, other human beings become nothing more than cogs in the machine of empty human existence. There is no basis for morality and the love of our neighbor in the absence of devotion to the Lord. Our vertical response to God is also rooted in the redemptive context of his deliverance of Israel from slavery in Egypt. If this context is missing, we have no gracious motive to love God and show mercy to humanity (Exod. 20:1-2; Deut. 5:6). Thompson remarks, "It was the responsibility of every Israelite in every age to identify himself with his ancestors and to participate in memory and in faith in their experience of God's deliverance."[4] The redemptive foundation provided in Israel's deliverance foreshadows the redemptive ministry of Jesus Christ on the cross and points to the gospel of grace as the motivating factor for following God's commandments (John 1:29; Rom. 6:15-23).

The primary vertical focus of the first four commandments calls for worship of the Creator and Redeemer in a way that honors and respects his name. Such respect for God, as the commandments call for, provides a basis for loving and caring for other human beings. The commandment are founded upon God's love for humanity through his acts of creation, providence, and redemption. One could also argue that the fourth commandment demonstrates not only a vertical emphasis but also includes a horizontal focus. Sabbath keepers are called to provide rest from work to their neighbors and animals which labor during the other six days of the week (Exod. 20:10; Deut. 5:14). Everyone in the household is encouraged to rest from their labor because God has set the seventh day apart as holy. The decision to make the day holy is based upon the Lord's gracious choice and redeeming work (Exod. 20:11; Deut. 15).

---

4. J. A. Thompson, *Deuteronomy: An Introduction and Commentary* (London: Inter-Varsity Press, 1974), 113.

The second half of the Decalogue primarily focuses upon the horizontal dimension. The fifth through the tenth commandments focus on how human beings should treat one another (Exod. 20:12-17; Deut. 5:16-21) in light of their relationship with God and calling to honor him on the Sabbath. These holy commandments cover the breadth of God's ethical demands and expectations between human beings. Reymond confirms this point when he states that "it is the Decalogue which is the ethical norm for the Christian's covenant way of life."[5] In the fifth commandment, the Lord addresses human authority as it is represented by parental authority. Such authority is ultimately grounded in God's cosmic rule. The Lord makes a promise to provide many days in the promised land if the Israelites honor their parents. The vertical dimension is mentioned as God tells his covenant people that he is the one who is giving them the land (Exod. 20:12; Deut. 5:16b). This reference to God's provisions recalls Israel's dependence upon God's grace and his ultimate authority. In other words, to honor one's parents is one way of honoring the Lord who has granted authority to parents.

In forbidding murder, Yahweh teaches his people to love life. The sixth commandment encourages the promotion and respect of human life. We cannot decouple the sixth commandment from the vertical reality of the fourth commandment which teaches us that God has created life (Exod. 20:11). As we consider our horizontal responsibility to honor life, we are driven to vertically recognize God as the giver and protector of life.

The Lord addresses the need for sexual purity (Exod. 20:14) in the seventh commandment (Exod. 20:14). This calling for holiness in our sexual relations flows from our calling to live holy lives in relationship with God who is a holy and jealous God (Exod. 20:5). The prophets fully understood this connection in their metaphorical admonition not to commit spiritual adultery with false gods (Isa. 1:21; 57:8; Jer. 9:2; Ezek. 6:9; 16:15-19, 30; Hosea 2:2-5; 3:1-5; 9:1). Just as God will not tolerate spiritual adultery neither will he endure sexual immorality among his people. The vertical informs the horizontal and vice versa.

---

5. Robert L. Reymond, *A New Systematic Theology of the Christian Faith* (Nashville: Thomas Nelson, 1998), 770.

The eighth commandment forbids stealing (Exod. 20:15; Deut. 5:19). It demands respect for our neighbor's property and indirectly encourages the principle of honorable work. Addressing the severity of stealing in Moses' day, Cole says, "In a peasant society where life is hard, any theft of property may lead to death, so theft is a very serious crime."[6] This horizontal commandment is supported in the fourth commandment which refers to the six days man is allowed to work in preparation for rest on the Sabbath Day. The reference to God's creation (v. 11) points to the giving nature of God who provides the blessings of creation, work, and Sabbath rest. The fruit of man's labor granted at the time of creation reveals the Lord's allowance for private property. The recognition in the fourth commandment of the possession of livestock illustrates God's approval of owning property. The Lord prohibits theft which is a violation of God's intended purposes for humans to enjoy the fruit of their labor. The positive side of this commandment would entail the promotion and respect of our neighbor's possessions. The provision of private property and prohibition against stealing from our neighbor are blessings from God. Such gifts provide human beings good reasons to work hard and give rather than to steal from their neighbor. Respect for our neighbor's property demonstrates respect for God who has given that property.

The ninth commandment forbids bearing false witness against our neighbor. In other words, people should speak truthfully to and about one another. God detests a lying tongue (Prov. 6:17, 19). This commandment is also grounded in the vertical commandments. God's distaste for idols reminds us that he will not tolerate devotion to lying false idols and images. He is the only God of truth worthy of worship. He despises that which is false and loves the truth because he is the truth. The Lord himself as the God of truth is the maker of reality. God's desire for truth is also represented in the third commandment. If we take God's name in vain, we allow and promote that which is false about God and all his works. Blaspheming the name of the Lord is something he will not tolerate. The God of truth demands that his people speak truthfully to and about one another if they desire to

---

6. R. A. Cole, *Exodus; an Introduction and Commentary* (Downers Grove, IL: InterVarsity Press, 1973), 160-61.

worship him as their faithful God of truth. If we love the God of truth, we will, in turn, love our neighbor by telling the truth.

The tenth commandment speaks against coveting (Exod. 20:17; Deut. 5:21). This commandment, like the eighth commandment, requires respect for our neighbor's property and belongings. It addresses not only outward theft but also the inward desire for what belongs to our neighbor. Indirectly, this command is connected to our vertical posture toward God and what he provides. Instead of being envious of or jealous of what belongs to others, we should be satisfied with what God has provided us. We should be happy about the blessings God has given to others because he is the giver of all good gifts (James 1:17). Human beings are called to work six days and rest with contentment in the Lord on the Sabbath (Exod. 20:8-11). Our contentment in God and Christ alone should replace our covetous desires (Exod. 20:3; Phil. 4:11-13). Idols of all kinds, especially the possessions of other people, are forbidden if we are devoted to the Lord (Exod. 20:3-5).

We have discovered that when the Ten Commandments are rightly understood, we develop a firm interdependent relationship between the horizontal and vertical. As we enter worship, the Ten Commandments with all their ethical considerations grounded in God and his grace must come to bear upon us. Regarding the worship of the Lord, we cannot just seek to focus on the first half of the Decalogue but leave the second half out when we come to meet with the Lord. The two foci must go together. All the commandments in principle should be on our minds, in our hearts, upon our lips, and demonstrated in our actions when we seek to engage God in worship. The commandments express our calling to love both God and our neighbor. The call to love both God and people is also demonstrated in the actions of King Saul.

1 Samuel 15:22-23

God had spoken through the prophet Samuel to King Saul telling him to go and destroy the Amalekites for the way they opposed Israel when "they came up out of Egypt" (1 Sam. 15:2). The Lord commanded Saul to totally destroy the Amalekites and everything in their possession including ox and sheep, camel and donkey (1 Sam. 15:3). The Hebrew word for the phrase "devote to destruction" in verse 3 is from the root *ḥrm* meaning to "dedicate to destruction."[7] God had called Saul to annihilate the Amalekites and their possessions without compromise. Saul summoned the people of Israel to fight against this enemy of God. King Saul even captured their king Agag but decided to spare his life. Saul allowed the troops to confiscate the spoils except for the things that were worthless. When confronted by the prophet Samuel regarding Saul's compromise, Saul used the excuse, "But the people took of the spoil, sheep and oxen, the best of the things devoted to destruction, to sacrifice to the Lord your God in Gilgal" (1 Sam. 15:21). Although Saul tried to explain why he did not listen to God with the excuse that the people kept the spoil to sacrifice to the Lord, God would not tolerate his attitude. Samuel tells Saul that God is not interested in the outward ritual acts of worship such as offering burnt offerings and sacrifices (1 Sam. 15:22). God was instead interested in Saul's obedience to his "voice." He compares Saul's disobedience to rebellion and calls such rebellion the sin of divination and idolatry (1 Sam. 15:23). This was a serious accusation against King Saul since the Lord highly detested divination and idolatry (Lev. 19:31; Deut. 18:9-15). In short, Saul had rejected the Word of God by emphasizing ritual over obedience to God's will (1 Sam. 15:23). He rejected God himself in his rebellious act of worship. Saul's ritual act of worship was actually a sacrifice based upon Saul's fear of the people (1 Sam. 15:24). His fear of them led him to seek their approval (i.e., "their voice") over the "voice" of God. It also involved Saul taking matters into his own hands as a leader rather than submitting to God's instructions through his prophet Samuel. His ritual was void of a heart committed to God and his will. This is a sober reminder that both the vertical and horizontal dimensions must comply with God's will regardless of a leader's position or the desires of the people. This act of defiance resulted in God rejecting Saul as the king of Israel (1 Sam. 15:23, 26). Woodhouse comments on the seriousness of the situation:

---

7. *A Concise Hebrew and Aramaic Lexicon of the Old Testament*, s.v. "חרם."

"Saul's disobedience was a rejection of the word of God, which was a rejection of God himself."[8]

It may be asked at this point, "What does this text have to do with the thesis of this project?" One of the things that people do when they overly focus on the vertical as they worship is to emphasize ritual in their worship. Ritual can apply to patterns that are followed either in the free church or more liturgical traditions. People can easily become comfortable or even smug in the belief that as long as they approach God with their particular tradition or ritual with either a vertical or horizontal posture, they will be right with God. This incident with Saul reminds us that we cannot dismiss from our thoughts God's calling to love our neighbor as we worship but it must be done in a manner that honors God. Just as God told Saul to act in a certain manner regarding the Amalekites, God also calls Christians to love their neighbor which is a command that cannot be left out of our worship. It also is not enough to have good intentions in our worship when God has commanded us to love our neighbor (Lev. 19:9-18). Although we may use the excuse, "I thought I was right with focusing solely upon God without consideration of my neighbor sitting beside me in worship," such an excuse will not satisfy God who desires obedience more than the sacrifice we offer and the rituals we follow when we worship him. The same principle applies to those who focus only on the horizontal dimension, forgetting that it is God alone whom they should worship. God will not tolerate giving our primary attention to men when we are called to honor him in our worship. This sadly occurs when worship leaders take matters into their own hands and shape their services primarily around the desires of those who attend. They choose to skip things that might cause offense or may be considered politically incorrect. When leaders make such decisions, they sound like Saul who excused his sin when he said, ". . . I feared the people and obeyed their voice" (1 Sam. 15:24). The severity by which God punished Saul should be a healthy reminder that the Lord wants us to follow his commands about how we approach him in our worship. God desires that we seek to please him rather than men. Loving our neighbor

---

8. John Woodhouse, *1 Samuel: Looking for a Leader* (Wheaton, IL: Crossway Books, 2008), 274.

involves more than fulfilling the desires of our neighbor. Love must always be qualified by what God reveals in his Word about what he desires for our neighbor. Our neighbor may not want us to say or do something that God has instructed us to say or do. If we follow the Lord's instruction in love, we have then loved our neighbor as God intended. This type of love is desperately needed today in a church culture that often caters to the whims of men versus the truths of the Word. Keil and Delitzsch wisely comment on the seriousness of worship without obedience as it pertains to the words of Samuel: "But it necessarily follows that sacrifices without obedience to the commandments of God are utterly worthless; in fact, are displeasing to God, as Ps. 50:8ff., Isa. 1:11ff., 66:3, Jer. 6:20, and all the prophets, distinctly affirm."[9] We will see later how serious God is about our horizontal treatment of others when Israel engages in corporate worship. We must never forget that God is watching the heart and the motivations of the worshipper just as he was watching the heart of Saul. Love of our neighbor, regardless of our ritual, must always comply with our love of God and his will expressed in Scripture. The Word is the "voice" of God, and we must listen to his voice in the way we worship. When Christians are listening to God's voice, biblical love will consequently be demonstrated in obedience to his word (1 Sam. 15:22-23, 26). As Scriptures direct us in worship, love of God and God's love for us (i.e., the vertical) should always guide us in the way we love our neighbor (i.e., horizontal) in our worship. Such love is also spoken about by the prophets. Let us consider the wisdom of Hosea about the love that God requires in our worship.

Hosea 6:6-8

The Lord does not find Israel's sacrifices acceptable due to her covenant unfaithfulness, especially with her neighbors. Hubbard notes that "The priests have disrupted social stability by murderous conspiracies which violated the terms of Yahweh's covenant (6:7-9)."[10]

---

9. Carl Friedrich Keil and Franz Delitzsch, *Commentary on the Old Testament* (Peabody, MA: Hendrickson, 1996), 2:468.

10. David Allan Hubbard, *Hosea: An Introduction and Commentary* (Downers Grove, IL: InterVarsity Press, 1989), 127.

One of the repeated themes throughout the Old Testament is that God is not satisfied through ritual and outward sacrifices which are devoid of love and the heart of worshippers. Hosea adds that the Lord desires *ḥesed* ("covenant love") and "the knowledge of God" (Hosea 6:6). Keil and Delitzsch say "*Chesed* is love to one's neighbour, manifesting itself in righteousness, love which has its roots in the knowledge of God, and therefore is connected with "the knowledge of God" here as in Hosea 4:1.[11] Their definition reminds us that God is always watching the hearts and minds of worshippers. He desires that believers offer their ritual acts of worship with lives that demonstrate covenant faithfulness informed by a true knowledge of God. Empty ritual does not please the Lord. God provides a wake-up call to those who often walk through the motions in their worship but do not think about what they are doing. The Lord will not allow his people to leave their ethical responsibilities and brains at the door as they seek to engage him. Mere emotional or cognitive ritual will not bring people to the throne of grace. God's desire for "the knowledge of God" demonstrates that vertical worship which is not informed about the person and work of God is unacceptable. The knowledge of God in the Semitic culture was never divorced from the application of that knowledge to life. Worshippers need to think about the true God of Scripture rather than fixate on fictional depictions of the Lord in their tradition or imaginations. In addressing their knowledge of God, the Lord is showing that he is interested in having his children understand him as he is revealed in Scripture. The best way to pursue an understanding of God is through a careful study of his Word and its application to life. The Scriptures reveal the character, person, work, and desires of the Lord (2 Tim. 3:16-17). They disclose the truth needed to understand the Creator.

A true knowledge of God always involves the cognitive and ethical. Those who know God strive to live for God according to his Word.

Regarding God's desire for *ḥesed*, the people are called to follow through with obedience to his commands and reflect that obedience in the way they treat others. God will not accept ritual devoid of ethics. Commenting on the ethics of the people, De Andrado states, "Their

---

11. Keil and Delitzsch, 10:66.

deficiency of values (such as knowledge of God) and consequent irreverent behavior make the people's offerings unacceptable to God and count as false worship. Clearly, for Hosea, authentic sacrifice requires not simply a technically proficient offering to God but ritual integrated with ethics."[12] Israel was unfaithful in obeying the covenant that God gave through Moses. The nation broke the covenant of creation God had made with Adam (Hosea 6:7). They did not respect their neighbor nor human life.

There are three interpretations of the phrase "like Adam." Some interpreters view this reference to "Adam" as pointing to a place called Adam, "a place identified with the ancient site Tell ed-Damiyeh on the Jordan River (Josh. 3:16), paralleling Gilead and Shechem (vv. 8, 9) and suggested by 'there' in the second half of the verse."[13] Robertson notes:

> This interpretation is difficult to support. Only pure supposition can provide a concrete occasion of national sin at Adam, located on the Jordan about 12 miles north of Jericho. The account of the rolling back of the Jordan to Adam makes no mention of a sin on Israel's part (cf. Josh. 3:16). Furthermore, this interpretation would seem to require an emendation of the massoretic text.[14]

Calvin translates the word *kĕ'ādām* "as men" rendering verse eight as "They as men have transgressed the covenant ... meaning, that they showed themselves to be men in violating the covenant."[15] The Hebrew does allow for this possible interpretation. A third interpretation is the more traditional view which sees "like Adam" as "an explicit reference to the sin of the first man."[16] Both the second and third interpretations are possible. Either way, one could argue that Adam, the first man, did break the covenant stipulation placed upon

---

12. Paba Nidhani De Andrado, "Ḥesed and Sacrifice: The Prophetic Critique in Hosea," *The Catholic Biblical Quarterly* 78, no. 1 (January 2016): 61.
13. R. C. Sproul, ed., *The Reformation Study Bible: English Standard Version (2015 Edition)* (Orlando, FL: Reformation Trust, 2015), 1504.
14. Robertson, *The Christ of the Covenants*, 22.
15. Jean Calvin, *Calvin's Commentaries*, vol. 13, *The Prophet Hosea* (Grand Rapids, MI: Baker, 1979), 235.
16. Robertson, *The Christ of the Covenants*, 22.

him in the garden of Eden by God thus breaking the covenant of works. Israel in a similar posture of disobedience broke the covenant God made with her in the way she "faithlessly" dealt with God. Robertson aptly summarizes the comparison: "As non-Israelite man has broken the covenant, so Israelite man has broken the covenant."[17] God will deal with those who have broken his covenant. The evildoers in verse eight include priests in Gilead who were no better than wicked criminals who kill and steal. They lay in wait to rob and murder others (Hosea 6:8-9). Hubbard believes this allusion to Gilead is a reference to at least one such plot that involved a *coup d'etat* against Pekahiah by Pekah with fifty men (2 Kings 15:25).[18] The wickedness of Israel was practiced by the very ones who were called to lead Israel to holy living. Wood remarks that what we find in verse nine "is that the very priests, appointed by Jeroboam from 'all sorts of people' (1 Kings 12:31), were robbing and murdering pilgrims."[19] The people of Israel are no better. Hosea calls the city of Gilead "a city of evildoers, tracked with blood" (Hosea 6:8). He further says, "In the house of Israel I have seen a horrible thing; Ephraim's whoredom is there; Israel is defiled" (Hosea 6:10). Although this wickedness was taking place in the nation of Israel, the people believe they are worshiping God through their sacrifices and burnt offerings (Hosea 6:6). The truth is that God warns that they will be judged (Hosea 6:5). The Israelites fool themselves into thinking that their worship was acceptable. They were hypocrites in preaching the Mosaic Law refusing to love their neighbor and the Lord as the Law demanded. Calvin puts it well: "The chief point is, that God desires to be worshipped otherwise than sensual men dream; for they only display their rites, and neglect the spiritual worship of God, which stands in faith and love."[20]

Israel would go on to live in this sinful state, and God would eventually judge the nation. He would allow Assyria to destroy the Northern Kingdom in 722 BC. The Southern Kingdom would not

---

17. Ibid.
18. Hubbard, *Hosea*, 129.
19. Leon J. Wood, *The Expositor's Bible Commentary*, vol. 7, *Hosea*, ed. Frank E. Gaebelein (Grand Rapids: MI: Zondervan, 1985), 195.
20. Calvin, *Calvin's Commentaries*, vol. 13, *The Prophet Hosea* (Grand Rapids, MI: Baker, 1979), 231.

take heed to his warning and would likewise fall to Babylon in 586 BC. God promises to Judah "a harvest" which is a reference to his coming judgment, but this promise also includes a time when the Lord will "restore the fortunes" of his people (Hosea 6:11). That restoration will not occur until "Israel as a nation shall be converted to Christ its Savior."[21] Such words encourage all believers that God will preserve a remnant for himself even when he allows judgment to fall upon his covenant people as a whole. He will be faithful to the faithful. It also encourages believers to repent when they discover that their worship is devoid of *ḥesed* and "the knowledge of God." Christians should not allow their vertical worship of God to be devoid of covenant love for their neighbor before, during, or after corporate worship. The vertical and the horizontal dimension must go together for our worship to be pleasing to God.

Calvin summarizes Hosea's concern that the vertical must be conjoined to the horizontal when he says,

> Faith by itself cannot please God, since it cannot even exist without love to our neighbor; and then, human kindness is not sufficient; for were any one to abstain from doing any injury, and from hurting his brethren in a thing, he might be still a profane man, and a despiser of God; and certainly his kindness would be then of no avail to him.[22]

This same message is preached by Jesus to the Pharisees who criticize the Savior since he expresses love to tax collectors and sinners.

Matthew 9:13

The Pharisees often criticized Jesus during his ministry. Matthew records an encounter with them that enlightens our understanding of what pleases God. Jesus sees a man named Matthew who is a tax collector sitting at his tax booth. He calls Matthew to follow him, and he becomes Jesus' disciple (Matt. 9:9). It appears that Jesus then goes

---

21. Keil and Delitzsch, 10:68.
22. Calvin, *Calvin's Commentaries*, vol. 13, *The Prophet Hosea* (Grand Rapids, MI: Baker, 1979), 231.

to Matthew's house to eat with him. In the first century "To share a meal was a sign of intimacy."[23] Many tax collectors and sinners go to Matthew's house to eat with Jesus and the disciples (Matt. 9:11). The Pharisees are disturbed at this association for they often seek to stay away from such people. They pride themselves on maintaining moral purity by avoiding sinners and people they consider spiritually unclean.[24] Tax collectors were viewed as some of the vilest sinners especially since they worked for the Romans. Ottenheijm remarks that they "were little loved due to the heavy burden of Roman taxes and the handling of coins that depicted the emperor."[25] Tax collectors were often hated since they were notorious for getting rich from collecting more money from the people than Roman taxes demanded.

Jesus responds to the Pharisees by disagreeing with their revulsion to his eating with sinners and tax collectors. The adversative *de* (but) that begins verse 12 sets Jesus "over against his Pharisaic critics."[26] He reminds them that "Those who are well have no need of a physician, but those who are sick" (Matt. 9:12). Considering the comparison to a physician, France points out that "A healer must get his hands dirty."[27] In other words, they had no reason to complain about his close association with sinners since he came to heal such people, and therefore, he was fulfilling his holy mission to reach them. The sick are not only the physically ill but also those who are soul sick with sin. Sinners need the healing grace of the gospel. Instead of despising such people, Jesus reaches out to them with love and grace. He seeks to heal them spiritually. Jesus then corrects the Pharisee's faulty perspective by telling them that what he is doing is in perfect accord with the teaching of the prophets. He tells them to, "Go and learn what this means, 'I desire mercy, and not sacrifice.' For I came not to call the righteous, but sinners" (Matt. 9:13). This quote is from Hosea 6:6.

---

23. R T. France, *The Gospel According to Matthew: An Introduction and Commentary* (Leicester, England: Inter-Varsity Press, 1987), 167.
24. John Nolland, *The Gospel of Matthew: A Commentary on the Greek Text* (Grand Rapids, MI: W.B. Eerdmans, 2005), 386.
25. Eric Ottenheijm, "The shared meal—a therapeutical device: the function and meaning of Hos 6:6 in Matt 9:10-13," *Novum Testamentum* 53, no. 1 (2011): 7.
26. Leon Morris, *The Gospel According to Matthew* (Grand Rapids, MI: Eerdmans, 1992), 221.
27. France, *The Gospel According to Matthew*, 168.

Jesus is saying that they have misread the Old Testament. Like the ungodly priests who are exposed by Hosea, they think that by their adherence to their traditions and rituals they are making themselves pure before God. They incorrectly misinterpret the meaning of biblical mercy. Edin remarks, "In the context of Hosea, the call for mercy rather than sacrifice is a call for righteousness that exceeds standard religious piety."[28] The Pharisees completely misinterpret the meaning of *ḥesed* (mercy) as expressed in Hosea 6:6. Calvin understands the horizontal requirement taught by Hosea which Jesus models. He states, "In the word *mercy*, note the synechote: the Prophet embraces under one part all that we owe to our brothers in humanity."[29]

Just like the priests and people of Israel, the Pharisees think they can worship God through meticulous attention to their rituals without showing love to their neighbors. They believe that they please God with their commitment to their traditions while neglecting and abusing their neighbors in Israel. The absence of covenant love for their neighbor makes their ritual null and void. It does not obtain God's favor nor his approval. The Pharisees "failed to recognize the connection between law observance and mercy."[30] Jesus, on the other hand, demonstrated true *ḥesed*. The Greek word used by Matthew for "mercy" is *eleos*. It is translated as, "kindness or concern expressed for someone in need, mercy, compassion, pity, clemency."[31] Jesus rightly understands that covenant faithfulness to God includes mercy for one's neighbor, even sinners, and tax collectors. This understanding of covenant faithfulness is a true "knowledge of God" (Hosea 6:6). Edin concludes: "Demonstrating both mercy and faithfulness, Jesus loves the way God loves, and Jesus loves the way Hosea announces that God intends God's people to love."[32]

How does this understanding relate to our discussion about the vertical and horizontal dimensions of worship? It drives us to ask some

---

28. Mary Hinkle, "Learning What Righteousness Means: Hosea 6:6 and the Ethic of Mercy in Matthew's Gospel," *Word & World* 18, no. 4 (September 1998): 358.

29. John Calvin, *Calvin's New Testament Commentaries*, ed. David W. Torrance and Thomas F. Torrance, trans. A. W. Morrison (Grand Rapids, MI: Eerdmans, 1989), 1:265.

30. Hinkle, "Learning What Righteousness Means," 360.

31. *A Greek-English Lexicon of the New Testament and Other Early Christian Literature*, 3rd ed. (Chicago: University of Chicago Press, 2000), s.v. "ἔλεος."

32. Hinkle, "Learning What Righteousness Means," 362.

key questions. How can we claim to worship the Lord God with a true knowledge of God as Hosea demands if we do not show grace, affection, and love for our neighbors in our worship services and our community? How can we expect to truly meet with God in worship when we despise, reject, or ignore our neighbor? It is easy for Christians to become ingrown in their attitudes toward others but forget the importance of reaching sinners who need the grace of God offered in the gospel. Christ's words to the Pharisees expand upon Hosea's teaching to remind the church to show love to unbelievers outside the church and those who attend their worship services. Jesus' example encourages Christians to invite unbelievers to their services so that they might experience the healing that only God can provide through Christ. Jesus demonstrates true covenant love and shows believers how they should strive to bring the gospel to sinners. Carson remarks, "His mission was characterized by grace, a pursuit of the lost, of sinners."[33] His model of mercy has profound implications for how we should conduct our worship services. Christ was interested in communicating the message of the gospel to sinners. Matthew Henry points out how important this work was to Jesus in his understanding of mercy. He remarks, "Christ's conversing with sinners is here called mercy: to promote the conversion of souls is the greatest act of mercy imaginable; it is saving a soul from death."[34]

As church leaders lead their people in worship, they should ask some important questions in their preparations. Are we striving to bring those in attendance to Christ? Are we seeking to show the mercy of God to sinners who need the grace of God or are we coldly focused upon running through established rituals and traditions? Jesus also sets the tone for our worship and interaction with people. He teaches us that we should worship the Lord, not as arrogant people who believe we are better than lowly sinners but people who likewise need God's grace and mercy because we are saved sinners by God's grace. We discover an attitude of humility in the ministry of Jesus. Unlike Christ in his moral perfection, Christian leaders in the church must realize that they are sinners who need the healing work of the Great Physician.

---

33. D. A. Carson, "Matthew," (Grand Rapids, MI: Zondervan, 1984), 8:225.
34. Matthew Henry, *Matthew Henry's Commentary on the Whole Bible: Complete and Unabridged in One Volume* (Peabody: Hendrickson, 1994), 1655.

Both believers and nonbelievers require the healing that only the Savior can provide.

It is also important to note that as Jesus reaches out to sinners, he does not skip over the truths of the Bible that describe the sinful condition of people. The Savior never excluded the topic of sin from the context of the gospel. He talked with people about their need for deliverance from sin so that they would understand their need for grace and mercy through the gospel (Matt. 1:21). Even in this passage, Jesus points out that the people are "sick" (Matt. 9:12) and "sinners" (Matt. 9:13). His model encourages Christians today to graciously show sinners that they need to go to the Savior who alone can heal their sin sickness. For people to be saved and sanctified, they must be told they need the mercy of God. Believers have drunk from the well of life and should offer Jesus, the one who has living water (John 4:14). Such truth reflects a true "knowledge of God" as Hosea puts it (Hosea 6:6). Calvin reminds us of the importance of this knowledge of God when he says, "We must get this into our heads, that faith and spiritual devotion are of themselves pleasing to God, and charity and the claims of humanity towards our neighbors are demanded on their own right, but sacrifices are nothing but auxiliary, as they say, deserving no reward or position unless they have a firm basis in truth."[35] Genuine knowledge of God will manifest itself through Christian love toward our neighbor. We see this love clearly demonstrated by Jesus when he meets with sinners and tax collectors. There is no favoritism with Christ. When believers gain a right understanding of Jesus' perspective of Hosea 6:6, they will exhibit covenant love toward others in worship. The knowledge of God and the Lord Jesus Christ should enrich our worship of the Lord. It should inform our attitudes toward our neighbors. Worship requires both love for God and mercy toward our neighbors. The liturgical attitudes and practices of believers should flow from hearts that desire to show mercy to others because they are in communion with the God who shows them mercy. Mercy is always an expression of love for our neighbor because we have been loved by God. It is deeply rooted in our love of God. Jesus speaks about this fact when he addresses a question about the Law.

---

35. Calvin, *Calvin's New Testament Commentaries*, 1:265.

Matthew 22:36-40

The Lord Jesus Christ was fully aware of the teaching of the Old Testament regarding God's commands. He knew that the Ten Commandments represented the essence of the Law. After Christ had astonished the crowds in answering a difficult question by the Sadducees, a Pharisee and "lawyer" of biblical law asked him a question: "Teacher, which is the great commandment in the Law?" (Matt. 22:36). The Greek word used in verse thirty-five for "lawyer" is *nomikos* which is used in the New Testament "always of those expert in Mosaic law."[36] The question seems to anticipate a one-directional answer. Nolland views this encounter as an attempt by the Pharisees to entrap Jesus. He notes, "Their hope is to put Jesus under pressure yet again, with a view to exposing his inadequacy in some way or other.[37] Considering the general attitude of the Pharisees in the Gospels, this lawyer likely expected an upward vertical response such as, "Love God with your whole being" or something similar. Jesus rather says, "You shall love the Lord your God with all your heart and with all your soul and with all your mind" (v. 37) and "You shall love your neighbor as yourself" (v. 38). Carson states, "From the viewpoint of biblical anthropology, 'heart,' 'soul,' and 'mind' (v. 37) are not mutually exclusive but overlapping categories, together demanding our love for God to come from our whole person, our every faculty and capacity."[38] Jesus' answer reveals that he would not give a one-directional answer. He fundamentally combines Deuteronomy 6:5 with a modified verse from Leviticus 19:18. France reminds us of the familiarity of Deuteronomy 6:5 among the Pharisees. He states that "Deuteronomy 6:4-9, from which this quotation is taken, was repeated twice daily by pious Jews as the opening of the Shema."[39] The Messiah teaches a view that fits with the bi-directional structure of the Ten Commandments. Hendricksen remarks, "Jesus here teaches that the whole duty of man, the whole moral-spiritual law, can be summed up

---

36. *A Greek-English Lexicon of the New Testament*, s.v. "νομικός."
37. Nolland, *Matthew*, 910.
38. Carson, *Matthew*, 8:464.
39. France, *Matthew*, 319.

in one word: *love*."⁴⁰ The Pharisees were quite comfortable focusing their sole attention on God (a vertical posture) while ignoring or refusing to show love to their fellow man (Matt. 9:11; 23:4, 15, 23, 34-35). This was an attitude that Jesus would not tolerate, nor would his heavenly father accept in daily life nor in worship.

Christ did not separate the calling to love both God and man in his understanding of the Law. He tells this Pharisee that the answer to his question is to love both God and his neighbor (Matt. 22:37, 39). The Savior points out that the calling to love God "is the great and first commandment" (Matt. 22:37). Jesus obviously knew that the commandments structurally prioritized the vertical love we should show to God (e.g., Exod. 20:3-11). The priority that we love God was essential for man's calling to love his neighbor. Without God, there is no reason to love others. Jesus knew that a biblical love of God is needed for a proper response toward other human beings. The Savior also does not separate this command from the calling to love our neighbor. As we ponder this calling, it is important to understand that Christ considered the neighbor to include not only one's fellow Israelite but also one's enemy (Matt. 5:43-47). Jesus proclaims the importance of the command to love others as ourselves by saying, "And a second is like it" (Matt. 22:39a). He elevates the command to love our neighbor to the status of loving God. Jesus adds that you should love your neighbor "as yourself." He surely knew about the horizontal emphasis of the second tablet of the Decalogue (Lev. 19:18), but he enlightens our understanding with the phrase "as yourself." This added phrase causes us to pause and contemplate how deeply personal is the calling to love our neighbor.

When we think about loving others, it is a challenge to consider how we should express love to our neighbor with the same intensity and love that we show daily to ourselves. Our love for our neighbor must take the same priority as caring for our daily physical, mental, and spiritual needs. The phrase "as yourself" reminds us that our treatment of and attitude toward others should always be informed by our constant desire to take care of ourselves. This perspective would by

---

40. William Hendriksen, *Exposition of the Gospel According to Matthew* (Grand Rapids: MI: Baker, 1973), 809.

necessity lead us to do and seek what is best for our neighbor rather than using or abusing them as the Ten Commandments forbid. Jesus will not allow the Pharisees nor anyone to treat the horizontal command to love others with contempt just because it is not the "great and first commandment." Even though it follows the first command, it must accompany that command. Hendricksen recognizes this fact when he says, "this love toward the neighbor, who is God's image-bearer, flows forth from the love toward God (1 John 4:21; see also Matt. 5:43, 7:12, 19:19)".[41] The Lord places this holy command to love our neighbor on par with the command to love God. It is so important that these two commands go together that Jesus declares, "On these two commandments depend all the Law and the Prophets" (Matt. 22:40). He understands them as two great pillars that hold up all biblical morality. Without conjoining them, the Law and the message of the prophets come crashing down. Acceptance of their unity and application are essential to pleasing God. Reflecting upon the importance of recognizing the unity of both commands Trueblood states,

> The love of God is of transcendent importance, but if it is not associated with the practical obligations to our fellow men, it is inevitably self-centered. The cultivation of inner spiritual life without constant social concern constitutes a heresy. On the other hand, the love of one's neighbor, without grounding in the love of God, easily becomes mere philanthropy and finally is superficial secularism. The only hope lies in involving both priorities in one living context. We must keep the roots and the fruit of our faith together, because they need each other."[42]

Jesus' use of the word "depend" (v. 40) conveys this truth. The question arises in light of this project: "What do these commands have to do with worship?" The answer is everything. These commands, which summarize the Law of God, cannot be limited to life before and after corporate worship. They should also be applied during our times of worship. The importance of combining the love of God and our

---

41. Hendriksen, *Matthew*, 810.
42. Elton Trueblood, *Confronting Christ* (New York: Harper and Brothers, 1960), 126.

neighbor is further described by Calvin: "Every man is self-centered—love for our neighbor will never flourish unless the love of God begins to reign. Love is a mercenary thing when the children of this world are attached to each other for the advantage each wants to gain. On the other hand, the love of God cannot reign without breeding a brotherly affection among men."[43] When we worship, we must come to God with all our heart, soul, and mind. We should seek him with our full devotion, but we must also love our neighbor as ourselves in the process. It is essential that we express our affection for God in a way that reflects consideration and care about those joining us in worship. We need to care about their souls, their progress in the faith, and their lives. Just as we seek comfort, compassion, the truth, peace, mercy, grace, change, salvation, and sanctification through our God, we should likewise seek the same for our neighbor. This perspective will affect our thoughts and actions toward our neighbors as we strive to worship God with them. We will consider at the end of this project what loving our neighbors may look like in our services, but for now, we must recognize the inseparable connection of the vertical with the horizontal. The very idea that the horizontal dimension is necessitated by Christ's teaching in this passage should open new avenues of discussion and consideration about how we can implement the horizontal dimension in our weekly worship services. It is not seeker-driven but rather God-driven when we strive to love our neighbor because it is God who commands us to show such love. This message of loving others is reinforced in the teaching of the apostle John.

John 13:31-35; John 15:12-17; 1 John 4:7-21

Many have described the apostle John as "the apostle of love" and for good reason. The apostle often combines the concept of loving God with loving others. There are numerous key Scriptures that John provides which reinforce this idea. One key passage is John 13:31-35 where Jesus teaches his disciples a "new command." The Savior gives this command in the upper room immediately after Judas left to do his treachery (v. 31). Christ addresses the disciples as "Little children" and

---

43. Calvin, *Calvin's New Testament Commentaries*, 3:36-37.

then gives his "new command" (vv. 33-34). He says, "A new command I give to you, that you love one another: just as I have loved you, you also are to love one another" (v. 34). This command is rooted in Jesus' understanding of the Law of God (Deut. 6:5; Lev. 19:18) and his future suffering on the cross. Morris comments, "The new thing appears to be the mutual affection that Christians have for one another on account of Christ's great love for them."[44] Carson adds,

> The new command is therefore not only the obligation of the new covenant community to respond to the God who has loved them and redeemed them by the oblation of his Son, and their response to his gracious election which constituted them his people, it is a privilege which, rightly lived out, proclaims the true God before a watching world. That is why Jesus ends his injunction with the words, *All men will know that you are my disciples, if you love one another.* Orthodoxy without principial obedience to this characteristic command of the new covenant is merely so much humbug.[45]

Jesus teaches that this command to love one another should be inseparably intertwined with his disciples' love of God. He further describes how this "love" is tied to their relationship with him. Christ says, "By this all people will know that you are my disciples, if you have love for one another" (v. 35). In other words, the world will know that you are a follower of Jesus by the way you show love to one another as evidence of your claim to know Christ. Jesus clearly teaches that his disciples' horizontal love toward one another will demonstrate the reality of their vertical love for him. The two dimensions (the vertical and the horizontal) must go together in the lives of Jesus' disciples. He later conveys a similar truth to the apostles in his instruction about the true vine (John 15:1-17).

Using the analogy of a vine, the Savior describes himself as the vine and the disciples as the branches (John 15:5). Commenting on the

---

44. Leon Morris, *The Gospel According to John: The English Text with Introduction, Exposition and Notes* (Grand Rapids: MI: Eerdmans, 1971), 633.
45. D. A. Carson, *The Gospel According to John* (Leicester, England: Inter-Varsity Press, 1991), 485.

context of the passage, Bruce notes that "This paragraph (verse 12-17) is an expansion of the new commandment of John 13:34 f; it begins and ends with the injunction to love one another."[46] Jesus calls his disciples to abide in him as the vine. He notes that when they obey his commands, their obedience indicates that they abide in him which is bearing fruit (vv. 7-10). He expresses the importance that his disciples bear fruit. Peterson recognizes that "The fruit of which he speaks is obedience to his commands (v. 10) and love for other believers (vv. 12-14)."[47] Many interpreters believe the fruit refers to witnessing the gospel (John 4:36). Carson sees the fruit as referring to "new converts."[48] Regarding verse sixteen, Morris comments, "In this place, the command to 'go' and bear fruit seems to show that winning people is at least partly what is meant. There would seem no point in their 'going' unless it was to be where people are and to do something about their lostness."[49] When we express love for Christ and choose to love that which he loves, we cannot help but seek to bring souls into the kingdom through the gospel. Witnessing was a key mission that Jesus gave his disciples (Matt. 4:19; Acts 1:8). When true believers worship God, they will express this same concern for others who join them in worship and those in need of Christ absent from worship.

For Christians to be fruitful in their witnessing and growth in Christian character, they must abide in Christ. Sproul remarks, "As Christians, we will bear fruit, but it will vary in degree. The closer we stay to Christ, the more fruit we will bear. The more we wander out from the center and neglect the means of grace that He has given to us, the less fruit we will produce."[50] Obedience to Christ demonstrates that believers abide in the love of Christ (v. 10). In verse twelve, Jesus repeats his earlier new command (John 13:34) but adds another reason for the disciples to love one another. He says, "love one another as I have loved you" (v. 12). These are profound words that call the disciples to express the sacrificial love that Jesus would demonstrate in

---

46. F. F. Bruce, *The Gospel of John* (Grand Rapids, MI: Eerdmans, 1994), 311.

47. Robert A. Peterson, *Getting to Know John's Gospel: A Fresh Look at Its Main Ideas* (Phillipsburg, NJ: Presbyterian and Reformed Pub. Co., 1989), 11.

48. Carson, *The Gospel According to John*, 523.

49. Leon Morris, *Expository Reflections on the Gospel of John* (Grand Rapids, MI: Baker, 1988), 526.

50. R. C. Sproul, *John* (Lake Mary, FL: Reformation Trust Pub., 2009), 288.

his death on the cross. These words ground their call to love one another (the horizontal) in Jesus' love for them (the vertical). In other words, the gracious vertical saving love of the Messiah should motivate Christians in their horizontal treatment of one another.

Jesus later reminds his disciples that their relationship with him occurred through God's sovereign choice. He says, "You did not choose me, but I chose you and appointed you that you should go and bear fruit ..." (v. 16). In recalling this gracious choice by Christ, the disciples learn that their calling to love one another was founded upon the unilateral gracious choice of Christ. Therefore, their call to love others was founded upon the vertical choice of the God-man Jesus. Believers should always recall the loving choice of Christ as they relate to one another. The Savior through his loving grace reached out to them, and they should likewise reach out to one another in love. We should also remember that Jesus did not choose perfect people but sinners to be his disciples. His love was faithful even though they would betray and abandon him at his arrest and during his crucifixion. Hendricksen puts it well: "Not only do we love *him* because he first loved us, but we also love *one another* because he first loved us. Our love for one another is an extension of Christ's love for us."[51] Jesus reinforces the importance of his teaching about love by repeating his earlier words: "These things I command you, so that you will love one another" (v. 17). If the disciples did not grasp his message at first, Jesus makes sure they fully understand that love for one another is the whole point of his commands. This lesson is something the Pharisees did not understand nor embrace in their teaching of the Law of God. Jesus, on the other hand, taught that obedience to his commandments is evidence of abiding in him (vv. 10, 14) and will produce Biblical love between believers. Therefore, the Savior understands that abiding in his and his Father's love (v. 10) should motivate his disciples to love one another (i.e., the vertical inevitably will produce the horizontal). This message of loving others is also repeated in 1 John.

The apostle John builds upon the teaching of Christ in 1 John 4:7-22. He links the vertical with the horizontal in noting that "whoever

---

51. William Hendriksen, *Exposition of the Gospel According to John* (Grand Rapid, MI: Baker, 1954), 309.

loves has been born of God and knows God" (v. 7). The apostle understands that love for our brothers must accompany our love of God. These two realities are inseparable. John also reveals the negative consequence if we do not love our brothers. He says, "Anyone who does not love does not know God, because God is love" (v. 8). In other words, we can claim to love God through our profession of faith or outward display of religiosity, but if we do not show love for our brothers, the truth is that we do not love God. Such a disconnect would demonstrate that we are false Christians. The phrase "God is love" (cf. 16) reminds us that our calling to love both God and our brothers is established in the nature of God. Those who abide in God will love their brothers because they are being transformed by their God of love. Marshall writes, "A person cannot come into a real relationship with a loving God without being transformed into a loving person."[52] The apostle John's words are serious and convicting. We need to hear them often today in the church, especially as they pertain to our corporate worship of God. Many people go to corporate worship claiming to love God in their vertical approach to God, but in their hearts, they hate their fellow believers or care little about them. Their worship is a mere show and lacks the spiritual substance the Lord demands. John provides the basis for why we should show love for our brothers. He grounds brotherly love in the love of God which is demonstrated in the person and work of Christ on the cross (vv. 9-11). Jesus brings together both our love for God and others just as Stott states: "The divine-human person of Jesus Christ, God's love for us, and our love for God and neighbor cannot be separated."[53] The grace of God provided in Christ and his saving work should motivate all Christians to love one another (v. 10). Drawing upon Jesus' teaching in the Upper Room about abiding in the vine, John proclaims that loving our brothers is an evidence of God abiding in us (v. 12). Calvin says, "wherever God abides, love must also flourish."[54]

In verse thirteen the apostle John points out that the presence of God's Spirit in believers will produce evidence that they abide in God.

---

52. I. Howard Marshall, *The Epistles of John* (Grand Rapids: MI: Eerdmans, 1978), 212.
53. John R. W. Stott, *The Letters of John: an Introduction and Commentary*, 2nd ed. (Leicester, England: Inter-Varsity Press, 1988), 168.
54. Calvin, *Calvin's New Testament Commentaries*, 5:294.

Stott describes the importance of the Spirit in enabling Christians to express Biblical love. He says, "Only the Holy Spirit can enlighten our minds to believe in Jesus and warm our hearts to love God and each other. So believing and loving are evidence that his Spirit is at work with us."[55] The apostle John sees these truths cemented in the person and work of Christ, the Savior of the world (vv. 14-15). For John, love for others is evidence that God abides in believers and they in him (v. 16). This reality of love for their brothers should give God's children confidence that they will not experience God's future judgment (vv. 17-18). Their love and confidence are based on God's sovereign and unconditional grace: "We love because he first loved us" (v. 19; cf. v. 10). John will not tolerate those who claim to be Christians and say they love God but yet they hate their brother. He calls them liars and concludes that they "cannot love God..." (v. 20). This is a convicting conclusion for those today who claim to love God in their worship while they hate their brethren in their hearts. Hate of our brothers should be understood within the context of what John says earlier. He states, "But if anyone has the world's goods and sees his brother in need, yet closes his heart against him, how does God's love abide in him?" (1 John 3:17). When we claim to love God in our worship but care little or nothing about the needs of our brothers who worship with us, how can we claim to truly worship God? The horizontal dimension must be present in our expressions of love toward God. Otherwise, our vertical efforts to meet with God are hypocritical and empty. Marshall warns us of the potential danger of settling for a pseudo-love for God. He states, "It is easy to have a kind of love for God which does not recognize the obligation to love one another."[56] Love for our brother must accompany real love for our loving God. Recalling the wisdom of Jesus, John closes his teaching about loving our brothers with these words: "And this commandment we have from him: whoever loves God must also love his brother" (1 John 4:21). There can be no doubt—Jesus' commandment is non-negotiable. In other words, our claim to love God (the vertical) must always include love for our brothers (the horizontal) and vice versa.

---

55. Stott, *The Letters of John: an Introduction and Commentary*, 171.
56. Marshall, *The Epistles of John*, 226.

Not only does John teach us about loving our neighbor, but the apostle Paul also addresses this topic in his first epistle to the Corinthians.

1 Corinthians 10:31-11:1

One of the foundational doctrines of Reformed theology is the view that we should glorify God. This important doctrine is highlighted in the first question and answer of the Westminster Shorter Catechism: "What is the chief end of man? Man's chief end is to glorify God and to enjoy him forever."[57] Many people often misunderstand this doctrine about how we should worship God in our services. First Corinthians 10:31-11:1 provides insights into the complementary relationship between the vertical and the horizontal as we seek to glorify God. In the Old Testament, the Hebrew word frequently used to refer to the glory of God is *kabōd* which is translated as "glory." The word refers to the honor, splendor, and magnificence of God.[58] It calls for great respect for God. Numerous Bible passages support the practice of glorifying God but perhaps the most often cited is 1 Corinthians 10:31: "So, whether you eat or drink, or whatever you do, do all to the glory of God." The Greek word used here for glory is *doxan*. The root *doxa* refers to "honor as enhancement or recognition of status or performance, fame, recognition, renown, honor, prestige."[59] When this verse is cited to speak about worship, most people think of it as solely addressing the vertical dimension with little attention to the horizontal. Of course, Paul's words encourage Christians to honor the Lord vertically since there is no one greater than God nor is there anyone more worthy of glory. It is right to think of God in this fashion when we worship corporately, but that is not all that we should contemplate. Even Paul in this passage has horizontal concerns as he utters these words. Fee draws our attention to Paul's horizontal concerns when he states, "He is currently addressing the question of conduct in nonessential matters, which began with the overarching principle that the Christian does not seek her/his own

---

57. WSC Q. 1.
58. *A Concise Hebrew and Aramaic Lexicon of the Old Testament*, "s.v. "כָּבוֹד."
59. *A Greek-English Lexicon of the New Testament*, s.v. "δόξα."

good but that of one's neighbor (vv. 23-24)."[60] Right after Paul calls believers to do all for God's glory, he addresses the attitude believers should have toward their neighbor: "Give no offense to Jews or to Greeks or to the church of God, just as I try to please everyone in everything I do, not seeking my own advantage, but that of many, that they may be saved" (1 Cor. 10:32-33). Notice that as Paul encourages believers to glorify God, he is also calling them to think about others horizontally by his admonition (v. 32) and example (v. 33). The apostle is ultimately concerned "that they may be saved" (1 Cor. 10:33). As he ponders glorifying God, the thought of others potentially coming to Christ is on his mind and in his heart. His call to "Give no offense to Jews or to Greeks or to the church of God" is not an imperative to compromise the gospel with a desire to sinfully please men. Fee comments, "Paul's concern is not that he himself be pleasing to them, but that his conduct be such that he may not stand in the way of their being saved."[61] The apostle provides the church with a proper perspective in his evangelistic concerns as he seeks to glorify God. His horizontal sensitivity to the lost is an expression of his passion for glorifying God in his witness. Paul's desire to bring others to Christ clearly presents a horizontal thrust that the apostle cannot decouple from his understanding of how to glorify God. The proclamation and the progress of the gospel inform his understanding of how to glorify the Lord. For the apostle, the horizontal is never far from the vertical. Paul's evangelistic orientation should not be surprising to us since he often expressed his drive for preaching the gospel (Rom. 1:15-17, 15:20; 1 Cor. 1:17, 23). Lest we dismiss Paul's teaching, the apostle closes his argument with a command for us to be imitators of him and Christ (1 Cor. 11:1). This imperative reinforces Paul's understanding of glorifying God primarily with an evangelistic goal. He does not permit the church to limit this perspective to himself alone. He encourages all believers to glorify God in a manner that follows his example. This calling must be applied to "whatever you do" (1 Cor. 11:31) which would surely include the practice of corporate worship. For Paul, seeking to glorify God in worship without a serious

---

60. Gordon D. Fee, *The First Epistle to the Corinthians* (Grand Rapids, MI: W.B. Eerdmans, 1987), 488.

61. Fee, *The First Epistle to the Corinthians*, 490.

evangelistic horizontal consideration of unbelievers in the service would be inappropriate.

It is easy to dismiss the horizontal and focus upon the vertical as we think about giving glory to God, but Paul has taught us that this is a mistake. However, when we ponder the idea of glorifying God, we often neglect this question: "If we seek to honor God in our worship, does God truly care what we think about others?" Better yet, "Does glorifying God include consideration of our neighbor?" Paul has shown in this passage that the answer to both questions is definitely yes. As we think more deeply about what it means to glorify God in our corporate worship, we need to ask, "What is God's disposition toward those attending the service?" God, throughout the Bible, is very mindful of human beings, especially those who come to corporate worship (John 4:23). We discover God's loving care for people when he commends the practice of hospitality within the body of Christ (Rom. 12:13; Titus 1:8; 1 Pet. 4:8-9). The Greek word *philozenoi* translated as "hospitality" literally means "love of strangers."[62] It demonstrates God's gracious disposition toward visiting strangers and his expectation that his people express love toward them. He is a deeply caring and loving God who is concerned about the lives of his people and the lost. The Creator is concerned for the salvation of unbelievers (2 Pet. 3:9) and the sanctification of his people (1 Thess. 4:3). He has, after all, decided to send his precious one and only Son Jesus to save humanity from their sins and eternal judgment (John 3:16). The Lord is also concerned about the needs of those attending worship. Yahweh is a compassionate God who wishes to comfort and bless his people (1 Pet. 5:7). He desires that people repent of their sins and come to him through Christ alone. We should also consider the fact that these concerns of the Father are the same concerns of the Son and Holy Spirit who are one with the Father (John 10:30; 1 Cor. 12:4-6; Eph. 4:4-6). If we decide to only focus on praising and honoring God with little to no concern for those sitting in the pews beside us, some of whom are heading to hell, backsliding, struggling in the faith, or simply needing encouragement, would that be honoring

---

62. M.J. Selman, "Hospitality," in *New Bible Dictionary*, 2nd ed., ed. J.D Douglas and N. Hillyer (Wheaton, IL: Tyndale, 1982).

our God who cares for them? If God cares about people attending the service, should not his people also care about their fellow worshippers as well? When we seek to glorify God, we should also think about what pleases him.

Emulating God's affections toward others is important. He commands Christians to imitate him (Eph. 5:1). What brings God pleasure? It pleases the Lord when we are biblically concerned about others' needs, salvation, and sanctification. As Paul encourages the believers at Corinth to glorify God and think about others, he calls them to follow his example as he seeks to follow Christ (11:1). Paul is a Christian leader who carefully considers whether his choices will either promote the salvation of others or get in the way of their spiritual progress. Christians who plan and attend worship in the church should follow the humble example of Paul. How often do people choose to do something in the worship service with little thought about how it will affect the sanctification and salvation of others in attendance? How frequently do those in corporate worship complain because they are more concerned about their personal preferences rather than the souls of those around them? We are quick to choose our preferences and styles with little missionary forethought or concern. It is easy to forget about God's desires in the way we worship with others. With such attitudes, we are not following Paul's gracious example, but rather giving in to our selfish desires and personal preferences. We could care less whether our preferences "give ... offense" to others (1 Cor. 10:32). Paul, however, seeks to follow the humble pattern of Christ in "placing the welfare of *'the other'* before that of oneself."[63] Unlike Paul, many Christians today use the excuse that they are seeking to follow God with their vertical focus, but actually, God and his desires are farther away from our choices than we are willing to admit. The apostle exhorts believers to look to the life, ministry, and desires of the God-man Jesus Christ as they strive to glorify God. In context, Paul is calling the church to glorify God in a way that models the life and heart of Christ as they express concern and love for one another (1 Cor. 11:1). The apostle is

---

63. Anthony C. Thiselton, *The First Epistle to the Corinthians: A Commentary On the Greek Text* (Grand Rapids, MI: W.B. Eerdmans, 2000), 796.

evangelistically concerned as he seeks to glorify God because Christ is also concerned that people be saved. This example of Paul encourages a biblical balance between the vertical and the horizontal. It expresses Paul's concern that souls "be saved" through Christ. The vertical informs the horizontal. If we are to glorify God in everything we do (1 Cor. 10:31), certainly we should strive to think about and treat others in a way that gives honor to our God even in our worship services. To do otherwise would dishonor his name and reputation as we claim the name of Christ. If we dismiss or minimize our horizontal concerns for others in corporate worship, this surely would dishonor the life and example of Jesus. It brings no true glory to God if we are not thinking about the spiritual and physical welfare of those in the pew beside us. At the heart of concern for others is biblical love for our neighbor. Regarding properly glorifying the Lord in worship with love, let us consider Paul's message on the chief importance of love.

1 Corinthians 13

In properly discerning the Lord's body (1 Cor. 11:29, 33) and showing due respect to every member in the church, Paul presents "the more excellent way" (1 Cor. 12:31). The apostle reminds the church that the best way they can express care for one another is to love one another. He addresses some of the practices witnessed in the worship services of the Corinthian church such as speaking in tongues and prophecy (1 Cor. 13:1; cf. 1 Cor. 14). Paul's emphasis on love in 1 Corinthians 13 prepares us for his teaching in 1 Corinthians 14 about how members of the church should treat one another in their services. His emphasis on the edification (i.e., horizontal dimension) of the body in 1 Corinthians 14 requires chapter thirteen's focus on love as the foundational principle for edification to become a reality in corporate worship. The reason the Corinthians were bypassing mutual edification in their worship was that they did not value their calling to love one another. They placed more importance on their own individual and dramatic experiences over their horizontal responsibility to love one another. The Greek word that Paul uses for love is *agapēn*. Thiselton remarks that it "denotes above all a *stance* or *attitude* which shows itself *in acts of will* as *regard, respect, and concern for the welfare of the other*. It is therefore profoundly *christological*, for *the cross* is the paradigm case of the act of *will* and *stance* which *places welfare of others above the interests of the self* [emphasis added by the author]."[64] Love is the most important character quality that believers can have toward their neighbor. Paul elsewhere teaches that it is the first fruit of the Holy Spirit (Gal. 5:22). Carson notes that chapter thirteen "emphasizes love so strongly that it is not hard to believe that the Corinthian church was singularly lacking in this commodity, again doubtless owing to factionalism."[65] The Corinthians seemed to have a serious problem with arrogance and a sense of spiritual superiority which contributed to divisions in the church. The apostle seeks to humble the arrogant before the Lord. One thing that they do not appear to cherish is "love." Paul writes that they may demonstrate many amazing gifts and powers reflective of a vertical relationship with God. If they could speak in tongues, utter prophecies, understand mysteries and knowledge, exhibit great faith, give away all they had, and even suffer martyrdom by being burned to death but lack love they would "… gain nothing" (1 Cor. 13:1-3). In other words, unless they express love to their neighbor their vertical posturing and claim to possess various powers are worthless and do not impress God. They can speak a thousand tongues and utter even more prophecies, but if they have not love for one another, their worship is meaningless to God. Religion without love is repugnant to God as Calvin articulates, "For without it the fairness of all virtues is mere veneer, it is empty jangling, it is not worth a straw, in short it is rank and offensive."[66] Paul goes on to describe what biblical love looks like (vv. 4-7) and proclaims its lasting quality saying "Love never ends" (v. 8). Lest we think there is something better than biblical love, the apostle concludes his discussion with "So now faith, hope, and love abide, these three; but the greatest of these is love" (1 Cor. 13:13).

This message about the importance of love repeats the teaching of Jesus in John 13:35 where he tells his followers that their love for one

---

64. Thiselton, *The First Epistle to the Corinthians*, 1035.
65. D. A. Carson, *Showing the Spirit: A Theological Exposition of 1 Corinthians 12-14* (Grand Rapids, MI: Baker, 1987), 9.
66. Calvin, *Calvin's New Testament Commentaries*, 9:276.

another will demonstrate to the world that they are his disciples. Paul elevates love above other gifts. Pratt reiterates this point when he writes, "The command to love one another is the second most important law of Scripture. It is no wonder Paul argued that without love for others all spiritual gifts are worthless."[67] Love was essential to the very health and definition of the body of Christ. Paul's instruction about love provides the church with a firm basis to encourage believers today to demonstrate and show love toward others when they attend corporate worship. The definition of love that Paul gives in verses 4-7 establishes practical considerations for how Christians should worship with one another. There is no room for being untruthful, manipulative, divisive, arrogant, dismissive, impersonal, selfish, envious, and unforgiving. As believers worship the Lord, they must express biblical love for one another. As they meet together in worship as one body, they must demonstrate their love for God in the way they love one another. Without love, they express nothing but obnoxious noise and present empty offerings that God considers worthless (vv. 1-3). This raises some questions about the way we worship. Do we love those who join us in worship? How should we show love for our neighbor in the way we worship?

It is our hope that a proper connection to loving one's neighbor and loving God has been established in relationship to the horizontal and vertical dimensions of worship. We should be convinced at this point in our study that the horizontal and vertical dimensions of worship are complementary rather opposing concepts. It should now be apparent that neighbor love is foundational to worshiping God in a manner that honors his Law, character, and expectations. Having read the above passages, we trust the reader will always consider the principles of biblical love in their preparation for and practice of weekly corporate worship. Having specifically addressed the horizontal dimension and its link to God's call to love our neighbor, we will now consider the horizontal in relation to the topic of justice.

God's demand for justice encourages believers to exhibit love for their neighbor in tangible and concrete ways. The Lord calls for

---

67. Richard L. Pratt, *I and II Corinthians* (Nashville, TN: Broadman & Holman, 2000), 229.

corporate worship to be done in the context of biblical justice. Without the presence of such justice, the worship of the God's people will be greatly hindered. Let us ponder whether God necessitates the presence and practice of justice when we engage in corporate worship and whether the principles of biblical justice demand our attention to the horizontal.

4

Worship with Justice for Your Neighbor

The concept of justice is often excluded from discussions about worship. Although some may claim to give thought to horizontal concerns in their worship, they may engage in unjust practices toward their neighbor(s). Perhaps this is one reason many people complain about the hypocrisy of professing Christian worshippers today who treat those outside the church poorly thus inviting criticism for rejecting Christ and the church. We will discover several biblical texts in which God requires justice among his people who expect to meet with him in worship. The Word of God is quite clear that those also who wish to properly exult the Lord in a respectful vertical posture must do so in the horizontal context of biblical justice. God's expectation of justice inherently connects his vertical demands for justice with the horizontal practice of justice. There are considerable insights provided in the Old Testament wisdom literature and the prophets. Let us examine some of the key passages that address this topic starting with Psalm 82.

Psalm 82

There is much to learn about the concept of justice in the context of worship from the wisdom of Asaph. The psalmist reminds the judges of Israel that they should be concerned about justice carried out among men (Ps. 82:2-4, 6-7). In verse one he presents a scene in which God takes his place as the Hebrew expresses in "the congregation of God" ("the divine council [ESV]). Some interpreters understand the phrase as referring to the heavenly council. Others believe it refers to the sons of Israel "which God has purchased from among the nations (Ps. 74:2), and upon which as its Lawgiver He has set His divine impress."[1] Either interpretation still applies to the congregation of Israel which should ultimately respect the just disposition of God in his heavenly high council. The word "unjustly" in Hebrew is *'āwel*. It is translated as "injustice, unrighteousness."[2] The concept of justice is inherently horizontal, and it is a moral expectation that cannot be dismissed by the people of God, even in worship. The judges of Israel were called to provide justice (Exod. 18; Deut. 18:16-20). We must remember that a psalm such as this would be read in the midst of Israel's congregational worship. It reflects a broad range of horizontal concerns that God desires his people (especially the leaders of Israel) to have in their corporate worship and daily life. It will not suffice that they carry on with their Sabbath day worship while injustice takes place in Israel. Asaph reminds Israel that God is a just Lord who sits "in the divine council" and "holds judgement" (Ps. 82:1). He will expect no less to be done among his chosen people than justice requires. The Psalmist cries out against the injustice done in Israel, "How long will you judge unjustly and show partiality to the wicked? Give justice to the weak and the fatherless; maintain the right of the afflicted and the destitute. Rescue the weak and the needy; deliver them from the hand of the wicked" (Ps. 82:2-4). Such horizontal concerns should be considered as the people corporately worshipped the Lord. The psalmist expects these sentiments to pervade the hearts, minds, and lips of all the people in worship. Asaph knows that such injustices anger the Lord because he is a just God (Exod. 20:16, 22:21-22, 23:6-8; Lev. 19:15; Deut. 16:19, 27:17; Ps. 12:5). The Lord expects his people to treat one another with justice and mercy. After all, he has been remarkably gracious and merciful to Israel in delivering the nation from slavery in Egypt. He specifically calls the judges of Israel to care about people in the country by defending the weak, the fatherless, afflicted, and destitute (Ps. 82:3). God calls Israel to avoid showing partiality to the wicked in their courts and judicial decisions.

---

1. Keil and Delitzsch, 5:549.
2. G. Herbert Livingston, "1580 עוֹל," in *Theological Wordbook of the Old Testament*, ed. R. Laird Harris, Gleason L. Archer Jr., and Bruce K. Waltke (Chicago: Moody Press, 1999), 652.

This demand for justice in no way exempts the average citizen of Israel who sits in worship with the judges. Boice addresses the practical application of the text to all Israel. He says, "But it is also a prayer that justice might be done by God through his people, who, whatever the failure of the civil rulers may be, nevertheless are called to show mercy and exercise justice in the sphere of their more limited influence and to the extent of their responsibility."[3]

Asaph asks God to carry out justice and to rescue the weak and needy (Ps. 82:8). He desires that God intervene among men who have woefully failed his desire for justice. This request to God connects the vertical with the horizontal. As he speaks vertically to God, he asks him to do the work that the judges should be doing horizontally. The vertical and horizontal dimensions of worship cannot be unlinked or disconnected. They are inextricably intertwined. Asaph asks God to do what men are not willing to do with the hope that the people will repent (Ps. 82:5-8). He strives to humble those in positions of authority by pointing to their mortal status before the "Most High" providing a wake-up call warning them that they "like men ... shall die and fall like any prince" (Ps. 82:7). Perhaps they will repent and bring justice again to the people. If not, in his conclusion, the Psalmist calls out to the Lord asking for him to "judge the earth" (Ps. 82:8). Such words remind us today of how important it is to the Lord that we pursue the horizontal requirements to love our neighbors and to administer justice. We cannot expect God to be pleased with the vertical dimension of our worship if we are not carrying out justice to others. The truth of Psalm 82 should be uttered in the congregation when the people of God gather for worship. The church should be encouraged to administer justice in their dealings with others as they seek to praise and honor God. The congregation should cry out for justice for the weak, the needy, the afflicted, and the destitute. The issue of justice is never far from the heart of God as we seek to offer him praise and adoration. If it is seemingly unattainable among men, we are encouraged to cry out to the Lord that he bring about the justice he desires. The topic of justice is also demonstrated in the wisdom of

---

3. James Montgomery Boice, *Psalms 42–106: An Expositional Commentary* (Grand Rapids, MI: Baker, 2005), 679.

Solomon. He declares the requirement of justice which should not only be applied to daily life but also in the lives of those who offer their worship to God.

Proverbs 18:5

Regarding the wicked and the righteous, Solomon advises, "It is not good to be partial to the wicked or to deprive the righteous of justice" (Prov. 18:5). We can draw insights about worship from this nugget of wisdom that also applies to all of life. One commentary notes that to "Be partial to is literally 'lift up the face of' and means to be biased or to favor one person or group more than the other."[4] We see that God does not consider it "good" to show partiality to the wicked. It's easy to show partiality when there is potential for personal gain or some advantage at stake. We are prone to show partiality if we feel that we can get away with it but still benefit in some manner. Waltke sees this verse as a synthetic proverb building upon previous verses that address the topic of injustice by the wicked. This was a common problem among many worshippers in Israel. Waltke remarks, "Its connection with Proverbs 17:23 suggest that the magistrate shows favoritism in exchange for a bribe (cf. Exod. 23:8), condemning himself along with the criminal."[5] Although this proverb directly speaks against corrupt judges who favor the wicked, we should apply this wisdom to our daily life. It also cannot be excluded from our thoughts or practices in the church, especially in our corporate worship (cf. James 2:1-13).[6] Solomon clearly presents us with a horizontal concern. If a worship leader takes to heart this principle against showing favoritism, he will not succumb to the practice of tailoring the worship service to the whimsical and ungodly desires of unbelievers. Such practices are a form of showing favoritism. Sadly,

---

4. William David Reyburn and Euan McG. Fry, *A Handbook on Proverbs* (New York: United Bible Societies, 2000), 385.

5. Bruce K. Waltke, *The Book of Proverbs* (Grand Rapids, MI: William B. Eerdmans, 2005), 2:72.

6. It is very likely that "James the Just" in addressing favoritism in the context of worship [Jas 2:1-13] had passages such as Proverbs 18:5 in mind which spoke against injustice among the people of Israel.

this is a popular trend in many churches today. Churches are constructing their worship services in ways that unbelievers would find appealing and inoffensive. In other words, they are planning their services in ways that unbelievers would find acceptable and thus dismissing what God says in his Word about edifying the church. In showing favoritism toward such church attendees, they are putting aside the teachings of Scripture to cater to the sensibilities of sinful men. This is an inappropriate application of the horizontal dimension. Such church leaders need to realize that they are violating Scripture when they choose to honor the desires of the wicked rather than the doctrines of the Word. They are showing favoritism to people who do not have the things of God in mind (Mark 8:33; Matt. 16:23; Rom. 3:10-18). The Creator will not tolerate his people showing favoritism to those who are ungodly and steering his children away from his desires for their lives.

The Lord also warns in this text that we are not to "deprive the righteous of justice." Again, we see the theme of justice which is close to the heart of God. Kidner remarks, "In 18:5 the man in the right loses his lawsuit."[7] This cry for justice is a call to do that which is right for those in the right. We should not favor the wicked over the righteous which would be an injustice. If we are worshiping the Lord but still do the things that this proverb forbids, we are not worshiping God in a manner that honors his name. The Lord expects his children to respond appropriately to the wicked and to deal fairly with the righteous. The principles of showing impartiality and administering justice do not stop when believers enter the sanctuary for worship. Principles of justice do not cease when the pastor gives the call to worship or when we sing the first song. Our vertical worship must always be informed by our conscious consideration and practice of the horizontal, especially in the area of justice. How dare we utter prayers for God's assistance and help in our worship if we are depriving the righteous of justice, lacking concern for injustice, or showing favoritism to the wicked? How can we expect to meet with God when we are indulging the wicked? How many Christians believe that they

---

7. Derek Kidner, *The Proverbs: an Introduction and Commentary* (Downers Grove, IL: InterVarsity Press, 1964), 126.

have met with God while they have deprived their neighbor of justice during the week or even on Sunday morning? Our concern for the wicked should be for their salvation rather than encouraging or condoning their sinful behavior. We should desire that the wicked repent and seek to obey the Lord. For the righteous, we should strive to build them up in the truths of God's Word. We are called to do what is right for their spiritual and physical benefit. We are encouraged to defend the cause of the righteous and to grant them justice. These horizontal concerns have various implications in how God's people conduct themselves and engage in corporate worship. It excludes wicked politicking that often happens in the church replacing it with doing what God considers right and true. Having a proper view of God's calling for justice should encourage the church to proclaim truths from the Word that promote the salvation of the wicked, preach repentance for unjust actions and attitudes, and uplift the cause of the righteous. Biblical justice should be in the minds, the hearts, and the prayers of God's people when they come together to honor his name. Just as Proverbs calls for justice, we hear similar concerns in the message of the prophet Isaiah. Let us consider his words to Israel.

Isaiah 1:10-20

Isaiah corrects many who cling to their rituals and traditions as reasons to believe that God will accept their worship. The prophet proclaims that the ritual of Israel is unacceptable to God in light of her disobedience and injustice (Isa. 1:21-23). The Lord is offended at her lack of concern for her neighbor, the oppressed, the fatherless, and the widow (Isa. 1:17, 21-23b). He is so angry at them that he compares them to the wicked when he says, "Hear the word of the Lord, you rulers of Sodom! Give ear to the teaching of our God, you people of Gomorrah!" (Isa. 1:10). For those who might wish to restrict God's rebuke only to the leaders of Israel, Oswalt wisely observes, "Verse 10 is a good example of parallelism. It indicates that no distinction is to be made between 'rulers' and 'people'—they are as one."[8] Repeating

---

8. John N. Oswalt, *The Book of Isaiah Chapters 1-39* (Grand Rapids, MI: Eerdmans, 1986-1998), 96, n 14.

his warnings in previous generations about empty and hypocritical worship, the Lord says he has had enough (Isa. 1:11). Their many sacrifices and burnt offerings are not acceptable to God due to their unjust treatment of others. God points to their violation of the judicial process, "When you come to appear before me, who has required of you this trampling of my courts?" (Isa. 1:12). Notice that they come to God in a vertical posture to worship him but their ill-treatment of others or lack of horizontal consideration of their fellow Israelites invalidates their worship as honoring to God. He sees what they do to others and knows how they have treated their neighbor. God is so tired of their vertical worship that he tells the people to stop bringing their sacrifices. He tells them that their worship is an "abomination" to him (Isa. 1:13). The Lord cannot "endure" their continued "iniquity and solemn assembly" (Isa. 1:13). It is all a sham. Oswalt remarks, "It is religion which leaves iniquity unchallenged and unchanged that the prophet, more importantly, God detests."[9] The Lord sees their heart and considers their worship a farce. Their frequent services, large offerings, many prayers, and expressive worship mean nothing to him. It is all conjoined with injustice toward their brothers (Isa. 1:14-15). The Lord says, "your hands are full of blood" (Isa. 1:15b). God has been watching their evil behavior. He clearly reveals why he rejects their worship. Calvin, commenting on why the Lord rejects their prayers and sacrifices says, "It is because they are cruel and bloody, and stained with crimes of every sort, though they come into his presence with hypocritical display."[10]

These are eye-opening warnings to Christians today who believe that they are offering acceptable worship to God through their worship attendance, emotional exertion, and commitment to tradition. Many today should heed these words, especially those who go to worship in support of sins such as abortion and unrepentant anger toward their fellow Christians. The Savior not only preached against outward murder but also rebuked those who murder their neighbor in their hearts (Matt. 5:21-24). It is easy to find false comfort in our ritual or belief that we are rightly focusing vertically upon the Lord while

---

9. Ibid., 97.
10. Jean Calvin, *Calvin's Commentaries*, vol. 7, *Commentary on the Book of the Prophet Isaiah* (Grand Rapids, MI: Baker, 1974), 61.

harboring wickedness in our hearts toward others. The people of Israel think that the sheer volume of their ritual sacrifices is worthy of God's praise. Motyer states, "The standing error of the ritualist is that if all depends on performing the ceremonial act, the more you do it the better."[11] The Lord will have nothing to do with outward expressions and ritual if we are not treating our brothers with love and justice. God will not stand for injustice against others, especially the most vulnerable among us. He commands Israel to do good and show justice to the oppressed, the fatherless, and widow (Isa. 1:17). Delitzsch reminds us of God's affection for such people when he says, "Widows and orphans, as well as foreigners, were the *protégés* of God and His law, standing under His especial guardianship and care."[12] Isaiah calls Israel to wake up and repent. He calls her to recognize her horizontal sins and her responsibilities to bring justice to the fatherless and widows (Isa. 1:16-17).

Amid his rebukes and commands, the Lord does not leave Israel's worshippers without hope. He promises cleansing and forgiveness if they will truly repent and obey the Lord (Isa. 1:18-19). He also warns the worshippers of Israel that if they do not repent, they "shall be eaten by the sword; for the mouth of the Lord has spoken" (Isa. 1:20). History records that the nation of Israel did not repent and went on to experience destruction and exile by the hand of the Assyrians. What do we learn from this passage? Worship is a big deal to God. He will not tolerate it when his people engage in vertical ritualistic worship to the exclusion of the horizontal dimension. He demands and expects his people to treat their neighbors justly before, during, and after worship. Their worship must be founded upon love for their neighbor. Otherwise, he will not accept it. In fact, he will judge such worship. The horizontal dimension is indispensable to the vertical.

Another encouraging lesson we learn from this passage is that if we discover that we are unbiblical with our horizontal treatment of others and truly repent, God will forgive us and accept our vertical worship (Isa. 1:16-19). These are valuable lessons for us today in the church, and we should strive to follow them. Ritual and tradition

---

11. J. A. Motyer, *Isaiah* (Downers Grove, IL: InterVarsity Press, 1999), 46.
12. Keil and Delitzsch, 7:64.

should always join with love for and justice toward our neighbor. Isaiah later brings up the importance of the heart in worship when he warns Israel of a future attack by her enemies.

Amos 5:10-15, 21-24; 2:6-7; 8:5-6

Like his message in Isaiah, God calls attention to the injustice practiced in Israel through his prophet Amos. He will not accept the worship of people who practice evil toward their neighbor. Not only will God refuse to accept Israel's worship, but he will judge the nation (Amos 5:27). The Lord speaks with strong language saying that he hates and despises Israel's feasts. The Hebrew word translated as "hate" is *śānē'tî* (Amos 5:21). This Qal perfect verb means to "1. hate . . . 2. be unable (or unwilling) to put up with, slight . . ." [13] This word conveys God's anger at the nation. The Lord takes no delight in Israel's corporate worship (Amos 5:21). It is impossible for the people to please God in their worship lest they repent (Amos 5:13-15). He will not accept Israel's burnt offerings, grain offerings, or peace offerings. Yahweh will not even look at the offerings the people bring to him in their worship (Amos 5:22). They think that they can please him with their music and songs of praise. Keil and Delitzsch note that "Singing and playing upon harps formed part of the temple worship (vid. 1 Chron. 16:40, 23:5, and 25)."[14] Perhaps they thought that a melody would appease God. Their singing brings no pleasure to the Lord. He considers their music to be nothing but "noise" (Amos 5:23). He will not listen to their musical instruments no matter how skillfully they may be played (Amos 5:23). There is no doubt that "they went in for religion in a big way in Gilgal."[15] However, no amount of religiosity would satisfy the Lord. These are important warnings for those today who think they will be heard by God because of their boisterous singing, fancy organs, choirs, praise bands, and professional singers.

---

13. *A Concise Hebrew and Aramaic Lexicon of the Old Testament*, s.v. "שׂנא."
14. Keil and Delitzsch, 10:193.
15. J. A. Motyer, *The Message of Amos: The Day of the Lion* (Leicester, England: Inter-Varsity Press, 1988), 131.

Musical offerings mean nothing to God if they are offered by people who treat their neighbor unjustly.

The Lord is so angry at the people that he considers their worship unacceptable and worthless? God conveys what he desires in verse twenty-four, "But let justice roll down like waters, and righteousness like an ever-flowing stream" (Amos 5:24). The chiastic structure of this verse places emphasis upon the metaphor of water as an image that conveys the ongoing administration of justice that God desires among those who wish to worship him. Hubbard points out that "Here Yahweh, acting as his own priest, pronounces Israel's offerings as unfit for him, not because of ritual impurity but because they are unaccompanied by acts justice and righteousness."[16] The Lord further demands that his people continually live righteous lives in accord with his word like an "ever-flowing stream." Israel has woefully failed in both areas of justice and righteousness. Motyer notes that "Broadly, therefore, justice is correct moral practice in daily personal and social life, and righteousness is the cultivation of correct moral principle (both for self and for society); justice is mainly outward, righteousness inward."[17] The nation has engaged in pagan syncretism with devotion to "*Sakkuth*, the Assyrian god of war, identified with the planet Saturn, called *Kaiwan*" (Amos 2:26).[18] Such wickedness and idolatrous devotion will bring God's judgment (Amos 5:27). The people may focus upon the Lord in their worship, but their wicked acts against their fellow Israelites create an impassable barrier between them and God. They hate those who reprove others and despise the person who tells the truth (Amos 5:10). They rip off the poor with taxes (Amos 5:11). Israel has mounted up many sins in their sinful behavior. They afflict righteous people by taking bribes and turn the needy away from receiving help (Amos 5:12). The powerful sell the righteous into slavery for financial gain and enslave the needy (Amos 2:6). They treat the poor like they are dirt and turn away those who are afflicted (Amos 2:7a). Men commit sexual sin that the Lord clearly forbids in his Law (Amos 2:7b). The Israelites show great disrespect for the Sabbath in

---

16. David Allan Hubbard, *Joel & Amos: An Introduction and Commentary* (Downers Grove, IL: InterVarsity Press, 1989), 181.
17. Motyer, *The Message of Amos: The Day of the Lion*, 132.
18. Ibid., 136.

their deceitful business schemes so that they may enslave the poor and needy (Amos 8:4-5). God will not tolerate such wickedness in the land. Amos teaches us today that God watches the way we live. He looks for righteousness and justice among his people. He requires that they treat others justly and with respect or he will not receive their worship. The Lord demands that Israel repent by living righteously and showing justice to their neighbors.

God's admonition reminds us today that as we seek to worship him vertically, our worship must coincide with the horizontal dimension. It cannot exclude or minimize justice toward our neighbor. We cannot seek to praise God without considering how we treat others. Worship that pleases God conjoins the two. This message is a great warning to believers in the church today who wish to please God in their corporate worship. They must treat their neighbor with justice and live righteously before them if they want to truly enjoy fellowship with God. In a culture of professing Christians who often live sinfully toward their neighbor, Amos provides convicting words. His prophetic call encourages a humble and repentant spirit as we seek to approach the Lord in worship. Our fellow man cannot be ignored or abused if we wish to please our Redeemer in our songs, praise, and offerings. God will not accept our worship if we live like pagans in our culture and treat our neighbors unjustly or unrighteously. The horizontal dimension regarding justice is always present in worship that pleases the Lord. This message of justice is also proclaimed by the prophet Micah.

Micah 6:6-8

One of the main texts we must keep in mind when we approach the Lord in worship is Micah 6:6-8. Its importance is similar to the messages of other prophets who call us to approach God with the right attitude and lifestyle. The prophet Micah poses key questions the people of Israel might ask God in defense of their approach to worship. The questions address their potential offerings and sacrifices. They ask about what "burnt offerings" they should bring (Mic. 6:6). They inquire whether the number of offerings would be acceptable by stressing large numbers like "thousands of rams" or "ten thousands of rivers of oil" (Mic. 6:7a). The people ask whether God would receive their most valuable sacrifice—their "firstborn" (Mic. 6:7b). To mention their firstborn recalls the great sacrifice that Abraham was willing to make (Gen. 22). Kaiser sees such a question as evidence of their attraction to pagan worship. He notes that "Only Molech-worship in Moab required such an awful sacrifice—that's how theologically unaware the nation was!"[19] Such extravagant sacrifices would easily be acceptable among the pagans or ritually-minded Israelites. God, however, is not pleased. Calvin rightly understands what God expects when he states, "for God did not command sacrifices, as though they were of themselves of any worth; but he intended to lead the ancient people by such exercises to repentance and faith."[20] The Lord will not find Israel's sacrifices acceptable due to their wicked living (Mic. 2:1-2, 3:1-3, 5-7, 6:10-12, 16a). He has observed the way they have treated their fellow citizens, the people of the covenant. Although they wish to bring their vertical worship to God, the Lord sees how far short they fall in the horizontal dimension. He knows how they are treating one another. God answers what he requires of the people. It is not mere outward sacrifices no matter how extravagant they may be. It is so much more.

Micah tells Israel in a nutshell what God requires. One scholar wisely called this verse "the golden rule of the OT."[21] Let us examine each requirement. First, God tells Israel that he has instructed them before about "what is good" (Mic. 6:8). Such instruction is provided throughout the Old Testament. Israel was taught what the Lord states briefly in this verse. He has given them past teaching about his requirements. They knew that he could see their hearts and observe their behavior outside their formal corporate worship. In other words, Micah informs Israel that what he is about to tell them is not something new. They should know better. Calvin wisely remarks, "It is evident that, in the two particulars, he refers to the second table of the Law; that is, *to do* justice, *and to love* mercy" [emphasis by the

---

19. Walter C. Kaiser, *Micah-Malachi* (Dallas, TX: Word Books, 1992), 73.

20. Jean Calvin, *Calvin's Commentaries*, vol. 14, *The Prophet Micah* (Grand Rapids, MI: Baker, 1974), 342.

21. C. Hassell Bullock, *An Introduction to the Old Testament Prophetic Books* (Chicago: Moody Press, 1986), 103.

author].[22] The first thing God requires is for each person in Israel "to do justice" (Mic. 6:8). Holladay notes that the Hebrew word *mišpāṭ* for "justice" refers to a "decision by arbitration > legal decision > legal case > justice, right > what is in conformity to a case."[23] Justice points to those "who are in a socially superior position and calls them to step in and deliver the weaker and wronged party by punishing the oppressor."[24] Frame writes, "In the Old Testament, God condemned formal worship that was not accompanied by a concern for compassion and justice."[25] Even if a worshipper offers a million sacrifices but still acts unjustly toward others, his sacrifices mean nothing to God. They are no more than hypocritical gifts given with empty platitudes. Justice is horizontal in nature but motivated by the vertical.

It is the justice of God toward men (i.e., the vertical) that they are called to emulate in their treatment of one another (i.e., the horizontal). The two, the vertical and horizontal, must go together. God demands justice be carried out among his people because he is a just ruler who is just with them. The Lord's demand for justice is a clarion wake-up call to Christians today who think that they can offer acceptable worship while cheating others or depriving them of justice. Justice must fill the minds and hearts of believers before they can expect God to accept their worship. As we ponder justice, we are reminded of the sacrifice of Christ. No greater act of justice was ever demonstrated. Mercy and justice met on the cross as Jesus sacrificed his life for sinners and endured the just wrath of the Father as a substitutionary atonement (Rom. 3:25). The concept of justice teaches us that God expects his people to show concern for the poor, underprivileged, widow, orphan, and needy (cf. Ps. 82:3; Jer. 22:3). He will not tolerate it if we care nothing for such people. God is their defender (Ps. 140:12). If we believe we can please God in our worship without demonstrating justice to others, we are deluded.

---

22. Calvin, *The Prophet Micah*, 343.

23. *A Concise Hebrew and Aramaic Lexicon of the Old Testament*, s.v. "משפט."

24. Bruce Waltke, *Obadiah, Jonah, Micah* (Downers Grove, IL: InterVarsity Press, 1988), 195.

25. John M. Frame, *Worship in Spirit and Truth* (Phillipsburg, NJ: P & R Publishing, 1996), 9.

The second requirement is "to love kindness" (Mic. 6:8b). The Hebrew word for "kindness" used here is *ḥesed*. Enhanced Brown-Driver-Briggs defines it as, "goodness, kindness... 2. *kindness* (especially as extended to the lowly, needy and miserable), *mercy* Pr 20:28 Jb 6:14."[26] This word refers to the covenant love that God expects among his people. Other versions translate it as "mercy" (e.g., NIV84, KJV, NKJV). It is grounded in the loving kindness that God has shown Israel through making a covenant with her and the kindness he expects his people to show to others. Kaiser points out that "It is the faithful, loyal love, mercy, and grace that binds a man to his Lord and to his neighbor or friend."[27] This kindness or mercy is an attribute that should be demonstrated in the lives of Christians today. It is horizontal by nature. The Lord requires this attitude in the lives of believers. It is, in fact, a fruit of the Holy Spirit (Gal. 5:22) and an expression of Christian love. Kindness is a form of compassion and reflects the very character of the Lord (Exod. 33:19; 34:5-6; 2 Kings 13:23; Neh. 9:19; Ps. 86:15; 103:8; 116:5; 119:156; 145:8). Allen states, "If *ḥesed* modelled upon their Lord's is cherished among them, then will the covenant purpose of God have reached its goal in the establishment of a society where theology and ethics are one."[28] God instructs believers to treat others with kindness if they wish to experience his kindness when they worship. No greater kindness was shown to humanity than when Jesus healed the sick, taught the outcast, ate with sinners, and forgave the lost upon the cross (Luke 23:34).

The third requirement was "to walk humbly with your God?" (Mic. 6:8b). The Hebrew concept of walking with God entails moral commitment and application of the Scriptures to one's life. God's people are called to humbly obey his laws in their daily lives. For God, talk is cheap. The Lord considers empty ritual meaningless without humble obedience to his Word. The Lord desires people to be completely dependent on him in their daily life. The Creator will not tolerate humans who are prideful and arrogant. When people are

---

26. *Enhanced Brown-Driver-Briggs Hebrew and English Lexicon* (Oxford: Clarendon Press, 1977), s.v. "חסד."

27. Kaiser, *Micah-Malachi*, 74.

28. Leslie C. Allen, *The Books of Joel, Obadiah, Jonah, and Micah* (Grand Rapids, MI: Eerdmans, 1976), 374.

prideful, they are foolish because they deny the reality that they are fully dependent on the Lord for their very existence and daily provisions. God is not against ritual, but he is against empty and heartless ritual. Many in Israel claimed to be recipients of the covenant. They expected blessing since they were born into a covenant family. They boasted in being children of Abraham. However, they did not desire to live for the Lord by humbly following his Word in the way they treated their neighbors. In their arrogance and selfish pride, they sought to take advantage of others, thwart justice, and abuse the less fortunate. They wanted to do what they wanted to do rather than God's will. God desires a humble submission to his Word in our daily lives. The wise man always trusts in the Lord, leans not on his own understanding, and acknowledges the Lord in all his ways (Prov. 3:5-6). This expectation, by implication, means that God desires continual repentance and faithful obedience in our lives, especially in the way we treat others. Believers must depend upon the Word of God and the Holy Spirit. This is what Jesus meant when He said, "Blessed are the meek, for they shall inherit the earth" (Matt. 5:5). If only the people in the churches today would walk humbly with their God, their country would be transformed. Many who worship the Lord would truly meet the living God in their praises and prayers as they engage in worship. Humility toward God would motivate believers to treat their fellow man and fellow worshippers with biblical love. Loving our neighbors would become a natural response emanating from humble hearts and attitudes. Families would experience renewal, marriages would enjoy blessing, relationships would be reconciled, the truths of God's Word would be honored, and the goodness of God would flow over their nation. Christians today must again renew their commitment to humbly walk with their Lord. Believers need a repentant and humble disposition toward God for the healing of their land (2 Chron. 7:14). Such are the kind of worshippers that the Father seeks. Micah teaches us that God expects a holy horizontal posture (justice and kindness) with the right vertical disposition (a humble walk with God) if we expect to offer acceptable worship to the Lord. There is no separating these two dimensions if we wish to meet with God.

We have traversed several key texts regarding the importance of the practice of justice as we seek to worship God acceptably. This theme of justice represents a tangible expression of the love that God requires in our treatment of the righteous as well as the wicked. It is loving to do that which accords with God's Word in our expression of love toward our neighbor when we include justice. For the wicked, we hope that justice will move them toward repentance and salvation. For the righteous, justice is meant to encourage them to continue to praise, honor, and trust in their God who is holy and just. Justice encourages all to consider the just demands of God ultimately poured out upon Christ on the cross, the only one who has fulfilled the just demands of the Law. In Jesus we see justice and mercy meet for the salvation of all those who believe in him. The idea that justice promotes the horizontal dimension of worship has been defended, and now we seek to encourage the horizontal dimension with passages that more directly address the topic of worship.

5

Worship with Your Neighbor

Many Scripture passages address the topic of worship directly and contain insights not only about the vertical dimension of worship but also provide wisdom on the horizontal aspect. We will look at some supporting texts that explicitly speak about worship in general. The reason 1 Corinthians 12 is included in this section is that it explains the call to "discern the body" that Paul speaks about in First Corinthians 11, a chapter that directly addresses the practice of the Lord's Supper. The Scriptures we will consider will uphold the premise that God is very concerned about the horizontal dimension when he specifically addresses the topic of worship. We will especially learn that he is particularly interested that his people worship in a manner that is edifying to their fellow worshippers. It should also become apparent that the Lord does not separate the vertical from the horizontal when he clearly talks about the topic of worship. An appropriate place to begin our study is with a Psalm of David, a man committed to worshiping God according to the Word from his heart and soul.

Psalm 40

David strives to please God in his worship. He is thinking about both the vertical and horizontal. David cannot help but give praise to God for his deliverance (Ps. 40:1-2, 9-10), greatness (Ps. 40:5), his law (Ps. 40:8), and his love and faithfulness (Ps. 40:10b-11). He calls out to God to deliver him as he faces his enemies (Ps. 40:13-17). Although Anderson classifies Psalm 40 as a lament Psalm, he notes that the psalmists are unlike "Greek tragedians who portray a no-exit situation of fate or necessity; rather, they raise a cry out of the depths in the confidence that God has the power to lift a person out of the 'miry bog' and to set one's feet upon a rock."[1] Futato classifies the Psalm as a Thanksgiving Psalm, but others scholars recognize that it contains features of both a Thanksgiving Psalm (vv. 1-11) and Lament Psalm (vv. 12-17).[2] Longman states, "The psalm opens the way an individual thanksgiving psalm would. It speaks of a past deliverance. Verse 4 has some wisdom connections. However, verse 11 and the verses following sound much like an individual lament."[3] However one classifies the Psalm, it is evident that David conveys an optimistic attitude throughout this Psalm. His words reveal a horizontal concern for others in corporate worship. As he sings new songs among the congregation, he is concerned that the people around him hear his praises to God. David says, "He put a new song in my mouth, a song of praise to our God." The phrase "song of praise" conveys the idea that David longs for the congregation to hear his praise to God. He then gives the reason for his praise which is that "Many will see and fear, and put their trust in the Lord" (Ps. 40:3). The shepherd-king plans to instruct those who join him in worship about the "wondrous deeds" and "thoughts" of God toward his people (Ps. 40:5a). David says, ". . . I will proclaim and tell of them, yet they are more than can be told" (Ps. 40:5b). Like Samuel's words to King Saul (1 Sam. 15:22-23), David again remarks that mere sacrifice and offerings do not delight the Lord (Ps. 40:6). God is not satisfied with ritual. He desires the hearts of his people (Ps. 40:8). David is concerned that God's "glad news of deliverance" will be declared in the congregation (Ps. 40:9-10). The congregation is worshiping the Lord. Bratcher and Reyburn note that "*The great congregation* (verses 9b, 10d) is the people of Israel assembled for worship in the Temple."[4] Calvin comments, "Accordingly, he declares that he had not concealed in his heart the

---

1. Bernhard W. Anderson, *Out of the Depths: The Psalms Speak for Us Today*, rev. ed. (Philadelphia: Westminster Press, 1983), 76.

2. Mark D. Futato, *Interpreting the Psalms: An Exegetical Handbook* (Grand Rapids, MI: Kregel Academic & Professional, 2007), 158. See also Robert G. Bratcher and William David Reyburn, *A Translator's Handbook on the Book of Psalms* (New York: United Bible Societies, 1991), 380.

3. Tremper Longman III, *How to Read the Psalms* (Downers Grove, IL: InterVarsity Press, 1988), 157.

4. Robert G. Bratcher and William David Reyburn, *A Translator's Handbook on the Book of Psalms* (New York: United Bible Societies, 1991), 386. Emphasis provided by authors.

righteousness of God, which it becomes us publicly to make known for the edification of one another."[5] This "glad news" is a precursor to the horizontal concerns that New Testament believers should have toward others in corporate worship who need to hear the message of redemption provided in Christ. David is thinking about the edifying effect upon his fellow worshippers as he sings praise (Ps. 40:3) and speaks forth praise to God (Ps. 40:9-10). He knows what the people need. They need God. As we ponder the horizontal dimension in the Psalms, let us consider the words of Isaiah as he addresses the worship of Israel.

Isaiah 29:13-14

After addressing the nation of Israel about the fact that God will send foreign foes against the country and also eventually defeat those nations, he addressed Israel's worship. He says,

> Because this people draw near with their mouth and honor me with their lips, while their hearts are far from me, and their fear of me is a commandment taught by men, therefore, behold, I will again do wonderful things with this people, with wonder upon wonder; and the wisdom of their wise men shall perish, and the discernment of their discerning men shall be hidden. (Isa. 29:13-14)

Oswalt states, "These verses take the form of a brief oracle of judgment."[6] One of the key reasons the Lord will eventually allow Israel to be defeated and exiled by her enemies is her unwillingness to obey the Lord in her worship. God calls out Israel for her heartless ritual. The people are so focused on the rules of worship that their ritual becomes spiritually empty. This type of worship easily sets in when the Israelites go through the motions of obedience to the Mosaic ceremonies while being heartless toward God and their neighbors (e.g. Isa. 1:2-23). They seek to draw near to God through their ritual and

---

5. Jean Calvin, *Calvin's Commentaries*, vol. 5, *The Commentary on the Book of Psalms* (Grand Rapids, MI: Baker, 1974), 105.
6. Oswalt, *The Book of Isaiah Chapters 1-39*, 532.

obedience to the law. They utter all the words outwardly that conform to the traditions they read in the law, but their mouths have no connection to their inner being. We can hear them utter their empty platitudes in their ostentation, but they are as cold as ice. It is nothing but a show. There is no power in their words and sacrifices. On the outside, everything appears to be in accord with God's Word, and onlookers may deduce that they are pleasing God, but he does not approve. He looks beyond the show into their hearts and sees their dead motivations that have nothing to do with the Spirit nor Yahweh's expectations. Jesus would later recall this passage. In pointing out the hypocrisy of the Pharisees and Scribes who scolded his disciples for not ceremonially washing their hands, Jesus exposes their heartless religion by quoting Isaiah 29:13-14 (cf. Matt. 15:7-19). The Pharisees and Scribes focus on their ritual but yet willfully break the fifth commandment deciding not to help their parents in need (Matt. 15:1-7). They refuse to honor their horizontal responsibilities to their parents with the excuse that they are honoring their tradition. Their hearts are far from God. Such hypocrisy is seen throughout the history of the church. Calvin compares the ostentation of Israel to the hypocrisy displayed in the Roman Catholic church during the time of the Reformation. He notes,

> We may easily conclude from this what value ought to be set on that worship which Papists think that they render to God, when they worship God by useless ringing of bells, mumbling, wax candles, incense, splendid dresses, and a thousand trifles of the same sort; for we see that God not only rejects them, but even holds them in abhorrence.[7]

Calvin's application of Isaiah's message is pertinent to those in every age within the church. People often tend to so focus on the outside demonstration and practices of their worship that they can easily fall prey to the same empty and heartless worship that Isaiah and Jesus condemns.

---

7. Calvin, *The Prophet Isaiah*, 324.

As we consider Isaiah 29:13, we can visualize the Jewish leaders in the worship service lifting up their hands and saying pious words void of any meaning to their souls. There is no affection, no concern, and no love of God in their hearts. It is all vanity. They possess no fear of the Lord. Their fear is false. It is a baseless reverence conjured up in their minds, "a commandment taught by men" (Isa. 29:13b). There is no Scripture-based faith undergirding their view of God and the reasons they claim to reverence, honor, and fear him. Idolatrous thoughts enamor the people. The great character of God and his wondrous deeds have nothing to do with their motives in worship. Many in Israel have become good at faking their affections for God, but the Lord sees through their scam. The Creator cannot be fooled. Motyer comments, "As the Sovereign reviews their worship, all he sees is conformity to human rules."[8] Isaiah reminds us that true worship of God is much more than mere ritual and ostentation. It is a matter of the heart. In fact, God wants the hearts of his worshippers. He desires that they draw near to him with their hearts, minds, and affections (James 4:8). This cold outward expression of worship on display in the temple courts is a type of vertical worship devoid of heartfelt love for God. The Lord gives us a glimpse into the type of worship he desires by pointing out the kind he rejects. When men do not give their hearts to God in their vertical worship, they will not be gracious and loving to those sitting beside them in the pews. Just as they care nothing for God, they will not care anything for their brother or sister in Christ. The vulnerable within the covenant community mean nothing to them. Their cold empty ritual toward God will be translated into a heartless and cold attitude toward others. If they are cold toward God they will not be biblically warm toward their brethren or the lost.

Verse fourteen reminds us that heartless worship will bring no spiritual benefit. Although Israel and especially her religious leaders may think they are wise, their supposed wisdom "shall perish" (Isa. 29:14). Those who engage in such cold worship think they are discerning, but their discernment shall cease. Isaiah says it "shall be hidden" (Isa. 29:14b). All the knowledge and wisdom they claim to possess will be shown to be empty and foolish. Delitzch describes the

---

8. Motyer, *Isaiah: An Introduction and Commentary*, 191.

severity of the situation: "This self-alienation and self-blinding, Jehovah would punish with a wondrously paradoxical judgment, namely, the judgment of a hardening, which would so completely empty and confuse, that even the appearance of wisdom and unity, which the leaders of Israel still had, would completely disappear."[9] The leaders of Israel are the blind who will lead their people into the ditch (Matt. 15:14). They have nothing from God to offer the people but the foolish wisdom of men. The Lord pulls back the veil to expose the Wizard of Oz. He is nothing but an old man full of smoke and mirrors with no substance. There is no mistake about it; God will have nothing to do with worship that is void of a heart that loves him or our neighbor. Biblical love for God and one's neighbor must motivate the heart. Let us now consider the words of Jesus about worship in the New Testament.

John 4:21-24

In talking with the Samaritan woman, Jesus provides insight into how believers should worship God. The Samaritans had placed great importance on the actual location of worship, but Christ reveals that it is not the physical location that matters but the manner in which God's children worship. Jesus explains that the time has arisen that all "true worshippers will worship the Father in spirit and truth" (John 4:23). He also notes that "the hour is coming, and is now here" (John 4:23). This "hour" points to "the hour of Jesus' cross, resurrection, and exaltation, or to events related to Jesus' passion and exaltation (as in 16:32), or to the situation introduced by Jesus' passion and exaltation (cf. notes on 2:4)."[10] Jesus' ministry changed everything. He confirmed that the Jews were right about the appropriate place to worship was Jerusalem (e.g., "for salvation is from the Jews" in John 4:22), but his coming meant worship would now happen everywhere true worshippers offered worship to God. Calvin's commentary sheds light on Jesus' stunning comments about Israel's worship. He states, "When He says that the hour cometh or will come, He teaches that the order

---

9. Keil and Delitzsch, 7:314.
10. Carson, *The Gospel According to John*, 223.

handed down by Moses is not for everlasting; when He says that the hour is now come, He puts an end to the ceremonies and so declares that 'the time of reformation' has been fulfilled."[11] The Savior clearly conveys what the Father desires when he adds, "for the Father is seeking such people to worship him" (John 4:23b). This phrase unveils what type of worshipper is pleasing to God. Jesus reiterates his point in verse twenty-four when he says, "God is spirit, and those who worship him must worship in spirit and truth" (John 4:24).

As we are dealing with the topic of how we should worship, we must ask what does Jesus mean by the words "in spirit and truth?" It appears that Jesus is trying to deemphasize the importance of mere externals such as the actual place of worship. Calvin points out that Jesus reveals that "In all ages God wanted to be worshipped by faith, prayer, thanksgiving, purity of heart and innocency of life."[12] This shift in perspective would straighten out the Samaritan woman's false impression that God is impressed by the outward externals of worship (e.g., the place of worship). We see a similar correction among some of the prophets in the Old Testament as has been noted previously in the various Old Testament passages. Jesus' words deemphasize the importance of externals in worship. The fact that God is "spirit" illustrates partially why God would not be impressed by outward things like the place of worship. Bruce explains, "it is not merely that he is *a* Spirit among other spirits; rather, God himself is pure Spirit, and the worship in which he takes delight is accordingly spiritual worship—the sacrifice of a humble, contrite, grateful and adoring spirit [emphasis by the author]."[13] The Lord, being a spirit, desires that his worshippers worship him in a manner that comes from the heart according to his Word in accord with his essence. Morris remarks, "Since God is spirit, our worship must be in spirit; it must be of a spiritual kind."[14]

Regarding the phrase "in spirit" in verses 23-24 there are fundamentally two interpretations. One view is that the phrase points to the spirit within a man. This view is held by various conservative

---

11. Calvin, *Calvin's New Testament Commentaries*, 4:99.
12. Ibid., 100.
13. F. F. Bruce, *The Gospel of John*, 111.
14. Leon Morris, *Expository Reflections On the Gospel of John*, 145.

theologians.[15] This interpretation incorporates the Old Testament theme that God desires worship from the heart rather than mere external rituals. It holds that there is a new emphasis on an unrestricted location for worship based upon God's work in the hearts of believers. One might argue that the second view offers a better interpretation in which the phrase "in spirit" is understood to refer to the second person of the Trinity. This view fits well with the Old Testament promises of a new covenant which predicted that the Holy Spirit would be given to believers (Ezek. 36:26-27; Joel 2:28; Acts 2:16-21). This understanding seems to more fully encompass the promise fulfillment motif in relation to God's covenant promises. It highlights the newness, so to speak, of the new covenant and the transformative benefits of being a New Testament worshipper in contrast to the Old Testament, especially with its emphasis upon the location of Jerusalem as the central place of worship. Ladd states:

> "Worship in spirit" does not mean worship in the human spirit in contrast to worship by the use of external forms and rites; it means worship that is empowered by the Spirit of God. The contrast here is not so much between the world above and the world below as between worship in the former time and worship in the new era inaugurated by Jesus. The contrast is between worship in spirit and truth as compared with worship in Jerusalem or Gerizim. Here is an "eschatological replacement of temporal institutions like the Temple." The "Spirit raises men above the earthly level, the level of flesh, and enables them to worship God properly." Here we meet for the first time the joining of the vertical with the horizontal. Because Jesus has come into the world from above, he has instituted a new order of things.[16]

---

15. See F. F. Bruce, *The Gospel of John*, 111; Arndt, Danker, and Bauer, 833; R. C. Sproul, *John* (Lake Mary, FL: Reformation Trust Pub., 2009), 64; Leon Morris, *The Gospel According to John: The English Text with Introduction, Exposition and Notes* (Grand Rapids, MI: Eerdmans, 1971), 270.

16. George Eldon Ladd, *A Theology of the New Testament*, rev. ed. (Grand Rapids, MI: Eerdmans, 1993), 261.

A dramatic change in worship has occurred through the ministry and presence of the Holy Spirit. Worshippers who are filled with the Spirit now include both Jews and Gentiles as one people (Eph. 2:11-22). In the new covenant, both races worship in the Spirit (Eph. 2:22). The promised hour has come with the outpouring of the Holy Spirit at Pentecost (Acts 2). Clowney remarks, "Worship in Spirit is worship in the Holy Spirit, given by Christ."[17] The Old Testament temple has been replaced with Christ as the church's new temple. Clowney adds, "Because Christ is our temple our worship is spiritual: the living power of his Spirit breathes life and joy into our hearts and brings to us now the living fellowship of Christ for which we have been re-created."[18] As new creations in Christ, all believers have also become temples of the Holy Spirit who resides in them as the children of God (1 Cor. 3:16, 6:19-20; 2 Cor. 6:16; Eph. 1:13-14). Christians in the new covenant are not limited to one location in their worship. There is a new freedom in New Testament worship. The presence of the Spirit has expanded the worship horizons of God's people. Commenting on John 4:23, Ladd says, "Because the Holy Spirit is to come into the world, people may worship God anywhere if they are motivated by the Holy Spirit. Only those born of the Spirit can worship God in the way he desires to be worshiped."[19]

The worship of God in "the Spirit" should be both horizontal and vertical. The presence of the Spirit will produce the fruit of the Spirit (Gal. 5:22-23). The fruit of the Spirit reflects both a vertical godliness toward God and horizontal focus upon others with the most important spiritual fruit being love. Believers are changed and filled with the Spirit with love for both God and their fellow man, especially their brethren. Spirit induced love is not the mushy or politically correct kind of love we see in the world. It is informed by the Word of God and seeks that which is best spiritually for our neighbor. It may include either correction or positive encouragement depending on what is most needed (John 16:8-15; 2 Tim. 3:16-17). It says what people need to hear versus what they want to hear. Joy will fill the souls

---

17. Edmund P. Clowney, "The Final Temple," *Westminster Theological Journal* 35, no. 2 (Winter 1973): 176.
18. Clowney, "The Final Temple," 177.
19. Ladd, *A Theology of the New Testament*, 328.

of Christians as the Spirit grants such joy in their salvation and relationship with God. That joy will become evident to others. Peace with God will soothe the souls of the saints and peace with others will be their desire. They will seek to patiently wait upon the Lord and exercise patience with others. The Spirit-filled believer will be kind to his neighbor since he has experienced the kindness of God in Christ through the gospel. The Spirit will move the believer to pursue and cherish that which is good because God is good. He will try to be good to others in the way God has been and is good to him. Christians will strive to be faithful to God and other people because their God is faithful. The believer will be gentle with their neighbor because Christ is gentle with them (Matt. 11:29). The saints will exercise self-control in the way they relate to others because their God demonstrates self-control. Worshiping "in spirit" changes the lives of those born of the Spirit (John 3:3). The Spirit takes that which belongs to God and translates it into holy actions and thoughts in the believer's life, particularly in the way they treat their neighbors. The horizontal and the vertical converge in the life of the Christian worshipper through the power and presence of the Holy Spirit.

The Lord Jesus also said that true worshippers would worship in "truth." The need to pursue truth means that believers should worship God in a manner consistent with his Word which is truth (John. 17:17). These are sobering words in a time when many Christians engage in worship that often encourages experimenting with the latest trend or fad rather than a careful consideration of what the Word says about worship. Sproul remarks, "Our worship must be based on God's self-revelation in Scripture. He is truth and His word is truth."[20] The Spirit within the believer will move him to seek to worship God according to the Word (John 16:13-15). Worship that is according to the Word will resonate with the hearts of Christians because of the Spirit inside them who loves the Word (Ps. 119; 2 Tim. 3:16-17). Worship driven by the Word will be Christ-centered since Jesus is the truth (John 14:6), the fulfillment of the Scriptures (Luke 24:27; John 5:39), and the Word made flesh (John 1:14). The truth of God's Word should direct all believers to love both God and their neighbor.

---

20. Sproul, *John*, 65.

In light of this passage, all believers should be encouraged to include the vertical and horizontal dimensions in their worship of God since their inclusion is in accord with the truth of God's Word. To diminish or negate either dimension from our worship would violate the principles Jesus provides in this text. If we wish to be the kind of worshippers the Father "is seeking" we will pursue God in a manner consistent with the Spirit and the truth. Our calling to pursue the truth of God's Word in the way we worship is reflected in the teaching of the apostle Paul in his dealings with the New Testament churches in their worship. Let us examine the words of Paul to the Corinthian church.

1 Corinthians 10:14-17; 11:22-33

The apostle Paul addresses the horizontal dimension in his treatment of the Lord's Supper in 1 Corinthians. Communion by its very nature encourages the horizontal dimension. It is a communal event that demands horizontal consideration of those present in worship. Paul's instruction to the Corinthians about the spiritual aspects of the supper should move believers to identify participation in the Lord's Supper as a visible demonstration of their horizontal connection to one another in Christ. The apostle teaches the Corinthians that when they eat "the one bread," this sacred act demonstrates that they are "one body" (1 Cor. 10:17). Paul says, "The cup of blessing that we bless, is it not a participation in the blood of Christ? The bread that we break, is it not a participation in the body of Christ? Because there is one bread, we who are many are one body, for we all partake of the one bread" (1 Cor. 10:16-17). The apostle draws a connection between the Lord's Supper and the unity of the body of Christ which is the Church, the people of God. Morris rightly notes, "Communicants are united to Christ and united to one another."[21] Both elements (the bread and cup) illustrate the horizontal reality that the people of God are joined in Christ as one community.

---

21. Leon Morris, *The First Epistle of Paul to the Corinthians: An Introduction and Commentary*, rev.ed. (Grand Rapids, MI: InterVarsity Press, 1985), 144.

Jamieson says, "Paul roots the church's unity in its celebration of the Lord's Supper. There is one body because there is one bread."[22]

As Christians in the local church participate in the Lord's Supper, they declare publicly that they are one with each other through their common faith in Christ. This unity is symbolized by the one loaf of bread and the cup. This oneness (a horizontal reality) should be on the minds and upon the hearts of all believers who partake together in the Lord's Supper. Jamieson believes that a covenantal renewal takes place when Christians experience communion. He states, "In the Lord's Supper, we renew our commitment to Christ and his people."[23] In their participation in the Supper, believers demonstrate to onlookers that they are in union with God vertically and unified horizontally with one another through their common faith in Christ as a covenant family. They are a people in communion with both God and one another covenantally. Paul's reference to "one bread" points to the oneness experienced by the people of God as they partake of that "one bread." Lenski describes this reality: "The one sacramental bread, which mediates the sacramental communion with Christ's body, makes all who partake of that bread, no matter how numerous they may be, one body."[24] When the Lord's Supper takes place, it represents the truth that the church is one covenantal people of God who are unified vertically with Christ and joined horizontally with each other through a common faith in Christ. The apostle Paul provides further support for the importance of both the vertical and horizontal dimensions in 1 Corinthians 11.

It is impossible to avoid the horizontal dimension when considering Paul's teaching about the Lord's Supper in 1 Corinthians 11:17-34. Morris says, "there is a marked stress throughout this passage on the corporate nature of the service, and on the responsibility of each to all."[25] The apostle addressed the church's abuse of the Supper when they gathered together (vv. 17-22). The

---

22. Bobby Jamieson, "How the Lord's Supper Makes a Local Church," *9Marks*, April 28, 2016, accessed March 26, 2019, https://9marks.org/article/how-the-lords-supper-makes-a-local-church/.

23. Ibid.

24. R. C. H. Lenski, *The Interpretation of St. Paul's First and Second Epistle to the Corinthians* (Minneapolis, MN: Augsburg Publishing House, 1963), 411.

25. Leon Morris, *The First Epistle of Paul to the Corinthians*, 161.

congregation has factions and people with self-serving attitudes (vv. 18, 21). These problems demonstrate that as the people engage in worship and participate in communion, many are more interested in being divisive than encouraging the unity of the body of Christ. Some of the people are not thinking about one another in a godly fashion when communion is served. They are more concerned about filling their own bellies and getting drunk (1 Cor. 11:21-22). They are arrogant in the way they treat the Supper and one another. Paul rebukes their sinful behavior when he says, "What shall I say to you? Shall I commend you in this? No, I will not" (v. 22b). They are not biblical in their horizontal concern for one another. Many do not express love for their brethren as Christ commanded. The apostle's reference to those "who have nothing" (v. 22) indicates that the rich are likely despising the poorer members of the congregation. Fee appears to understand the issue at hand when he states, "… Paul's present concern is *not* with penury or gluttony but with their being truly together at the common table, with no class distinctions being allowed on the basis of the kind and amount of food eaten."[26] Paul will not allow the Corinthian believers, especially the more economically privileged members, to treat one another poorly at the Table. His corrective instruction should encourage Christians today to love and care about one another in their worship without prejudice, especially during their communion services.

The apostle goes on to describe the meaning of the Supper (vv. 23-26) but also calls for self-examination before taking the elements. Reformed theologians have historically used verses 27-32 to support the idea of fencing the Lord's Table which involves warning those in worship to beware of eating judgment unto themselves. This process would include both a vertical and horizontal concern. First, the person needs to examine their vertical relationship with God and make sure they are Christians and also repentant. Secondly, communicants need to establish whether they are in good fellowship with others in the church. This examination involves the horizontal dimension since fellowship includes the relationships in the church. Paul's concern that they consider others horizontally is also supported by his rebuke of

---

26. Fee, *The First Epistle to the Corinthians*, 544.

selfish attitudes (vv. 21-22) and his admonition that they "wait for one another" (v. 33b). There is no room for smug individualism in participating in the Supper as Calvin wisely remarks, "each person may not celebrate his supper on his own."[27] As he fences the Table, the pastor should encourage all penitent believers to partake in the Supper. He should clearly instruct unbelievers and the unrepentant to exclude themselves from eating and drinking the elements lest they be judged by God (vv. 27, 29-32). This is a serious horizontal concern. The minister should fence the Table by instructing believers in the kind of concern they should have for one another. People should not partake of the Lord's Supper if they harbor unforgiveness in their hearts toward fellow Christians or treat their neighbor in a sinful manner. True believers should also be concerned for the salvation of any unbelievers who are present. They should pray for souls to trust in Christ.

One very important criteria for celebrating the Lord's Supper is to discern the Lord's body which likely involves a horizontal concern. Many interpreters misunderstand what Paul is saying when he warns the Corinthians about "discerning the Lord's body." They think Paul is addressing the idea of discerning the presence of Christ in the Supper (e.g., transubstantiation, consubstantiation, etc.). This perspective seems to insert an outside theological agenda versus looking more carefully at the surrounding context and focus of the passage. Witvliet in his discussion on the phrase "discerning the Lord's body" in verse 29 believes Paul is calling for a horizontal self-examination. He states,

> the phrase means primarily 'to determine, perceive, and practice what it means to be the church—a community who embodies Jesus' love.' The central application of this discernment action is beautifully summarized in verse 33: 'wait for, receive, and welcome one another' as you gather at the table. It is a powerful antidote to individualism, inhospitality, and arrogance.[28]

---

27. Calvin, *Calvin's New Testament Commentaries*, 9:257.
28. John D. Witvliet, "Psalm Singing, Discerning the Body, and Projected Song Texts," *Reformed Worship*, no. 90 (December 2008): 45.

It appears that there were some in the church who thought more highly of themselves than their brethren and consequently were selfishly taking the elements and forgetting that they should take them with others in mind. They did not discern the body of Christ with a spirit of grace and biblical love. Many did not recognize and respect the church as the body of Christ, a people unified through a common faith in Jesus and cleansed by his blood. They did not acknowledge the Table as representing their unity in Christ. Fee describes God's expectations:

> The Lord's Supper is not just any meal; it is *the* meal, in which at a common table with one loaf and a common cup they proclaimed that through the death of Christ they were one body, the body of Christ; and therefore they are not just any group of sociologically diverse people who could keep those differences intact at this table. Here they must "discern/recognize as distinct" the one body of Christ, of which they all are parts and in which they all are gifts to one another. To fail to discern the body in this way, by abusing those of lesser sociological status, is to incur God's judgment [emphasis by the author].[29]

As the people examined their relationship with God vertically, they were not properly examining their relationship with one another horizontally as the body of Christ. They needed to understand that they could not engage in the Supper vertically without respecting one another horizontally. God's blessing required an appreciation of both dimensions. We need to recognize that this passage clearly addresses a common subject of worship—the Lord's Supper. The truths that we have considered above regarding this portion of the worship service provide us with clear vertical and horizontal principles and attitudes that should be present in every corporate worship service. Paul continues to address the concept of the body of Christ in chapter twelve of First Corinthians.

---

29. Fee, *The First Epistle to the Corinthians*, 564.

1 Corinthians 12

After Paul calls the church to properly engage in the Lord's Supper by "discerning the body" (1 Cor. 11:29) he provides a thorough theological treatment of the body of Christ in 1 Corinthians 12. Chapter twelve is an excellent explanation about what one should think concerning the body of Christ as they engage in worship and the general life of the church. The apostle begins by describing the importance of spiritual gifts that are given to Christians by the Spirit of God (v. 3). Calvin interprets this verse to teach us that "men have nothing good or praiseworthy except what comes from God alone."[30] Before Paul speaks about the horizontal dimension, he addresses the vertical connection believers have with God. He notes that church members are established upon a biblical confession of Christ (v. 3) and teaches that the source of their gifts is the Spirit of God (vv. 3, 7-9, 11). The Corinthians learn that there is no possibility of the horizontal dimension without a vertical foundation. Paul begins the section on the church by using the metaphor of the human body. He points to the vertical connection that the body has to the "one Spirit" in which the Corinthian believers "were all baptized into…" (v. 13). Picking up his earlier communion theme from chapter eleven, the apostle says, "all were made to drink of one Spirit" (v. 13b). This teaching about their unity in Christ through the Holy Spirit provides a basis for Paul's further instruction concerning the unity and diversity that exists in the local church at Corinth. The unity of church members is founded upon a common Spirit, but their diversity is rooted in the unique spiritual gifts that the Holy Spirit gives to each member of the body. The horizontal dimension is shown by the apostle's emphasis upon the importance of every member of the church. Paul's teaching that the members of the body should appreciate one another corrects the divisive, arrogant, and selfish attitudes he describes in chapter eleven, especially toward those who had nothing (1 Cor. 11:18, 23, 33). He says the Spirit has given spiritual gifts to each member of the church for the "common good" (v. 7). Fee remarks that in making this point Paul "anticipates the concern of chaps. 13 and 14, that the gifts are for

---

30. Calvin, *Calvin's New Testament Commentaries*, 9:261.

the building up of the community as a whole, not primarily for the benefit of the individual believer."[31] The gifts that the Spirit bestows pave the way for the members of the body to work together for the common spiritual good of the whole church in its worship and work.

Using the analogy of a body, the apostle encourages an attitude of unity, respect, and mutual concern for everyone in the church (i.e., the body) (vv. 16-27). Calvin comments on Paul's focus upon mutual concern: "But in this passage Paul is urging believers to bind themselves together by pooling their gifts for the benefit of each other; for their gifts were given them by God, not for every individual to nurse his own to himself, but so that they might help one another."[32] Nine times Paul uses the word "member" to describe individual Christians within the church providing a biblical reason for the concept of church membership (vv. 12, 14, 18-19, 25-27). The apostle teaches the church that those members of the body who have been treated with contempt by the stronger members are vital to the health of the whole church. Paul says,

> ... the parts of the body that seem to be weaker are indispensable and on those parts of the body that we think less honorable we bestow the greater honor, and our unpresentable parts are treated with greater modesty which our more presentable parts do not require. But God has so composed the body, giving greater honor to the part that lacked it, that there may be no division in the body, but that the members may have the same care for one another. (1 Cor. 12:22-25)

For Paul, "discerning the body" (11:29) of Christ means not only to understand who Christ is but to also care about and respect every member of the church which is Christ's body. This means that Christians should appreciate the usher as well as the soloist, pray for the organist as much as the preacher, respect the person running the sound board as much as the elder leading in prayer, and encourage the

---

31. Fee, *The First Epistle to the Corinthians*, 589.
32. Calvin, *Calvin's New Testament Commentaries*, 9:264.

greeter as much as the person in the pew. There is no room left for an individualized and tier-oriented perspective of worship.

The apostle reinforces his doctrine on the body of Christ by further stating, "If one member suffers, all suffer together; if one member is honored, all rejoice together" (1 Cor. 12:26). Such words encourage the church to appreciate its corporate unity as a body versus its tendency toward individualism. Carson notes, "No Christian is to think in individualistic terms but in terms of the body. Where this attitude dominates the believers, there can no longer be any place for spiritual one-upmanship, self-promotion, or an unbalanced stress on select gifts."[33] Paul's concern for the horizontal dimension in the attitudes of believers in the church toward their fellow believers is unavoidable. This concern and care applies not only to their daily treatment of one another but also in their corporate worship. Corporate concern leads to edification in the church when the members discern their unity as one body granted spiritual gifts for the common good. We discover how vital this theological viewpoint becomes when Paul explicitly addresses the way the Corinthians worship in chapter fourteen. Chapter twelve provides foundational presuppositions about the horizontal that are vital for biblical corporate worship that is pleasing to God. Christians cannot expect to focus on God vertically and claim union with Christ while treating one another poorly or avoiding the call to care for one another as members of the body of Christ-given gifts for mutual edification. Their common unity in the Spirit with his accompanying spiritual gifts demands that they give attention to the horizontal while claiming to worship God vertically.

After the apostle lays the groundwork for why Christians should show respect and care for one another as the body of Christ, the very body they are called to discern (11:29), he later addresses the Corinthians' abuse of some spiritual gifts exhibited in their worship. In chapter fourteen, Paul develops the idea of the horizontal by stressing the importance of edification in the context of biblical worship by addressing specific spiritual gifts.

---

33. Carson, *Showing the Spirit*, 49.

1 Corinthians 14

One of the problems in the church of Corinth was its overemphasis upon the extraordinary gifts and especially the gift of tongues. In chapter fourteen Paul addresses this problem by focusing on the inadequacy of tongues as a gift in comparison to prophecy. He notes that the gift of tongues is not the superior gift that the church believes it to be. Paul especially addresses the attitude we should have in corporate worship since the Corinthians were engaging in the practice of speaking in tongues in their services to the neglect of better gifts. Paul argues for the superiority of prophecy over tongues based primarily on the need for edification in the church. The word he uses for edification is *oikodomēn* (v. 3). It refers to the "process of building, *building, construction* ... figurative of spiritual strengthening (s. οἰκοδομέω 3) *edifying, edification, building up* [emphasis by the author]."[34] Paul sees tongues as a gift that primarily edifies the individual unless there is an interpreter who explains what the tongues speaker is saying. Morris rightly understands the apostle's emphasis upon building up the body when he remarks, "Paul insists that edification must be the prime consideration. Does one's gift help other people? That is the important thing."[35] Although the apostle understands the importance of individual edification (a vertical orientation in worship) (vv. 2, 15, 17-18, 39), he is far more concerned that worshippers strive to edify others as they worship (a horizontal concern). Contrasting a vertical orientation with the horizontal, Paul says, "On the other hand, the one who prophesies speaks to people for their upbuilding and encouragement and consolation. The one who speaks in a tongue builds up himself, but the one who prophesies builds up the church" (vv. 3-4). The Corinthians' overemphasis on tongues clouds their understanding of how important the horizontal is in their worship. Calvin grasps Paul's emphasis on the horizontal dimension in verse four stating "anything that is done in the Church ought to be for the good of all."[36]

---

34. *A Greek-English Lexicon of the New Testament*, s.v. "οἰκοδομή."
35. Morris, *The First Epistle of Paul to the Corinthians*, 186.
36. Calvin, *Calvin's New Testament Commentaries*, 9:287.

The reason Paul finds prophesy to be the greater gift is that it is intelligible and builds up listeners by enabling them to understand God's truth (vv. 4, 17, 19, 31). Tongues, on the other hand, without an interpreter, hinders intelligibility (vv. 9, 11, 14, 16) and edification (v. 17). Carson is correct in his analysis that "edification demands intelligible content, and tongues, by themselves, cannot provide it."[37] The unintelligible nature of tongues is why Paul requires an interpreter if tongues are spoken during corporate worship (vv. 13, 27-28). Paul's stress upon having an interpreter expresses his horizontal concern that everyone in the service understands what is happening and be edified. He calls the church to "strive to excel in building up the church" (v. 12). In verse sixteen, the apostle points out that if one gives thanks in tongues with their "spirit" (a vertical experience), an outsider who listens will not be able to say Amen to the thanksgiving that is offered because he will not know what is being said. His concern that hearers understand the words uttered in worship is a key reason Paul concludes, "Nevertheless, in church I would rather speak five words with my mind in order to instruct others, than ten thousand words in a tongue" (v. 19). Paul's concern about edification and intelligibility leads him to prefer prophecy to tongues when God's people assemble.

The apostle also expresses great concern for unbelievers who may attend corporate worship. He notes that if they come to a Christian meeting and hear people speaking in tongues, they will conclude that the congregation is crazy (v. 23). Carson comments, "Because the flow of the argument in these verses contrasts believers with unbelievers, newcomers with the established Christian community, it seems best to see in 'outsiders and unbelievers' a double description of the non-Christian visitor to the congregation."[38] So Paul concludes that prophecy is the preferred gift in worship because it is intelligible and therefore may convict the listener (v. 24), expose the secrets of his heart, and lead him to fall on his face, induce him to worship God and "declare that God is really among you" (v. 25). Paul's care for unbelievers clearly conveys his horizontal concern not only for Christians but also the unsaved. The apostle's instruction corrects

---

37. Carson, *Showing the Spirit*, 103.
38. Carson, *Showing the Spirit*, 116.

those today who wish to say that our services are not for unbelievers. Christian worship services should address the souls of both believers and unbelievers. Paul's comment that unbelievers will be "convicted" when the church comes together likely means that the message of the gospel will be conveyed. This is the message that Paul has already said should be preached (1 Cor. 1:17-18, 23; 2:2). Reflecting upon the evangelistic thrust of verses twenty-four through twenty-five, Matthew Henry wisely comments, "Religious exercises in Christian assemblies should be such as are fit to edify the faithful, and convince, affect, and convert unbelievers. The ministry was not instituted to make ostentation of gifts and parts, but to save souls."[39]

In his continued discussion on worship, the apostle provides further encouragement for believers to consider one another in the expression of their gifts, teaching, and singing in order to build up the body of Christ (v. 26). His instruction about how to conduct worship conveys additional support for the horizontal dimension. Paul corrects the individualized mentality among the Corinthians. Commenting on verses twenty-six to forty, Fee states that Paul's "antidote is to offer guidelines for regulation that, taken together, suggest orderliness, self-control, and concern for others."[40] The Corinthians are called to think about how they are building up one another in their worship. Paul promotes an orderly use of the gifts "so that all may learn and all be encouraged" (v. 31). Gifts are not given by God just to bless the individual but to also spiritually encourage the whole church. Understanding Paul's emphasis upon the body versus the individual Schweizer remarks, "The goal of the service is by no means the comfort, the happiness, or even the salvation of the individual taking part in it. It is always the upbuilding of the church."[41] Order should also be maintained for the spiritual growth and blessing of everyone in the worship service. Such concerns for order are based upon a wise understanding of the orderly character of God (a correct vertical

---

39. Matthew Henry, *Matthew Henry's Commentary on the Whole Bible: Complete and Unabridged in One Volume* (Peabody: Hendrickson, 1994), 2271.

40. Fee, *The First Epistle to the Corinthians*, 688.

41. Eduard Schweizer, "Service of Worship: An Exposition of 1 Corinthians 14," *Interpretation* 13, no. 4 (October 1959): 404.

understanding). Paul states, "For God is not a God of confusion but of peace" (v. 33, cf. v. 40).

In summary, all things should be done in worship for the praise of God in an intelligible, clear, and encouraging manner for the upbuilding of the body of Christ and the salvation of souls. If the church today would apply Paul's teaching in 1 Corinthians 14 on worship, it would surely foster the pursuit of love toward God and our neighbor (v. 1). Now let us consider Paul's instruction in the pastoral epistles about the horizontal dimension.

Ephesians 5:19

During his Roman imprisonment, the apostle Paul wrote a letter to the Ephesian church to encourage them in a biblical understanding of the doctrine of the church. As Paul calls the church to "walk in love" (5:2) and walk "as wise" (5:15) Christians, he provides insight on the dynamic that should take place in their worship services. His words steer us away from an individualistic perspective on worship in which our attention is solely upon the Lord and ourselves. Although there is no one else they can worship other than God, the believers in Ephesus are encouraged to minister to one another in their worship. Stott notes that "the mention of 'psalms, hymns and spiritual songs' ... indicates that the context is public worship."[42] Although worship is the primary subject at hand, we should not limit the application of this text to worship alone. Paul conjoins the worship of God with attention to ministering to our neighbor. This text clearly presents support for the horizontal dimension of worship. Chapell observes:

> In contrast to some contemporary teaching that says that our worship is to be directed entirely to God, Paul presumes that there is a horizontal dimension to our worship. In praising God we consciously should be directing our worship to the edification of others. As Christ ministers to others by extending himself for them, when we worship with the needs of others as

---

42. John R W. Stott, *The Message of Ephesians: God's New Society* (Leicester, England: Inter-Varsity Press, 1986), 205.

our concern, then we are ministering Christ and consequently being filled with his indwelling Spirit.[43]

After telling the church to "be filled with the Spirit," the apostle describes what this should look like when the believers are together. Foulkes remarks, "the fullness of the Spirit will find manifestation in fellowship when Christians are found together and will be given joyful expression in song and praise."[44] When the Spirit fills the people of God, they cannot help but sing. As the Spirit does his work of filling, Paul declares that the Corinthians will engage in "addressing one another in psalms and hymns and spiritual songs, singing and making melody to the Lord with your heart" (v. 19). The participial phrase "addressing one another" supports the idea of the horizontal dimension. The Greek is *lalountes heautois*. It is literally translated as "speaking to one another." Christians should not simply engage in worship for their own benefit and edification. They should seek to edify one another in their worship by speaking words that "build up the lives of others and bring glory to the living and true God."[45] This principle is reminiscent of Paul's emphasis on edifying the body of Christ in 1 Corinthians 14. Paul goes on to describe how the Ephesians should speak to one another in their worship. This should happen through their singing of psalms, hymns, and spiritual songs. We can be sure that Paul is not excluding the primary focus for their singing which is the praise of God (i.e., "making melody to the Lord") but here he is highlighting the horizontal responsibility of believers to minister to one another in their singing. It is important to note that not all singing in the Bible directly addresses God, but there are songs which are sung for "mutual exhortation" (i.e. Psalm 95).[46] We sing horizontally when in our songs we testify to one another, stir others to praise God, encourage thanks to the Lord, instruct each other in the

---

43. Bryan Chapell, *Ephesians*, Reformed Expository Commentary (Phillipsburg, NJ: P & R Publishing, 2009), 163-4.
44. Francis Foulkes, *The Letter of Paul to the Ephesians: An Introduction and Commentary*, 2nd ed. (Leicester, England: Inter-Varsity Press, 1989), 159.
45. F.F. Bruce, *The Epistles to the Colossians, to Philemon, and to the Ephesians* (Grand Rapids, MI: W.B. Eerdmans, 1984), 380.
46. Stott, *The Message of Ephesians*, 206.

truths of the Word, and testify to the world that the gospel is true and God is great. Singing is a practical way to express being filled with the Holy Spirit. There is much debate as to what Paul means regarding the different types of songs. Some interpreters say that the different terms that Paul uses simply refer to the psalms of the Old Testament Psalter. The fact that Paul uses different musical terms likely indicates that he is distinguishing different types or styles of music that Christians may have sung with or without instruments. Martin provides a helpful explanation regarding this debate:

> It is hard to draw any hard-and-fast distinction between these terms; and modern scholars are agreed that the various terms are used loosely to cover the various forms of musical composition. 'Psalms' may refer to Christian odes patterned on the Old Testament Psalter. 'Hymns' would be longer compositions and there is evidence that some actual specimens of these hymns may be in the New Testament itself. 'Spiritual songs' refer to snatches of spontaneous praise which the inspiring Spirit placed on the lips of the enraptured worshipper, as 1 Corinthians 14:5 implies. These 'inspired odes' would no doubt be of little value, and their contents would be quickly forgotten.[47]

When Christians sing to the Lord, it is important for them to ponder how and what they are communicating to their fellow worshippers. Sadly, many people who attend church today do not sing but rather watch others perform the music during worship. This kind of non-participatory worship happens too often regardless of whether the liturgical style is contemporary, traditional, low-church, or high church. Such services look more like a concert or symphony than the type of worship we observe in the New Testament. This approach encourages people to view worship more as entertainment rather than a time to honor God and edify our neighbor. There is little attention given to mutual edification when the people of God refuse to speak to

---

47. Ralph P. Martin, *Worship in the Early Church*, rev. ed. (Grand Rapids, MI: Eerdmans, 1975), 47.

one another in song as Paul promotes. They forget their calling to encourage and minister to one another as they worship. Singing is not just a personal vertical experience between the individual and God, but it is also an opportunity to build up others through the melody and message of praise to the Lord. It encourages the congregation when people sing out loud from hearts that are committed to God with thanksgiving "in the name of our Lord Jesus Christ" (v. 20). The hearers experience the truth of God's Word and the gospel expressed through the body of Christ. Participatory singing demonstrates that God has saved not only individuals but his covenant people: the church. Paul's words of wisdom should encourage all Christians to participate in singing to the Lord for the edification of the body of Christ. The content of such music should be accessible and understandable. O'Brien states, "the fact that believers address one another in these psalms and songs shows that Paul has intelligible communication in view, not meditation, unknown speech, or glossolalia."[48] The normal direction of singing in worship should be for the praise and glory of God for the edification of the body and salvation of sinners. The focus on glorifying God and building up the body of Christ means that the content of the songs in worship should be theologically consistent with the doctrines of the Word (1 Tim. 4:16). Paul provides similar instruction in his letter to the Colossians.

Colossians 3:16

The apostle Paul uses similar words to those he used in Ephesians 5:29 with some notable variations. Moo states, "This verse is one of the very few that provide us with any window at all into the worship of the earliest Christians."[49] Here the apostle adds the importance of the Scriptures, "Let the word of Christ dwell in you richly…" In Ephesians, he emphasizes the work of the Spirit, but now he gives attention to the necessity of the Word. Paul reminds us that when the

---

48 Peter Thomas O'Brien, *The Letter to the Ephesians* (Grand Rapids, MI: W.B. Eerdmans, 1999), 395.

49. Douglas J. Moo, *The Letters to the Colossians and to Philemon* (Grand Rapids, MI: William B. Eerdmans, 2008), 290.

Spirit is doing his work of "filling" the believer, the Word of God is always present. The "word of Christ" either refers to the very words that Jesus spoke or those words spoken about Christ and his work. Dunn comments, "As such it can denote both the word (gospel) of which (the) Christ is the content (so most; "the mode of Christ's presence in the community," Wolter 189), and the word which (the) Christ spoke (Jesus tradition); there is no reason why the genitive form should be pressed to an either-or decision (either objective or subjective).[50] It is a mark of godly wisdom for the believer to dwell upon the Scriptures and to have them dwell in him. As the Christian gives way to the peace of Christ and submits to his rule (v. 15), he is compelled to store the Word "richly" in his heart. When this submission occurs, the believer considers the importance of the Word and gives considerable thought to its meaning and application in his life. Once this takes place, there is no room for complacency. Paul declares that believers should then engage in "teaching and admonishing one another in all wisdom, singing psalms and hymns and spiritual songs with thankfulness" in their "hearts to God." Regarding the different musical terms Paul uses, Wright remarks, "Together these three terms indicate a variety and richness of Christian singing which should neither be stereotyped into one mould nor restricted simply to weekly public worship."[51] Similar to his comments to the Ephesians, Paul again encourages the horizontal dimension by calling believers to teach and admonish one another, and singing is one of the ways they can do this. Commenting on the construction of verse sixteen, Bruce notes, "Whatever view is taken of the punctuation or construction of the sentence, the collocation of the two participial clauses (as they are in the Greek text), 'teaching and instructing . . .' and 'singing . . .,' suggests that the singing might be a means of mutual edification as well as a vehicle of praise to God."[52] Paul reminds us that a clear presentation of the Word of God should inform their ministry to one another in worship. They should also seek to carefully

---

50. James D. G. Dunn, *The Epistles to the Colossians and to Philemon: A Commentary on the Greek Text* (Grand Rapids, MI; William B. Eerdmans; 1996), 236.

51. N T. Wright, *The Epistles of Paul to the Colossians and to Philemon: An Introduction and Commentary* (Leicester, England: Inter-Varsity Press, 1986), 145.

52. Bruce, *The Epistles to the Colossians, to Philemon, and to the Ephesians*, 158.

interpret and apply the Word in their words and song. There is no room for the wishy-washy political correctness that is often seen in churches today which hide the clear truths of God's Word for fear of offending those who listen. The singing of believers should include the horizontal dimension since it provides a way to admonish and teach others the Word of God. Calvin remarks, "all our words should be disposed to edification."[53] Singing in the service should not be limited to the personal experience that is often sought today in many churches. Detwiler states:

> As Christians assemble for worship, they are not merely individuals expressing personal worship to the Lord; they are also members of one congregation who have the responsibility of encouraging each other through music. Both of these dimensions must be kept in mind. Believers may benefit from asking themselves, "What am I communicating to those around me during our times of singing to the Lord?" And, "How am I building up others as we worship in song together?"[54]

As Christians address one another Paul adds the phrase "in wisdom." Bruce suggests this might mean that "The Colossian Christians, like those at Rome, should be able to instruct one another; but such instruction should be given wisely and tactfully. If wisdom or tact be absent, the instruction, however well-intentioned, could provoke the opposite reaction to that which is designed."[55] The phrase "with thankfulness in your hearts to God" indicates the ultimate vertical direction and attitude that Christians should adopt when they admonish and teach one another in their singing during corporate worship. All things should be done from the heart with thankfulness toward the Lord. He desires sincere worship according to his Word (Isa. 29:13; John 4:23-24). It is a recurrent biblical theme that God desires worship from the heart rather than empty ritual and tradition. Christians should remember that God is always watching their heart.

---

53. Calvin, *Calvin's New Testament Commentaries*, 11:353.
54. David F. Detwiler, "Church Music and Colossians 3:16," *Bibliotheca Sacra* 158, no. 631 (July 2001): 365.
55. Bruce, *The Epistles to the Colossians, to Philemon, and to the Ephesians*, 158.

He desires both love for their neighbor and heartfelt thankfulness to God. It is important to understand that love as God defines it always includes doing that which may lead those we love to give thanks to God from their hearts. Such love will not hide or distort God's Word to please men at the cost of truth. When believers express thanks to God in their hearts they are pondering the goodness of the Lord, his saving work in Christ, and his continual providential care through Christ (vv. 16b-17). Such considerations should affect the music we choose to sing and the attitude in which we sing in worship. This attitude in worship should also overflow from the way we worship into the way we live and treat others every day of the week (v. 17). What and how we sing should encourage all those who listen to give "thanks to God the Father through him [Christ]." Not only does Paul encourage Christians to consider others in worship but James likewise addresses the horizontal dimension by providing instruction on how to avoid favoritism and inconsistency when believers come together.

James 2:1-13; 3:9

James calls our attention to the way believers should act toward those who attend their assemblies. Adams remarks that James "teaches that from God's perspective poverty is not evil and riches are no advantage."[56] The setting of James 2 appears to be a worship service where favoritism is taking place. James' reference to the "assembly" of the brothers likely means that the Christians are meeting in a house church. The apostle begins this passage by calling believers to "show no partiality" as they "hold the faith in the Lord Jesus Christ" (v. 1). The Greek word translated "partiality" is *prosōpolēmpsiais*. Zerwick translates it as *"partiality, respect/favouring of persons on the ground of social standing, wealth, or influence* [emphasis by the author]."[57] James' reference to "the faith" likely refers to the apostolic doctrines of the Christian faith that have been passed down to the church through the Scriptures especially their interpretation according to the

---

56. Jay E. Adams, *A Thirst for Wholeness* (Wheaton, IL: Victor Books, 1988), 66.
57. Max Zerwick and Mary Grosvenor, *A Grammatical Analysis of the Greek New Testament* (Rome: Biblical Institute Press, 1974), 694.

Lord Jesus. Regarding "the faith," Davids notes that "True faith has no place for the social distinctions of the world."[58] James' reference to Jesus in verse one grounds the apostle's horizontal concerns in the vertical position that believers possess in Christ. James highlights Jesus' exalted status by calling him "the Lord of glory" (v. 1). The appeal to Jesus' glory reminds us of the fact that he left the glory of heaven to humble himself for our salvation on the cross (Phil. 2:1-11). Jesus' descent from heaven and humiliation upon the cross exemplified immense grace and mercy toward humanity, an attitude foreign to the practice of idolizing riches or favoring the wealthy over the poor. James hints at the incompatibility of favoritism with Christianity when he mentions their "holding the faith" in Christ (v. 1). Faith in the Savior who demonstrated love to all should encourage his followers to follow in his footsteps. The Scriptures teach that God shows no favoritism for people (cf. Deut. 10:17; Gal. 2:6). Therefore, his children should avoid showing partiality as they strive to imitate their heavenly Father (Eph. 5:1).

The apostle presents a hypothetical situation that may be based on experience or information he has learned about the church's treatment of a poor man in comparison to a rich man. Both the wealthy and poor man come to a Christian assembly. It appears that they are strangers or visitors to the church since they need to be directed to where they should sit. In verse three, James presents the scenario of favoritism shown to the rich man. He is given "a good place" (v. 3) in the assembly while the poor man is directed to a less important seat (e.g., "Sit down at my feet" [v. 3b]). One of the church members sees the gold ring and expensive clothing of the rich man and gives him preferential treatment. Another person sees the other man dressed in "shabby clothing" and judges him less worthy of special attention (v. 2). The word "shabby" is the Greek word *rhypara* which pertains "to being dirty, *filthy, soiled* [emphasis by the author]."[59] We can envision one of the church members walking up to the rich man, happy to see such a well-dressed and important man entering the place of worship. Then the member escorts him to one of the best seats in the house.

---

58. Peter H. Davids, *The Epistle of James: A Commentary on the Greek Text* (Grand Rapids, MI: Eerdmans, 1982), 105.

59. *A Greek-English Lexicon of the New Testament*, s.v. "ῥυπαρός."

The rich man can see everything from his vantage point while the poor man remains at a distance sitting on the floor barely able to see or hear what is happening in the service. The church member is not too excited about whether the poor man is noticed or treated well. In fact, he is probably thinking the less others see this poorly dressed man the better it is for the image of the church. He probably thinks that the poor man will not protest since he obviously lacks influence. Favoritism is taking place because some in the church are judging the rich man by his outward appearance and considering him more worthy of special treatment. Such ill-treatment of people demonstrates how the horizontal dimension can be distorted because the vertical expectations of God are ignored or misunderstood. Those who are showing favoritism are not thinking about how their Lord Jesus Christ would want them to treat those who enter their worship services regardless of their socio-economic status or appearance.

The apostle condemns the behavior of those who show favoritism. James says that those who practice such things have "become judges with evil thoughts" (v. 4). Showing favoritism is no small thing. The Greek word used for "evil" is *ponērōn*. It means "to be morally or socially worthless, *wicked, evil, bad, base, worthless, vicious, degenerate* [emphasis by the author]"[60] After clarifying the seriousness of showing favoritism James then provides a proper vertical understanding of God and his attitude about the poor. Motyer comments, "It has always been the case that the Lord's true people are predominantly less well-off, the prey for stronger, more ruthless forces, and subject to less than justice from those who know how to manipulate the system."[61] The Lord blesses the poor in this world by making them rich in faith and heirs of his kingdom (v. 5). They are not lowly or unimportant to him, and so they should not be mistreated or disrespected. They bear God's image just as much as those who possess many riches. James provides practical advice about the foolishness of favoring the wealthy. The rich are often the ones who use their influence to oppress others (v.6) and blaspheme God (v. 7). Giving them preferential treatment is simply unwise and a misunderstanding about their importance in comparison

---

60. Ibid., s.v. "πονηρός."
61. J. A. Motyer, *The Message of James: The Tests of Faith* (Leicester, England: Inter-Varsity Press, 1985), 89.

to the poor. James goes on to encourage a horizontal focus that believers should have by loving their neighbor as themselves (v. 8). Loving one's neighbor is the fulfillment of "the royal Law" (v. 8). Ladd states, "The Law is royal because its author is none other than the King of the universe."[62] Jesus, the King of Kings, taught his disciples to love God and their neighbor (Matt. 22:37-40). James repeats the teaching of the Savior about loving others (v. 8b). When the church shows partiality to the rich, they are not showing love to their neighbor. Christ's doctrine of love for our neighbor is firmly grounded in the truths of the Old Testament (Lev. 19:9-18). The apostle exclaims that showing favoritism is sin and clear evidence of transgression of the Law of Moses (v. 9). Stulac says:

> Favoritism is sin because it violates Christ's law of love. Loving your neighbor as yourself requires an openness to friendship with any neighbor – regardless of that neighbor's wealth, position, status, influence, race, appearance, attractiveness, dress, abilities or personality. The follower of the royal law will reach out to any neighbor.[63]

James speaks about God's commandment against murder to illustrate the fact that showing favoritism is a form of murder (cf. Matt. 5:21-22). Davids notes, "Murder, however, is frequently associated with discrimination against the poor and failure to love the neighbor (Je. 7:6; 22:3; Sir. 34:26; Test. Gad 4:6–7; 1 Jn. 3:15; Am. 8:4; cf. the literature cited on 2:9)."[64] The Lord expects his people, especially in their assemblies, to show mercy to the poor who attend their services just as they acknowledge the mercy of God toward themselves (vv. 12-13). Mercy toward others is the demand of the "law of liberty" which refers to the Law of God as taught by Christ and the church. To God, the Law must always be interpreted with a commitment to the priority of Biblical mercy (Matt. 9:13; Hos. 6:6). Jesus taught the Law in light of a biblical understanding of love for God and our neighbor, a love

---

62. Ladd, *A Theology of the New Testament*, 638.
63. George M. Stulac, *James,* vol. 16 (Downers Grove, IL: InterVarsity Press, 1993), 102.
64. Davids, *The Epistle of James*, 117.

steeped in mercy. Favoritism for the rich over the poor was a clear violation of Christ's understanding of the Law. Christians are called to speak and act with careful consideration of Jesus' interpretation of the Law. Those who were unwilling to show mercy toward others without favoritism could expect the judgment of God (v. 13). After all, Jesus taught in the Sermon on the Mount, "Blessed are the merciful, for they shall receive mercy" (Matt. 5:7). James gives a warning to the church to avoid unmerciful acts and attitudes toward others, especially the poor who attend their assemblies. Davids states, "Certainly the connection must be that in humiliating the poor (whom God honors) and in transgressing the law of love (thus breaking the law) they are also failing to show mercy. As such they could expect no mercy in the final judgment. Yet showing mercy reminds one primarily of helping the poor materially."[65] James concludes his pericope, James 2:1-13, with a positive axiom to encourage the congregation to show mercy, "Mercy triumphs over judgment" (v. 13). This theme of mercy is a repeated Old Testament and New Testament teaching exemplified in the example of God the Father and the Son toward humanity. Mercy is what Christians receive from God vertically through Christ and an attribute the Father expects Christians to exhibit in their horizontal relationships, especially in their worship services. James presents a familiar doctrinal theme that the vertical and horizontal dimensions are inextricably intertwined in the life and worship of the church. If one is going to worship the Lord as they should, they cannot choose one dimension over the other.

Having spoken about how we should treat people without favoritism in our services, James later discusses the topic of taming the tongue (James 3:1-12). In this passage, he presents the inconsistency in which we use our tongue in relation to our worship of God (vv. 9-12). One minute we praise God with our tongue, but then we also use it to curse other human beings. James is not forbidding the correct use of the tongue in a biblical sense but "What James appears to be referring to is the use of a curse in anger, especially in inner-church party strife."[66] In addressing the tongue, James clearly communicated

---

65. Davids, *The Epistle of James*, 119.
66. Ibid., 146.

the necessity of joining the vertical with the horizontal. Speaking of the tongue, he says, "With it we bless our Lord and Father, and with it we curse people who are made in the likeness of God" (v. 9). Commenting upon the text, Davids states, "this blessing is undoubtedly a liturgical blessing of God in the church services and private prayers rooted in the emergence of the church services from the synagogue (which may not have been complete at the time James was written)."[67] It appears that this brother of Christ is calling the brethren to be consistent in their praises to God with due respect for their fellow man. He draws our attention to the absolute incompatibility of such inconsistent uses of the tongue by saying "these things ought not to be so" (James 3:10). He illustrates the ridiculous nature of this scenario by comparing such speech with a few impossible examples.

James presents rhetorical questions that demand negative responses (vv. 11-12). Using the tongue for praise and cursing would be like a spring pouring forth fresh water while at the same time pouring out salt water, an utterly ludicrous thought (v. 11). It would also be like a fig tree bearing olives, a horticultural fantasy. Such talk would be comparable to grapevines producing figs, something that would never happen. He summarizes his line of argument with the assertion: "Neither can a salt pond yield fresh water" (James 3:12)." This summary statement punctuates the absolute incompatibility of using our tongues to praise God in our worship (i.e., a vertical act) while cursing other people (a horizontal act). Stulac remarks, "He is exposing the hypocrisy of speaking praise to God with the worshiping church or in private prayer while abusing people with ridicule, insult, and attacks through the rest of the week."[68] The grave concern that James has for such inconsistency in the way we use our tongue in worship should convict and inform us all. He is encouraging believers to be consistent in their praise of God and their respect for others who are made in the image of God (Gen. 1:27; 9:6). Moyter comments that this passage addresses "the way we speak inwardly about a brother or sister, the way we speak to somebody else about a brother or sister, the

---

67. Ibid.
68. Stulac, *James*, 128.

way we speak to a brother or sister. If we are in earnest as we sit before the Word of God, then we admit what seems far more than our powers, but we can start here with a new respect for the image of God seen in the members of his family."[69] James challenges believers today to seek to combine their vertical praise to God with an equally respectful horizontal consideration of the people they both live and worship with each week. Believers should use their tongues to both praise God and bless others. In short, James calls for worship that combines the vertical with the horizontal.

Summary

We have covered much ground regarding both the vertical and horizontal dimensions of worship. Key passages have been discussed that represent a sufficient sample of scriptural teaching on the subject of the horizontal dimension's interdependence with the vertical dimension. We have discovered that the concept of the horizontal dimension is founded upon God's Trinitarian being. His relationship within the Trinity demonstrates a firm basis for the horizontal relational dynamics that he expects among his people, especially in worship. It has been argued that the horizontal is also rooted in covenant theology and God's covenantal expectations in corporate worship. Various Scriptures, both in the Old and New Testaments, demonstrate that the Lord calls his people to include both the vertical and horizontal dimensions in their corporate worship. We have learned that the Law of God at Sinai supports the premise that the vertical and horizontal dimensions are intertwined. The vertical and horizontal dimensions should apply not only to daily life but also to corporate worship. We should never leave the Law's demands that we love both God and neighbor at the entrance to the sanctuary. God longs for his people to love others as they express their love for God in their worship. The Lord also will not tolerate empty and ritualistic worship that is devoid of the heart and soul of the believer. He desires mercy rather than outward sacrifice. Mercy always includes love for our neighbor. Without love, our sacrifices and ritual are worthless to

---

69. Motyer, *The Message of James*, 126.

God. Love for God and our fellow worshippers must always go together. Love is the most "excellent way" and must inform our vertical and horizontal expressions of worship. When it comes to the horizontal expectations of God, he expects his people to love their neighbor before, during, and after their corporate worship.

The Lord also watches how his people are treating the poor, needy, orphans, widows, and the sojourner. He considers whether their love for their neighbor includes justice and mercy. Are they treating their neighbor fairly, according to the Word of God? There is no room for favoritism or despising one's neighbor because of their outward appearance, race, or socio-economic status. Justice is essential to biblical worship. We have discovered that justice includes the vertical and the horizontal. If we do not treat our neighbor in a just manner, God will not accept our worship. The Lord demands that we maintain justice for both the righteous and the wicked. This teaching challenges Christians today to avoid the hypocrisy of claiming to praise Christ while treating their neighbors unjustly with contempt and disrespect. God corrects those who claim to worship him acceptably, but yet they act wickedly toward their fellow man doing such things as cheating, stealing, committing murder, taking bribes, coveting their possessions, thwarting the due process of the law, and taking advantage of the weak. When we consider the God of justice, we should be moved to pursue justice with our neighbor before, during, and after of our regular worship.

Lastly, we have considered Scriptures that explicitly address the topic of worship and have found that God demands worship be done "in Spirit and truth." This means that our worship should be done according the work of the Holy Spirit and in line with the truth of Scripture. The Spirit moves believers to praise God and love their neighbor. The Spirit produces the fruit of the Spirit, fruit that specifically addresses how believers view and treat their neighbors. It has been shown that the Lord is deeply concerned that our worship be done in such a way that it convicts unbelievers unto salvation and edifies Christians in their sanctification (two important horizontal concerns). The Lord's Supper reveals that God demands that believers see their worship as communal rather than individualistic. In other words, Christians need to consider their connectedness with the body of Christ and worship in a way that promotes repentance, faith, encouragement, growth, and unity unto the praise of the Father through his Son Jesus. We have learned that musical praise to God is not just meant to bless us individually. Christians should minister to one another in the way they sing to God in worship. The Lord calls believers to worship with respect for their fellow worshippers without showing favoritism. Christians are taught to be biblically consistent in their worship. This means that as they praise God, they should also respect their neighbors who have been made in the image of the God they praise. To do otherwise makes no sense in light of the spiritual transformation that has taken place in the lives of Christians.

In short, the theme of biblical love for God and others in corporate worship runs throughout the Scriptures. The horizontal dimension is upheld by the Lord and cannot be separated from the vertical. If we wish to worship God acceptably, we must also love our neighbor. The principle of the horizontal dimension of worship is firmly established throughout the Bible and is inseparable from a vertical posture toward God in accord with Scripture. We must always worship God with love for our neighbor.

One of the essential teachings of the Reformation was to ground everything that the church does and believes in the Bible. This sentiment is represented by the Latin motto, *Sola Scriptura* (Scripture alone). We have confirmed above that the horizontal dimension is well founded upon the authority of Scripture and should be carefully considered in the construction and practice of corporate worship. We now turn to the theological teaching and practices of the Reformation. Let us examine some of the major Reformers, creeds, and Reformation guidelines for worship to determine whether the Reformation provides sufficient support for the horizontal dimension of worship.

Part 2

HISTORICAL CONSIDERATIONS

In considering the historical basis for the horizontal dimension of worship, it is important to understand the fundamental practices and thinking of the early church. Harkening back to the first century, we find limited documentation regarding the exact elements used in first-century Christian churches. Carson notes, "we have no detailed *first-century* evidence of an entire Christian service."[1] The details are primarily those we find in Scripture. As Christendom progressed, services in the Roman Catholic church became primarily clergy driven, vertically oriented and less horizontal. By the time of the Reformation, there was much to be done to reform the corrupt and heretical practices of the church, especially in its worship. Many church historians view the time of the Reformation as a movement that was greatly influenced by a desire to reform the church's worship. The Reformers were concerned with reforming worship practices according to the Word of God with a careful consideration of the practices of the early church and the early church fathers. The Latin phrase *ad fontes* (meaning "to the sources") was a motto of Reformed biblical scholars who sought to bring the church back to its scriptural roots and early historical practices which were in conformity with the Word.[2] As we look to some of the key Reformers and the Reformed confessional standards, we are reminded of several concerns of the Reformation that call for a consideration and practice of the horizontal dimension in congregational worship. Not only will we ponder the thoughts of some major Reformers but we will also consider the supporting views of key Reformed confessional standards that provide additional support for the horizontal dimension. One of the key

---

1. D.A. Carson. "Worship Under the Word," in *Worship by the Book*, ed. D. A. Carson (Grand Rapids, MI: Zondervan, 2002), 21.

2. Terry L. Johnson. *Worshipping with Calvin: Recovering the Historic Ministry of Worship of Reformed Protestantism* (Welwyn Garden City, UK: EP Books, 2014), 40.

documents strictly related to the practice of worship, the *Westminster Directory of Worship*, will also be given special attention in our consideration of this project's thesis.

In this chapter, we will limit our survey to two individuals who many historians consider the most influential Reformed theologians on the Protestant view of worship—Luther and Calvin. We will also focus upon certain early post-Reformation doctrinal standards that introduced significant landmark changes to Roman Catholic worship during the Reformation and early post-Reformation era. Due to the direct historical connection of the modern Protestant and Evangelical church to these Reformed leaders and doctrinal statements we will give little attention to the time prior to the Reformation except for corrections suggested by the Reformers to the practices of Rome. The Reformers' desire to go back to the Scriptures and the early church fathers in their attempt to reform worship gives us no reason to survey the prior centuries since it is the intent of this project to prove that the Reformers and the Protestant Reformed standards support the horizontal dimension. It is the purpose of this chapter to clearly convey the fundamental and significant changes that occurred among Reformed Protestants to the practice of worship and how those changes particularly paved the way for a renewed appreciation and practice of the horizontal dimension in corporate worship. It will be shown that those who state that the practice of the horizontal dimension is not Reformed are incorrect in their assessment when we carefully examine the actual statements and practices of the Reformers and doctrines of their post-Reformation children.

Since Luther and Calvin were so instrumental in the changes made during the Reformation, we will focus upon their significant contributions. Albeit, the phrase horizontal dimension might not necessarily appear in Reformation writings, we cannot dismiss the concept of the horizontal in the theology and practices of the Reformed church. Using the Reformed principle "by good and necessary inference" we will discover that the Reformers indeed supported the horizontal dimension in their desire to glorify God in their worship.

The first place to begin our survey is at the feet of the great Martin Luther, the Reformer who ignited the fire of the Reformation in

Germany. He helped to lay a foundation for integrating a passion for the vertical while expressing concern for the horizontal. Luther and other Reformers were deeply committed to worshipping in a God honoring manner while simultaneously showing concern and love for his neighbor.

6

Martin Luther

General Issues

Luther brought his keen mind and theological insights to bear upon many subjects during the Reformation. Although worship was one area in which he expressed great concern his writing on the topic of liturgy is somewhat limited. Luther was distraught over the unbiblical worship of the Roman Catholic Church wherein the people were given a back seat to the priest who was believed to be the primary mediator between God and man. Worship was often reduced to a perfunctory ritual in which the people were encouraged to think about worshiping God vertically through an earthly, priestly mediator or trained professional rather than encouraged to engage the Lord corporately. This approach focused on the individual via the liturgical ritual of the priest thus reducing most congregants to mere spectators. Lange remarks, "Worship had become a performance for the people who did not participate but simply watched."[1] Luther, however, believed the people had a significant role to play in the church and especially in the worship of God. One might argue that this shift in emphasis upon participating in worship was not necessarily a promotion of the horizontal versus the vertical dimension, but we cannot deny that a biblical understanding of participation in worship would undeniably lead not only to participating with God but also with our neighbor as we engage in corporate worship. This is a de facto result from the Christian's double union with Christ and his fellow believers. When we are united to Christ, we are also united to other Christians. This mysterious union is demonstrated in the way we treat

---

1. Dirk G. Lange, "Martin Luther's Reform of Worship," *Oxford Research Encyclopedia of Religion,* March 2017, accessed July 15, 2017, http://dx.doi.org/10.1093/acrefore/9780199340378.013.357.

one another in daily life and in our worship of God. If Christians truly participate in loving God in worship, they cannot decouple participating with others in their corporate worship. As has been noted in chapter two, participation with God in worship will flow over into loving our neighbors and translate into some form of participation with them in our worship. Otherwise, we are not truly participating with God as we claim. He will not accept worship that participates with him only in worship but ignores our neighbor. His commands demand that we both love God and our neighbor in corporate worship. The Lord expects and demands that we participate with others with an attitude of love and concern, a love that is motivated by our love for God. It is possible that Luther did not fully grasp the horizontal implications of promoting participatory worship, but we should understand that this emphasis upon participation provides a clear stepping stone toward horizontal participation in the service and thus paves the way for a more biblical understanding of worship in Reformed churches. Luther's emphasis upon the role of the laity as priests of God would encourage the people to acknowledge their participatory role in ministering in worship not only to God but also to their neighbors.

Luther promoted the doctrine that the people were ministers of the Lord as well as the clergy. This view introduced the importance of each member's role horizontally in ministering to one another during corporate worship. As priests of God, the people were expected to participate rather than act as mere spectators in worship. Luther said, "For thus it is written in 1 Pet. 2 [:9]: 'You are a chosen race, a royal priesthood, and a priestly royalty.' Therefore we are all priests, as many of us as are Christians. But the priests, as we call them, are ministers chosen from among us."[2] At the time, worship services were primarily conducted in Latin—a language that most people could not understand. Consequently, corporate worship lost its communal and covenantal nature in the Roman church. Aniol comments, "Beyond the Eucharist, however, Roman worship had moved from the 'work of the people' (liturgy) to the work of the clergy. The language of the

---

2. Martin Luther, "On the Babylonian Captivity of the Church," in *Three Treatises*, ed. Frederick C. Ahrens and Abdel Ross Wentz, 2nd ed. (Philadelphia: Fortress Press, 1978), 244.

Mass was entirely in Latin, the elements of the Table were withheld from the 'laity,' and even music was performed only by approved singers."[3] As Luther sought to reform worship, he argued that the laity should be more engaged in the service. He believed that worship should be practiced in the language of the people rather than only in Latin. Often the people had no clue what was being said or sung since they only spoke German. In his treatise *The Babylonian Captivity of the Church* Luther voices his concerns about the incommunicable nature of the Roman priest's presentation of the mass:

> And would to God that as he elevates the sign, or sacrament, openly before our eyes, he might also sound in our ears the word, or testament, in a loud, clear voice, and in the language of the people, whatever it may be, in order that faith may be the more effectively awakened. For why may Mass be said in Greek and Latin and Hebrew, but not in German or any other language?[4]

Luther's horizontal concerns were matched with his passion for the church to engage in worship with a scriptural understanding of the vertical dimension. He sought to honor the Lord in corporate worship and all of life. Early in the Reformation, Luther exhibited a strong commitment to the authority of the Word of God over the church and its worship. The Reformer expressed a high view of the preaching of the Word which was hidden for many years in the Roman liturgy. He rejected five of the seven sacraments in the Catholic church since he believed that only baptism and the Lord's Supper were "divinely instituted" sacraments.[5]

Luther recommended changes in the order of the church's liturgy to establish a biblical balance between the horizontal and vertical dimensions of worship. Lange states that Luther's "liturgical order communicates through the means of preaching and sacrament an

---

3. Scott Aniol, "Martin Luther's Worship Reforms," Religious Affections Ministries, October 30, 2010, accessed July 13, 2017, http://www.religiousaffections.org/articles/articles-on-worship/martin-luthers-worship-reforms/.

4. Luther, "On the Babylonian Captivity of the Church," 174.

5. Ibid., 258.

encounter with the living God that re-orients life in this world, moving the believer away from self-centeredness to God- and neighbor-centeredness."⁶ The Reformer was not against using a liturgical order but sought to rid church services of Roman rituals and accruements that were unbiblical and did not promote the gospel. He detested the many superstitious practices that had crept into the church and rejected the emphasis in the Mass on the sacrifice of Christ. It was his goal to return worship to its evangelical purpose. Luther completely removed the Roman canon of the Mass from his liturgies. He is not shy about his distaste for it: "Let us, therefore, repudiate everything that smacks of sacrifice, together with the entire canon and retain only that which is pure and holy, and so order our Mass."⁷ Leupold remarks, "Much offense has been taken at his complete excision of the canon of the Mass, but this ruthless operation freed the Words of Institution from the rank growth around them and placed the gospel squarely in the center of the Eucharistic rite."⁸ Although he did not embrace the regulative principle that everything in worship should be explicitly prescribed, Luther did move the church toward the principle of reforming worship according to the Scriptures. This conviction would become a fundamental belief in the reformation of the church which would develop into the regulative principle among other Reformers. We see his progression toward biblical changes from the typical elements of the Roman Mass to a more evangelical order of service for the church at Wittenberg (Formula Missae) in 1523 and later with his German Mass and Order of the Liturgy in 1526.⁹ Luther decided to conduct services in the language of the people while removing repetitive prayers. He included corporate music, asserted the importance of preaching, and conducted communion more inclusively. The Reformer removed the restriction of the cup to the laity and gave back all the elements of the Lord's Supper to the people. He firmly believed the people should engage in worship from their heart and soul. For Luther worship was a corporate experience meant

---

6. Lange, "Martin Luther's Reform of Worship," 11.
7. Martin Luther, *Luther's Works*, vol. 53, *Liturgy and Hymns*, ed. Ulrich S. Leupold (Philadelphia: Fortress Press, 1965), 26.
8. Ibid., XVII.
9. See Appendix A for consideration of Luther's recommended liturgical order.

to help God's people meet with God which should equip them to love others. He declared his horizontal concerns about worship after an incident in which the people had vandalized the church and destroyed sacred pictures in response to Carlstadt's preaching. When Luther came back to town and discovered this vandalism, he preached a series of eight sermons to encourage moderation. He voiced concern for the horizontal by admonishing the congregants to show love and sensitivity toward the weaker members in the church. Thompson observes that Luther wanted to "know what had happened to the love of these innovators who had pursued rash and impatient action without regard for the conscience of their weaker brethren."[10] The great Reformer always thought of Christ's calling to love others as he passionately preached the necessity of reform. Luther further displays a horizontal concern in the promotion of intercessory prayer in worship after the preaching of the sermon. He encouraged the paraphrasing of the Lord's Prayer. Conforming one's prayer to the Lord's Prayer would engage the congregation in the horizontal dimension as they prayed with the pastor not only for their own needs but also for the needs of others. They would also be encouraged to pray for the forgiveness of those who trespassed against them. This manner of prayer would unite their horizontal concerns with their vertical calling to honor and glorify God. It pleases the Lord when his people pray for one another. Although prayer was important to Luther, the use of music in worship was also very dear to his heart.

Music

Luther was not against using liturgical forms, but he was concerned about making the worship of God more accessible to the people in their own language especially in the area of music. The Reformer firmly believed music plays an important role in worship. In the *Preface to Georg Rhau's Symphoniae iucundae* (1538) he says, "next to the Word of God, music deserves the highest praise."[11] In his

---

10. Bard Thompson, *Liturgies of the Western Church* (Philadelphia: Fortress Press, 1980), 96.

11. Luther, *Liturgy and Hymns*, 323.

comments on the German Mass Luther states, "I also wish that we had as many songs as possible in the vernacular which the people could sing during Mass."[12] In reshaping the Mass, Luther comments on the need to use the indigenous language of the people:

> But I would very much like to have a true German character. For to translate the Latin text and retain the Latin tone or notes has my sanction, though it doesn't sound polished or well done. Both the text and notes, accent, melody, and manner of rendering ought to grow out of the true mother tongue and its inflection, otherwise all of it becomes an imitation, in the manner of the apes.[13]

As the Reformation moved forward, Luther would come to incorporate the German language in the Mass along with corporate singing. He would substitute German hymns and psalms in place of Latin. He strongly encouraged the people to sing praises to God believing that intelligibility was essential to biblical worship. Bainton comments on Luther's contribution to congregational singing, "The last and greatest reform of all was in congregational song. In the Middle Ages, the liturgy was almost entirely restricted to the celebrant and the choir. The congregation joined in a few responses in the vernacular. Luther so developed this element that he may be considered the father of congregational song."[14] Barber reflects upon Luther's changes to the liturgy of the Mass: "The existential emphasis of the Mass is evident in the fact that it stressed the simple marriage of text and tune so that all people, especially the uneducated laity, could participate."[15] Luther felt so strongly about incorporating music that he wrote at least thirty-seven hymns (that we know of) and encouraged the writing of hymn books by those gifted in musical composition. Resultantly, hymn writing and participatory singing in

---

12. Ibid., 36.
13. Martin Luther, *Luther's Works*, vol. 40, *Church and Ministry II*, ed. Lehmann, Helmut T., and Conrad Bergendoff (Philadelphia: Fortress Press, 1958), 141.
14. Roland H. Bainton, *Here I Stand: A Life of Martin Luther* (Peabody, Mass.: Hendrickson Publishers, 2009), 355.
15. John Barber, "Luther and Calvin on Music and Worship," *Reformed Perspectives*, June 25, 2006, 3.

the church under Luther flourished. Regarding God's use of music and its ability to affect the church horizontally Luther states,

> For whether you wish to comfort the sad, to terrify the happy, to encourage the despairing, to humble the proud, to calm the passionate, or to appease those full of hate—and who could number all these masters of the human heart, namely, the emotions, inclinations, and affections that impel men to evil or good?—what more effective means than music could you find? The Holy Ghost himself honors her as an instrument for his proper work when in his Holy Scriptures he asserts that through her his gifts were instilled in the prophets, namely, the inclination to all virtues, as can be seen in Elisha [2 Kings 3:15]. On the other hand, she serves to cast out Satan, the instigator of all sins, as is shown in Saul, the king of Israel [1 Sam. 16:23].[16]

Luther himself was known as an excellent musician and gifted tenor. He was greatly concerned that all the hymns and songs of the church be based upon the truth of Scripture. This was a vertical concern in Reformed worship meaning that the service should conform to the Word of God which was the will of God. Barber states, "Luther wanted scripture itself put to music; he wanted worship songs to contain or to adhere as closely as possible to the ideas expressed in the Bible."[17] He sought to reform the music of the church in both its musical content and musical style. This understanding gave way to new hymnody and the singing of psalms in the church. In comparison to Luther, Calvin did not emphasize the singing of hymns. He was more convinced that the singing of the Scriptures themselves was permissible, but psalm singing should be the primary type of music in worship.

Regardless of their positions on the types of music for worship, both Luther and Calvin believed that God's people should engage individually and corporately in musical praise to God. This very fact was a departure from the common liturgical practices in the Roman church that minimized the importance of corporate singing. Luther's

---

16. Luther, *Liturgy and Hymns*, 323.
17. Barber, "Luther and Calvin on Music and Worship," 11.

horizontal concerns are also revealed in his admonition that edification should be a primary consideration in preparing services. He declares, "Now even though external rites and orders—such as masses, singing, reading, baptizing—add nothing to salvation, yet it is unChristian to quarrel over such things and thereby to confuse the common people. We should consider the edification of the lay folk more important than our own ideas and opinions."[18] The Reformer believed that the order of the service was not as important as showing love to one's neighbor for their edification. He says, "But you are bound to consider the effect of your attitude on others. By faith be free in your conscience toward God, but by love be bound to serve your neighbor's edification, as also St. Paul says, Romans 14 [15:2]."[19] He strongly believed the purpose of music, as well as all the elements of worship, were to include the horizontal function of edification in praise of God.

Luther does not demand a rigorous order of service but rather encourages freedom in the order of worship. However, many in his day sought his wisdom and advice on how to conduct their services. Luther's concern for the horizontal was always present as his comments on the *German Mass and Order of Service* attest, "But while the exercise of this freedom is up to everyone's conscience and must not be cramped or forbidden, nevertheless, we must make sure that freedom shall be and remain a servant of love and of our fellow-man."[20] Luther cautions against the heartless liturgical practices of the Roman church. He knows that an overemphasis upon liturgical form and order are real dangers that can lead to empty ritualistic worship even in Protestant Churches. He warns:

> For the orders must serve for the promotion of faith and love and not be to the detriment of faith. As soon as they fail to do this, they are invalid, dead and gone; just as a good coin, when counterfeited, is canceled and changed because of the abuse, or as new shoes when they become old and uncomfortable are no longer worn, but thrown away, and new ones bought. An order is an external thing. No matter how good it is, it can be abused.

---

18. Luther, *Liturgy and Hymns*, 47.
19. Ibid.
20. Luther, *Liturgy and Hymns*, 61.

Then it is no longer an order, but a disorder. No order is, therefore, valid in itself—as the popish orders were held to be until now. But the validity, value, power, and virtue of any order is in its proper use. Otherwise it is utterly worthless and good for nothing. God's Spirit and grace be with us all. Amen."[21]

Not only was Luther instrumental in providing foundational teaching on worship during the Reformation, but John Calvin also made significant contributions. He produced the systematic theological structure for many of the doctrines of the Reformation. His theological genius helped establish biblical principles on worship that built upon the views of Luther and influenced Protestant liturgical theory and practice for centuries.

---

21. Ibid., 90.

7

John Calvin

A close study of Reformed worship reveals the historical fact that John Calvin had a significant influence upon the Reformed church's view of worship. Rayburn comments, "It is no exaggeration to say that John Calvin is the most pivotal figure in the development of the worship of the Reformed tradition. His influence is still felt today in those churches which have retained a consciousness of and emphasis upon their historic roots."[1] Much of Calvin's views on worship developed while he was pastoring briefly in Strasbourg from 1538-1541. Johnson astutely comments, "Calvin's liturgy should be seen not as the product of a single individual, but as the culmination of decades of reform."[2] He was particularly influenced by Martin Bucer especially regarding his views on the sacraments and the Lord's Supper. Like Luther, Calvin had a profound belief in the authority of God's Word. Along with many of the Reformers, he was deeply concerned about the abuse of the Roman Catholic Church and how it had drifted from the teachings of Scripture, especially in the area of worship. The Reformer sought to bring glory to God in all his teachings and application of the Word. When Calvin entered Geneva to lead the city in its transformation, he first set about reforming its worship. He held to the principle that everything we do in worship should be founded upon the Bible. In other words, the Scriptures should regulate the why and what in worship. The Reformer realized that man-made ideas had corrupted many of the Roman Catholic churches in their worship. The Catholic church had filled its worship with practices often done for

---

1. Robert Gibson Rayburn, "Worship in the Reformed Church," *Presbyterion* 6, no. 1 (1980): 17.

2. Terry L. Johnson, *Leading in Worship: A Sourcebook for Presbyterian Students and Ministers Drawing from the Biblical and Historic Forms of the Reformed Tradition,* rev. ed. (Power Springs, GA: Tolle Lege Press, 2013), 187.

ostentatious reasons. For Calvin, worship was not meant for entertainment nor show. Kelly comments, "For Calvin, the public worship of God is not some light-hearted, entertainment-driven, flippant affair. It is a sobering encounter with the triune God mediated through the presence of the resurrected Christ in the power of the Holy Spirit."[3] In warning the church, Calvin remarks, "God rejects and even abominates everything devised for worship by human reason."[4] The Reformer sought to go back to the practices of the early church. Gore states, "The formative principle in Calvin's liturgical renewal was fidelity to the Scriptures, as understood by the early church. Essential to Calvin's thinking is man's sin. Because of that sin we would be unable to worship God unless he told us how we should worship and serve him."[5] Calvin understood that the New Testament did not provide a specific order of worship. This perspective allowed for freedom to a certain extent in forming liturgies. He did, however, seek to structure his services in a fashion that promoted God's glory and the gospel of Christ.

During the Reformation, there were fundamentally two approaches to worship. Some focused on a fixed liturgy while others promoted a type of free worship. The first group was primarily represented by the Anglican Church. The second approach was represented primarily among the Anabaptists and many Puritans. Calvin and Knox, as key proponents of the Reformation, neither promoted a strict liturgy nor advocated absolute liturgical freedom. They did produce recommended liturgies for the churches. Rayburn notes that "Calvin was especially resistant to the practice of allowing freedom to ministers to formulate their own prayers for their services of worship. He wrote the prayers for use in the churches of Geneva himself."[6] Calvin's emphasis upon such liturgical restrictions was

---

[3]. Joe Wayne Kelly, "Seated in the Heavenlies: Integrating John Calvin's Principles of Worship in a Baptist Context" (Doctor of Ministry diss., Reformed Theological Seminary, 2010), 96.

[4]. John Calvin, "The Necessity of Reforming the Church," in *Calvin: Theological Treatises*, Vol. 1, Edited and Translated by J. K. S. Reid (Louisville, KY; London: Westminster John Knox Press, 1954), 192.

[5]. R. J. Gore, Jr., "Reviewing the Puritan Regulative Principle of Worship," *Presbyterion* 21, no. 1 (1995): 42.

[6]. Rayburn, "Worship in the Reformed Church," 19.

loosened later by the Puritans who became averse to mandating the use of form prayers especially those of the *Book of Common Prayer*, commonly called "Laud's Liturgy," named after its creator, Archbishop William Laud.[7] Nevertheless, Calvin's thoughts on devising a thoughtful and planned liturgy lived on among many Presbyterians who embraced the biblical principle of conducting worship in a decent and orderly manner (1 Cor. 14:40).

Calvin's liturgical structure had two foci. His worship order included the following:

Liturgy of the Word
Scripture Sentence (e.g., Ps. 121:2)
Confession of Sins
Prayer for Pardon (Calvin used words of Pardon only at Strasbourg. Such words were not allowed in Geneva)
Metrical Psalm Sung
Ten Commandments (sung with Kyries at Strasbourg)
Prayer with Lord's Prayer (called a Collect) for Illumination
Scripture Reading (called a Lection)
Sermon
Prayer of Intercession ending with a paraphrase of the Lord's Prayer
Aaronic Blessing[8]

Liturgy of the Upper Room (Practiced Quarterly in Geneva)
Collection of Alms
Intercession
The Lord's Prayer
Apostle's Creed (sung as elements were prepared)
Words of Institution

---

7. Bishop Laud (1573-1645), was the Archbishop of Canterbury during the time of King Charles I of England. He revised Thomas Cranmer's *Book of Common Prayer* and sought to impose it upon the Presbyterians in Scotland to promote liturgical uniformity. His efforts were strongly resisted by the Scottish church. Laud was eventually beheaded by the Parliamentarians of the English parliament in 1645.

8. Thompson, *Liturgies of the Western Church*, 191, 203. Thompson adds the elements of prayer (intercession) and an Aaronic Blessing to the normal service which are two elements that Chapell leaves out when listing the elements of Calvin's typical service.

>Exhortation (form of fencing the Table)
>Fraction (breaking of the bread)
>Communion (with Scriptures read)
>Psalm Sung
>Thanksgiving Prayer (Post-Communion Collect)
>Aaronic Blessing[9]

We do not mention this liturgical order to force it upon the church today, but it is informative to see how Calvin stresses certain elements that accord with both the vertical and horizontal dimensions. The Reformer drew upon the practices of the second- and third-century church fathers who used similar orders of service. By the time he first arrived in Geneva, Calvin inherited the liturgy of William Farel. Farel's liturgy was similar to Zwingli's in "its infrequency of Communion and the absence of singing."[10] After Calvin left Geneva to serve in Strassburg with Martin Bucer, he developed additional liturgical insights which he would later bring back to Geneva to influence its reformation. The Reformer disagreed strongly with the Roman Catholic practice of withholding certain elements from the people in the Supper and condemned the practice of taking communion once a year. Kelley remarks, "The common practice of withholding the cup from the laity, in Calvin's estimation, was an invention that came out of the devil's workshop."[11] Calvin's desire to celebrate the Supper weekly expresses a horizontal concern for the congregants. He says, "The Lord's Table should have been spread at least once a week for the assembly of Christians, and the promises declared in it should feed us spiritually."[12] Calvin believed that every repentant Christian had a right to all the elements in the Lord's Supper. The Reformer wished to practice the Lord's Supper each Sunday viewing the Liturgy of the Upper Room as an expression of the gospel presented in the Liturgy of the Word. The council of Geneva, however, chose not to follow his

---

9. Bryan Chapell. *Christ-Centered Worship: Letting the Gospel Shape Our Practice* (Grand Rapids, MI: Baker Academic, 2009), 52; Robert Gibson Rayburn, "Worship in the Reformed Church," *Presbyterion* 6, no. 1 (1980): 25.

10. Chapell, *Christ-Centered Worship*, 47.

11. Kelly, "Seated in the Heavenlies," 81.

12. John Calvin, *Institutes of the Christian Religion*, ed. John T. McNeill, trans. Ford Lewis Battles (Louisville, KY: Westminster John Knox Press, 2011), 4.17.46.

preference for weekly communion. Calvin was left to a quarterly practice.

The Reformer also voiced his concerns over the use of unknown languages such as Latin in Roman worship. In his letter to Emperor Charles V, he explains the horizontal concern of the Reformers that they educate the people regarding the Lord's Supper "as in the case of Baptism, so also in the case of the Lord's Supper, we explain to the people faithfully and as carefully as we can its end, efficacy, advantages, and use."[13] The Reformer embraced both the vertical and horizontal emphases in Communion. Blocher quotes Calvin on the topic of Communion in the *Short Treatise (on the Supper)* (1541) and draws attention to the Reformer's view that the sacrament is both vertically and horizontally useful. Calvin says the Supper "induces us to render thanks to him [God], and, as it were, by *public confession*, protest how much we are indebted to him. The third benefit consists in our having a vehement incitement to holy living, and above all to observe charity and *brotherly love among us* [emphasis mine]."[14] Notice in Calvin's comments that biblical love is one of the guiding principles in determining the conduct and practices of the church in its life and worship. One could argue that Calvin's inclusion of Christian love in his thinking regarding worship was grounded carefully in his view of the Law of God. He embraced the two-fold division of the Ten Commandments. Calvin accepted the vertical direction of the first table of the Decalogue believing it focused upon God and that the second table of the Law as horizontal focused upon the duties of people to their neighbor. He viewed the two tables of the Law as interdependent rather than mutually exclusive. Commenting on their relationship and the importance of the first table to the second, Calvin states, "We call it source and spirit because from it men learn to live with one another in moderation and without doing injury, if they honor God as Judge of right and wrong."[15] Calvin felt strongly that loving one's neighbor was as an application of obedience to the Law

---

13. Calvin, "The Necessity of Reforming the Church," 205.

14. John Calvin, "Short Treatise on the Holy Supper of our Lord and Savior Jesus Christ," in *Calvin: Theological Treatises*, Edited and Translated by J. K. S. Reid (Louisville, KY; London: Westminster John Knox Press, 1954), 149.

15. Calvin, *Institutes*, 2.8.3.

and one's true love for God. The reformer cannot separate loving God from loving our neighbor. He says, "our soul should be entirely filled with the love of God. From this will flow directly the love of neighbor."[16] Calvin would never agree with the vertical-only mentality in which the worshipper thinks only about himself and what he might get out of his time in corporate worship. Such a view would have violated Calvin's view of Christian love. He confirms this point when he states:

> Hence it is very clear that we keep the commandments not by loving ourselves but by loving God and neighbor; that he lives the best and holiest life who lives and strives for himself as little as he can, and that no one lives in a worse or more evil manner than he who lives and strives for himself alone, and thinks about and seeks only his own advantage.[17]

The Reformer did not separate the love of God from the love we must show for our neighbor whom Calvin "includes even the most remote person."[18] He further comments about this perspective:

> Therefore, if we rightly direct our love, we must first turn our eyes not to man, the sight of whom would more often engender hate than love, but to God, who bids us extend to all men the love we bear to him, that this may be an unchanging principle: whatever the character of the man, we must yet love him because we love God.[19]

Christian love for Calvin was a pivotal link in a healthy relationship with God and others. He could not envision a worship service without love for one's neighbor (i.e., horizontal) and the love for God (i.e., vertical) no more than one could envision a fish without water.

---

16. Calvin, *Institutes*, 2.8.51.
17. Ibid., 2.8.54.
18. Ibid., 2.8.55.
19. Ibid.

Later in book four of his *Institutes,* Calvin speaks about what the church is bound to versus its freedom in worship. He comments about the importance of edification and love:

> the Lord has in his sacred oracles faithfully embraced and clearly expressed both the whole sum of true righteousness, and all aspects of the worship of his majesty, and whatever was necessary to salvation; therefore, in these the Master alone is to be heard. But because he did not will in outward discipline and ceremonies to prescribe in detail what we ought to do (because he foresaw that this depended upon the state of the times, and he did not deem one form suitable for all ages), here we must take refuge in those general rules which he has given, that whatever the necessity of the church will require for order and decorum should be tested against these. Lastly, because he has taught nothing specifically, and because these things are not necessary to salvation, and for the upbuilding of the church ought to be variously accommodated to the customs of each nation and age, it will be fitting (as the advantage of the church will require) to change and abrogate traditional practices and to establish new ones. Indeed, I admit that we ought not to charge into innovation rashly, suddenly, for insufficient cause. *But love will best judge what may hurt or edify; and if we let love be our guide, all will be safe*[20] (emphasis added).

For Calvin, love for one's neighbor must guide the church in its application of the Word as it carries out corporate worship. As he focused on the Lord's Supper, he could not separate the vertical from the horizontal. In Calvin's mind, this divinely given sacrament brings the vertical and the horizontal together in one harmonious stream with love being the guiding principle. Commenting upon the importance of both honoring God and the importance of love for one's neighbor in the administration of the Lord's Supper, the Reformer states:

---

20. Calvin, *Institutes,* 4.10.30.

Rather, it was ordained to be frequently used among all Christians in order that they might frequently return in memory to Christ's Passion, by such remembrance to sustain and strengthen their faith, and urge themselves to *sing thanksgiving to God and to proclaim his goodness*; finally, by it to *nourish mutual love, and among themselves give witness to this love*, and *discern its bond in the unity of Christ's body*. For as often as we partake of the symbol of the Lord's body, as a token given and received, we reciprocally *bind ourselves to all the duties of love* in order that none of us may permit anything that can harm our brother, or overlook anything that can help him, where necessity demands and ability suffices[21] (emphasis added).

Notice that Calvin does not separate praise to God and the love demanded by God for one's brother (in the body of Christ) in his consideration of the Lord's Supper. Concerning this passage, Moore states, "I note that Calvin expresses a 'horizontal' concern in the Supper: it 'nourishes' and 'witnesses' to love, and invariably represents a 'binding' awareness on Calvin's part of the value in religious worship of expressing and facilitating brotherly relationships with the church."[22] The call to love others in the Supper should inspire Christian love within the congregation. Calvin notes that it should "nourish mutual love" meaning that believers who participate in the Supper should contemplate how they are bound together in love through Christ and are also called to show love to one another in various and tangible ways. This is a beautiful perspective on the Lord's Table and its purpose in the lives of the saints. The principles that Calvin espouses in the practice of the Lord's Supper provide insight into his thinking about the prominence of the horizontal dimension in corporate worship.

The Reformer also provides wisdom on the inclusion of the horizontal dimension in his commentary on Acts 2:42. He points out that when the church gathered together, it included the apostles' teaching, breaking of bread, prayers, and fellowship. In his *Institutes*,

---

21. Ibid., 4.17.44.
22. Peter Charles Moore, "The Spirit of Calvin and 'Intimations' in 'Religious Worship,'" *The Reformed Theological Review* 69, no. 2 (August 2010): 92.

Calvin comments on Acts 2:42 concluding, "Thus it became the unvarying rule that no meeting of the church should take place without the Word, prayers, partaking of the Supper, and almsgiving. That this was the established order among the Corinthians also, we can safely infer from Paul [cf. 1 Cor. 11:20]. And it remained in use for many centuries after."[23] The context of Calvin's remarks in light of the Lord's Supper seems to strongly suggest that his phrase "no meeting of the church" indicates that he is referring to "what we in the Westminster tradition call 'religious worship.'"[24] Calvin believes that the word *koinōnia* in Acts 2:42 includes "mutual association, alms, and other duties of brotherly fellowship" and he considers it to be one of the four marks of the "true and genuine church."[25] For Calvin, fellowship is an essential expression of Christian love within the body of Christ and one of the key elements in biblical worship.

The Reformer also recognizes that an important expression of brotherly love and fellowship in the New Testament is demonstrated in the practice of giving "the holy kiss" (Rom. 16:16; 1 Cor. 16:20; 2 Cor. 13:12; and 1 Thess. 5:26). He believes it was a customary symbol of friendship among the Jews (Rom. 16:16). In his commentary on 1 Corinthians 16:20, Calvin says, "But Paul is probably speaking here about a ceremonial kiss, with which they greeted each other when they gathered for worship. For I could well believe that from the time of the apostles a kiss was already used in connexion with the administration of the Supper"[26] Calvin further states that the holy kiss was a "sign of mutual love . . . meant to cultivate goodwill among themselves . . . so long as it was holy, that is to say, not lustful or sham; although 'holy' can also be taken as referring to an of act of worship."[27] Therefore, the Reformer acknowledges this horizontal practice in the context of worship since it was often mentioned in the New Testament. One might argue in light of Calvin's recognition of the importance of love and the inclusion of a holy kiss in New Testament

---

23. Calvin, *Institutes*, 4.7.44.
24. Moore, "The Spirit of Calvin and 'Intimations,'" 94.
25. Ibid., 94.
26. John Calvin, *Calvin's New Testament Commentaries*, ed. David W. Torrance and Thomas F. Torrance, trans. A. W. Morrison (Grand Rapids, MI: Eerdmans, 1989), 9:356.
27. Ibid., 9:356-57.

worship that his understanding of the regulative principle is more principial than strictly prescriptive. His approach leaves open the possibility of various ways in which to demonstrate brotherly love in corporate worship.[28]

In Calvin's theology, the worship service was not an opportunity to be entertained by professionals. The Reformer considered it essential to involve the body of Christ in singing praises to God. He promoted corporate singing mainly of the psalms as well as some Scripture set to music. In Strasbourg, the Reformer encouraged the congregation to sing the Decalogue. He "wrote the rhymed version himself."[29] His singing of the Ten Commandments after the Confession and Pardon for Sin demonstrated that he believed obedience to God was a product of grace rather than a means to earn it. Calvin's focus upon the Scriptures as God's authoritative and inspired Word led him to primarily sing the Psalms. He was concerned that music that was created by men could lead people astray. He believed the singing of the Psalms was the most ancient practice of the church. He advocated the writing of metrical psalms and also promoted the creation of the *Genevan Psalter* which became a beloved songbook for the Reformed church inspiring many future revised editions. He championed the practice of worshiping in the language of the people. Calvin was appalled by the use of Latin in the church since most could not understand it. He said, "Thus is a very great impudence on the part of those who introduced the Latin language in the Church where it is not generally understood. And there is neither subtlety nor casuistry which can excuse them, because this practice is perverse and displeasing to God."[30] Believing that singing was a form of public prayer, Calvin expressed the strong opinion that "prayers should be

---

28. This perspective may allow for various expressions of the horizontal dimension such as: announcements, greetings, missionary reports, etc.

29. Chapell, *Christ-Centered Worship*, 49.

30. John Calvin. *Preface to the Psalter*, 1543. From the facsimile edition of: "Les Pseaumes mis en rime francoise par Clément Marot et Théodore de Béze. Mis en musique a quatre parties par Claude Goudimel. Par les héritiers de Francois Jacqui" (1565); Published under the auspices of La Société des Concerts de la Cathédrale de Lausanne and edit, in French, by Pidoux, Pierre, and in German by Ameln, Konrad. (Baeroenreiter-Verlag, Kassel, 1935), accessed March 21, 2019. https://www.ccel.org/ccel/ccel/eee/files/calvinps.htm

made in a language commonly known to the people."[31] He believed that all things should be conducted in the worship service for the edification of the people. We should note that such horizontal concerns represent a desire to help the congregation glorify God through mutual ministry in offering praise to the Lord. It is clear in the Genevan liturgy that Calvin seeks to help the people properly focus on the Lord from a gospel-centered perspective. He begins the service with a scriptural sentence to focus the people on God. This is meant to encourage their praise, awe, and humility as they begin their time of corporate worship. It was essentially a scriptural call to worship. Like the encounter of Isaiah (see Isa. 6) who was convicted of his sin when he saw a vision of God, Calvin wishes to move the people toward confession and repentance early in the service. He then offers hope and grace in Christ through a prayer of pardon. The people are then prepared to join together to sing a Psalm of praise and thanksgiving to God for his pardoning grace. Calvin then encourages a humble reliance upon God for his illumination to understand the Word. He leads the worshippers to listen to God's Word through a reading of Scripture in the language of the people. Afterward, the minister is called to preach a sermon that seeks to explain, illustrate, and apply the Word of God to the lives of the hearers. Calvin's high view of Scripture means that the reading and preaching of the Word were the highlights of the service. The preaching of the Word was the apex of worship since it was the time when God spoke to his people (God's horizontal concern) and directed them in the way they should think and live.[32] The preached Word calls for the people to exercise humility, eagerly desire God's direction, and give their fullest attention to his will (2 Tim. 3:16-17). The preaching of the Word is where the vertical and horizontal meet in one harmonious symphony of worship to the praise of God.

We also discover the vertical and horizontal in Calvin's Liturgy of the Upper Room. First, we see the vertical and horizontal represented in the collection of Alms. Chapell states,

---

31. John Calvin. *Preface to the Psalter*, 1543.
32. Preaching demonstrated the pastor's horizontal concern for the people in light of God's horizontal concerns for the hearers.

Almsgiving demonstrates that the Lord's Supper has both horizontal (believer-to-believer) and vertical (believer-to-Redeemer) dimensions in Calvin's theology. The horizontal dimension of the Lord's Supper is also reflected in Calvin's reminder that the sacrament is a shared meal. New Testament believers were to share nourishment and serve one another in their observance of Christ's ordinance (see 1 Cor. 11:33). So the church's meal (as well as baptisms) and Intercessions of prayer come after the Sermon. In this way congregational members can care for one another in light of the grace received from instruction in God's Word. The community also bound itself together in a mutual profession of its beliefs and dependence on God by singing together the Apostle's Creed as Calvin brought the bread and wine to the table. The vertical aspect of the sacrament is its promotion of the "mystical union."[33]

Regarding the practice of prayer, the great Reformer calls attention to both the vertical and horizontal dimensions during his prayers that followed the sermon. He opens his prayers to the glory of God and intercedes for authorities, pastors, the lost, and the saved. One cannot accuse Calvin of forgetting the horizontal during corporate worship. Consider some of the wording of a sample collect (i.e., prayer) that Calvin encourages ministers to pray that includes references to the vertical and horizontal:

> Almighty God, heavenly Father, thou has promised to grant our requests which we make unto thee in the name of thy well-beloved Son, Jesus Christ our Lord: by whose teaching and that of His apostles we have also been taught to gather together in His name, with the promise that He will be in the midst of us, and will be our intercessor with thee, to obtain all those things for which we agree to ask on earth.
> First, we have thy commandment to pray for those whom thou hast established over us as rulers and governors; and then for all the needs of thy people, and indeed of all mankind.

---

33. Chapell, *Christ-Centered Worship*, 53.

Wherefore we pray thee, O heavenly Father, for all princes and lords, thy servants, to whom thou hast entrusted the administration of thy justice, and especially for the magistrates of this city.

We pray thee also, O faithful Father and Savior, for all those whom thou hast ordained pastors of thy faithful people, to whom thou hast intrusted the care of souls and the ministry of thy holy Gospel. Direct and guide them by thy Holy Spirit, that they may be found faithful and loyal ministers of thy glory, having but one goal: that all the poor, wandering, and lost sheep be gathered and restored to the Lord Jesus Christ, the chief Shepherd and Prince of bishops, so that they may grow and increase in Him daily unto all righteousness and holiness. Will thou, on the contrary, deliver all the church from the mouths of ravening wolves and from all mercenaries who seek their own ambition or profit, but never the exaltation of thy holy name alone, nor the salvation of thy flock.

We pray thee now, O most gracious and merciful Father, for all men everywhere. As it is thy will to be acknowledged the Savior of the whole world, through the redemption wrought by thy Son Jesus Christ, grant that those who are still estranged from the knowledge of Him, being in the darkness and captivity of error and ignorance, may be brought by the illumination of thy Holy Spirit and the preaching of thy Gospel to the straight way of salvation, which is to know thee, the only true God, and Jesus Christ whom thou hast sent. Grant that those whom thou hast already visited with thy grace and enlightened with the knowledge of thy Word may grow in goodness day by day, enriched by thy spiritual blessings: so that all together we may worship thee with one heart and one voice, giving honor and reverence to thy [Son Jesus] Christ, our Master, King, and Lawgiver.

Likewise, O God of all comfort, we commend unto thee all those whom thou dost visit and chasten with cross and tribulation, whether by poverty, prison, sickness, or banishment, or any other misery of the body or affliction of the spirit. Enable them to perceive and understand thy fatherly affection which doth chasten them unto their correction, that they may turn unto thee with their whole heart, and having turned, receive full consolation and deliverance from every ill.[34]

This recommended intercessory prayer should inform and inspire all pastors and their congregants during worship to pour out their hearts and souls to God on behalf of their fellow believers, the unsaved, the needy, the sick, and those in authority. Such prayer was meant to apply the message of God's Word in the lives of the hearers. The Reformers like Calvin were concerned that the Word of God shape the lives of those sitting under biblical preaching. This horizontal intercessory prayer was also intended to move God's people to engage in such prayer during the week and meant to instruct them on how to treat their neighbors.

Calvin also promotes the horizontal by including the corporate singing of the Apostle's Creed to signify the unity of God's church in a common faith and doctrine. During the fencing of the Table, an exhortation is given which addresses both the vertical and the horizontal. The fencing of the Table encourages the faithful to confess their sins and seek reconciliation with their brethren. It calls them to address their relationship with both God and man. They are exhorted to rely on the Lord's grace and to trust in God's promises of forgiveness through true repentance and faith in Christ alone. It is made clear that one cannot be right with God unless he is right with his brethren (Matt. 5:24). This Old Testament theme of the need to love both God and one's neighbor is repeated in a proper administration of the Lord's Table. The Consecration Prayer and Fraction remind participants that the Supper is God's vertical institution for the benefit, blessing, and edification of the church. It is an institution given by Christ himself. The shared communion and partaking of the elements demonstrate both the spiritual union of believers with Christ and their union with fellow members in the body of Christ—the church (1 Cor. 10:16-17). The members of the

---

34. Thompson, *Liturgies of the Western Church*, 199-200. Note that this sample prayer or one like it would have been prayed shortly after the sermon at either a normal non-communion or communion service. In other words, intercessory prayer was a fixed feature of Calvin's liturgy.

congregation edify one another in singing praise to God who has given them his grace, union with Christ, and oneness through the Spirit (Eph. 4:4-6). The closing of the service with a Thanksgiving Prayer and an Aaronic Blessing represent the vertical dependence upon God that his people have in Christ. Calvin clearly sees that both the vertical and horizontal are essential dimensions of biblical worship. Thompson recalls Calvin's union of the horizontal with the vertical referencing Calvin's thanksgiving prayer prior to his Aaronic Blessing, "Thus may we order and pursue all of our life to the exaltation of thy glory and the edification of our neighbor; through the same Jesus Christ, thy Son, who in the unity of the Holy Spirit liveth and reigneth with them, O God, forever, Amen."[35]

Having considered two monumental Reformers and their views related to the vertical and horizontal dimensions, we now will examine the teachings on the matter among some of the great Reformed confessions, catechisms, and standards for worship. We will seek to determine if the horizontal dimension is supported in these foundational documents.

---

35. Thompson, *Liturgies of the Western Church*, 203.

8

Reformed Creeds & Catechisms

Belgic Confession

The Belgic Confession was one of the earliest Reformed confessional standards. Authored by Guido de Brès in 1561, it became a confession of both the north and south regions of the Netherlands, which today is divided into the Netherlands and Belgium. "In 1566 the text of this confession was revised at a synod held at Antwerp. In the Netherlands, it was at once gladly received by the churches, and it was adopted by national synods held during the last three decades of the sixteenth century."[1] Although the Belgic Confession says little explicitly about the subject of worship, there are principles it lays down that support the concept of the horizontal dimension. This highly respected doctrinal confession would have been thoroughly applied to the life of the Reformed church. We contend that if we carefully examine the confession, we should come to appreciate its important doctrinal statements that support the horizontal dimension in corporate worship. We should also note that the clergy of the church who vowed to uphold this doctrinal statement would be duty bound to expound upon and encourage church members to apply the confession's teaching in both their daily lives and gatherings on the Lord's Day. This brings us to consider what the confession says about the obligations of church members.

Article twenty-eight addresses the "The Obligation of Church Members." In this section Christians are called to join and unite with the church. It states, "... keeping the unity of the church by submitting to its instruction and discipline, by bending their necks under the yoke

---

1. *Ecumenical Creeds and Reformed Confessions* (Grand Rapids, MI: CRC Publications, 1987), 79.

of Jesus Christ, and by serving to build up one another, according to the gifts God has given them as members of each other in the same body."[2] Note that the confession calls us to recognize the horizontal role that believers possess in "serving to build up one another." This is founded upon the gifts God has provided to the members of the church. This principle of building up one another is a principle that was dear to the apostle Paul (e.g., 1 Cor. 14) and the Reformers (e.g., Luther, Calvin, etc.). This principle of edification should apply in the way believers treat one another both during and outside of worship.

The idea of considering one's neighbor is also mentioned in Article twenty-nine which speaks about "The Marks of the True Church." After speaking about the marks of the church, the article addresses the marks of those who can belong to the church. It says, "They love the true God and their neighbors, without turning to the right or left, and they crucify the flesh and its works."[3] The confession clearly addresses both the vertical and horizontal evidence of true believers in that they "love the true God and their neighbors." The mention of these two directions for love repeats the requirements of Christ for keeping the Law and reflects a right understanding of the Law (Matt. 22:36-40). Such love will be exercised by true believers when they seek to worship God. This kind of love would be encouraged in the sanctuary as God's people gathered together. This brings us to the confession's remarks about the Lord's Supper.

Article thirty-five describes a biblical view of the sacrament of the Lord's Supper. After explaining several details about how to understand the Supper, the confession points to the practical implications of taking it correctly. It states, "In short, by the use of this holy sacrament we are moved to a fervent love of God and our neighbors."[4] This statement provides a clear reference to the attitude we should have in our worship of God when we partake of the Supper. The confession notes that it should evoke "fervent love of God and our neighbor" (i.e., the vertical and horizontal). This view fits well with what we see in Paul's teaching (cf. 1 Cor. 11 and 13) as well as in

---

2. *Belgic Confession*, Ecumenical Creeds and the Reformed Confessions (Grand Rapids, Mich.: CRC Publications, 1987), Art. 28.
3. *Belgic Confession*, Art. 29.
4. *Belgic Confession*, Art. 35.

comments made by Calvin on the same subject. Love is again seen as vital to biblical worship. There can be no doubt that this early confession viewed a correct administration of the Supper as a provocation to biblical love for one's neighbor. This would encourage church members to ponder their relationships, consider the lost, love their enemies, pray for the brethren, and engage in almsgiving.

Let us consider another early Reformed catechism that supports the principle of the horizontal dimension.

Heidelberg Catechism

Perhaps one of the most beloved confessional standards during the Reformation is the Heidelberg Catechism. Its pastoral treatment of numerous topics has endeared it to the hearts of many who love the teachings of the Reformation. In 1559, the catechism was published by Elector Frederick III in Heidelberg, Germany. He sought to provide instruction to the people under his rule with the doctrinal teachings of the Reformation. It is believed that Zacharias Ursinus was the major contributor to its construction with contributions by Caspar Olevianus.[5] A synod in Heidelberg approved the catechism in January 1563, while "a second and third German edition, each with small additions, as well as a Latin translation were published the same year in Heidelberg."[6] Soon after, the catechism was divided into fifty-two Sundays, and pastors of the Reformed church were instructed to read the corresponding portion of the catechism before preaching their sermon each Lord's Day.[7] The catechism became a popular doctrinal statement of faith for Reformed churches and has been translated into "most of the European languages and into many Asian and African languages as well."[8] This rich doctrinal statement of faith was especially embraced by the Reformed churches of the Netherlands and remains

---

5. G. I. Williamson, *The Heidelberg Catechism: A Study Guide* (Phillipsburg, NJ: P & R Publishing, 1993), ix.

6. *Heidelberg Catechism*, Ecumenical Creeds and the Reformed Confessions (Grand Rapids, MI: CRC Publications, 1987), 12.

7. Ibid.

8. *The Heidelberg Catechism with Scripture Texts* (Grand Rapids, MI: CRC Publications, 1989), 5.

a favorite standard of Dutch Reformed Christians till this day. It is often called one of the "Three Forms of Unity" among Reformed churches.[9]

Although the catechism does not use the phrase "horizontal dimension," it does support the idea in various doctrinal statements. We need to understand that the corresponding sections addressed in this survey of the catechism were read in a congregational setting, and the passages that called for loving one's neighbor would have been applied to all of life, including worship. It is important to recognize this fact when we ponder relevant passages from the catechism and their application to the church and her worship. Pastors were also encouraged to read and preach through the catechism each Lord's Day. If a pastor were to carry out his duty in expounding upon the catechism's doctrinal statements, he would consider their pertinence and seek to apply its truths in the context of worship as well as to other areas of life. Let us consider some passages that support the principle of the horizontal dimension.

Question and answer fifty-five regarding the communion of saints teaches that "each member should consider it a duty to use their gift readily and cheerfully for the service and enrichment of the other members."[10] This teaching addresses the horizontal responsibilities of believers to serve and enrich their fellow believers with their Christ-given gifts. Visscher remarks, "there is the communion which believers have among each other in which they use Christ's gifts for mutual edification. Some speak of this first part as depicting a vertical relationship since it looks up to Christ and of the second part as a horizontal relationship seeing that it looks to those who stand beside you in the fellowship."[11] The catechism's emphasis on serving and enriching other members would apply not only to daily living but to the worship of the Lord when the saints gather together. Service and enrichment cannot be limited to times outside of worship. As we worship the Lord, we should think about the spiritual and physical

---

9. The three forms of unity are considered: the Belgic Confession, the Heidelberg Catechism, and the Canons of Dort.

10. *The Heidelberg Catechism*, Q. & A. 57.

11. James Visscher, *I Belong: A Course of Study On the Heidelberg Catechism*, Teachers ed. (n.p.: Premier Printing Ltd, 1998), 53.

needs of our fellow worshippers. This attitude among the saints should evoke acts of service and consideration of ways to edify others in the church and its weekly worship.

In dealing with the topic of good works, the catechism speaks to why we do them: "... so that he [God] may be praised through us. And we do good so that we may be assured of our faith by its fruits, and so that by our godly living our neighbors may be won over to Christ."[12] First of all, our works are done for the praise of God (i.e., the vertical). Believers also do good works with the hope of leading to Christ those who see and experience their good works (i.e., a horizontal concern). Kuyvenhoven wisely applies this teaching in the catechism:

> The gain from our works is supposed to go to Christ, or to God. Many of us are inclined to do nice deeds to gain points with other people. Then we are the ones to whom our neighbors are 'won over.' *But the catechism speaks of winning neighbors over to Christ. Evangelism is not only different from but the opposite of proselytizing or group extention.*[13]

Good works, whether they are exhibited with words or actions, demonstrate the truth of the gospel at work in the lives of believers. This principle should inform Christians to realize that the way they worship and their attitudes in worship are examples of the good works that God can use to lead others to Christ. This may happen through their prayers, songs, confessions, reading of Scripture, attentiveness to the gospel, hunger for the Scriptures, hospitality, and loving kindness.

Following the classic Reformed understanding of the commandments, the catechism in question ninety-three divides the commands "Into two tables. The First has four commandments, teaching us what our relation to God should be. The second has six commandments, teaching us what we owe our neighbor."[14] As with previous arguments noted in the second chapter about the Ten Commandments, we discover that the Reformed church represented

---

12. *The Heidelberg Catechism*, Q. & A. 86.
13. Andrew Kuyvenhoven, *Comfort and Joy: a Study of the Heidelberg Catechism* (Grand Rapids, MI: CRC Publications, 1988), 193.
14. *The Heidelberg Catechism*, Q. & A. 93.

by the catechism clearly views the Law as including both the vertical and horizontal dimensions. The application of the horizontal would apply to worship as well as to all of life. We cannot leave the commandments that primarily address the horizontal duties we have toward our fellow man at the entrance of our sanctuaries. God's Law must be brought into the place of worship.

In question and answer ninety-three we also find that the Heidelberg Catechism in its dealings with the fourth commandment on the topic of the Sabbath includes a horizontal concern stating that it is God's will that we "regularly attend the assembly of God's people" and that we "bring Christian offerings for the poor."[15] Consideration of the poor with almsgiving was a common element in Reformed services, and this concern is reinforced by the catechism. Ursinus remarks, "it has always been the practice of the church to bestow alms upon the Sabbath day, and to perform acts of charity towards those who need our help and sympathy."[16] If we are to bring offerings for the poor into our worship services, this means that we should think about their needs and pray for them during our time of worship. In giving our offerings to help the poor, we are taking steps that are horizontal to assist them. This should happen because of our respect for God and commitment to obey his will (a vertical concern).

As we examine the sixth commandment, we discover that the catechism encourages the practice of biblical love in its positive application. In question and answer one hundred and seven it states, "By condemning envy, hatred, and anger, God tells us to love our neighbors as ourselves, to be patient, peace-loving, gentle, merciful, and friendly to them, to protect them from harm as much as we can, and to do good even to our enemies."[17] This doctrinal statement is a strong admonition to exercise biblical love for our neighbor and should be applied in how we treat one another every day of the week, especially on the Lord's Day. If we could treat one another with such love in our worship services God would be pleased. We could apply this instruction in several ways, but perhaps most importantly our

---

15. *The Heidelberg Catechism*, Q. & A. 103.
16. Zacharias Ursinus and G. W. Williard, *The Commentary of Dr. Zacharias Ursinus on the Heidelberg Catechism* (Cincinnati, OH: Elm Street Printing Company, 1888), 569.
17. *The Heidelberg Catechism*, Q. & A. 107.

services ought to be constructed in an understandable manner with thoughtful consideration of our hearers. A biblical view of the sixth commandment would also enrich the way we pray for our neighbors. We would ponder their physical and spiritual needs asking God to save, bless, heal, help, and restore them. This leads to the Lord's Prayer.

The catechism in question and answer one hundred twenty-six instructs Christians on how they should pray for forgiveness. It says, "Forgive us just as we are fully determined, as evidence of your grace in us, to forgive our neighbors."[18] Visscher gets to the heart of the meaning of the catechism, "If we do not forgive others the wrongs that that they have done us, the Father will not forgive us the wrongs we have done Him."[19] This section deals with our vertical relationship with God based on how we are treating others (i.e., the horizontal). We are asking God to forgive us in the way we are forgiving others. This has tremendous ramifications in our horizontal relationships when we worship. If we hold grudges and hate our fellow Christians in our worship we are asking God to withhold his forgiveness for us. How often do Christians hate others while they sing praises to God and write down sermon notes and put money in the collection plate? Such activity does them no good. Their vertical posture and activity mean nothing to God who holds them accountable. He will forgive if they forgive. Kuyvenhoven affirms, "A forgiving spirit is the evidence of being forgiven."[20] Spykman says it another way, "Our forgiving is not the measure of God's. If our forgiving were the measure, we would be doomed. For we are stingy about forgiving—reluctant to forgive the wrongs others have done us. Rather, our forgiving others is an expression of our appreciation for God's forgiving us."[21] Our forgiveness of others reflects the forgiveness we have received from God through Christ. It demonstrates our understanding and acceptance of the forgiveness we have experienced through the gospel

---

18. Ibid., Q. & A. 126.
19. Visscher, *I Belong: A Course of Study On the Heidelberg Catechism*, 110.
20. Kuyvenhoven, *Comfort and Joy: a Study of the Heidelberg Catechism*, 304.
21. Gordon J. Spykman, *Never On Your Own: a Course of Study On the Heidelberg Catechism and Compendium*, rev. ed. (Grand Rapids, MI: Board of Publications of the Christian Reformed Church, 1984), 187.

of Christ. Like we have seen before, the vertical (our desire for God's forgiveness) and the horizontal (our willingness to forgive others) are inseparable in the eyes of our Creator and Redeemer.

Now that we have examined the Heidelberg Catechism let us turn to consider what the Westminster Confession has to say about the horizontal dimension.

Westminster Confession

Many critics today of the Westminster Assembly would claim that the writers of the confession were a group of cold and indifferent Puritan theologians. Such an assessment would not only be unfair but far from the truth. The Divines were men who respected and revered the Lord, but they were also ministers of the gospel and sought to convey the Word of God in a way that ministered to both the souls and lives of people. When we carefully consider their doctrinal statements, we must concur that they cared deeply for people. Their vertical direction concerning God affected their horizontal concerns for men. As we look at the Westminster Confession of Faith, we discover many statements that support the horizontal dimension. Numerous passages within the Confession provide horizontal propositions that if applied would directly affect worship. Let us examine these doctrinal statements.

The first place we see evidence of the horizontal is in chapter one which deals with the subject of Holy Scripture. Like the Reformers before them, the Divines note that the Old Testament was written in Hebrew, a language that was a "native language of the people of God of old" and the New Testament was written in Greek which was "most generally known to the nations."[22] These facts demonstrate God's gracious concern that people understand his Word which is inherently a horizontal concern. Understanding God's desire to reach men in a way they can understand the Divines state:

> But, because these original tongues are not known to all the people of God, who have right unto, and interest in the

---

22. WCF 1.8.

Scriptures, and are commanded, in the fear of God, to read and search them, therefore they are to be *translated into the vulgar language of every nation* unto which they come, that the Word of God dwelling plentifully in all, they *may worship* Him in an acceptable manner; and, through patience and comfort of the Scriptures, may have hope[23] (emphasis added).

The Divines make it known that they are thinking about communicating the Word of God in a way that people can understand. They affirm this viewpoint in their footnote that provides Scripture proofs supporting their comment that the Bible should be translated into the vulgar (vernacular) languages. The Divines cite numerous supporting texts by Paul in 1 Corinthians 14 in which the apostle emphasizes the importance of worshiping God with understanding versus unintelligible words.[24] Commenting on the Confession's reference to the "right" of men to have access to the Word in their language Dixhoorn states:

> It is not often that the Westminster assembly spoke of the 'rights' of Christians. But the men gathered there were convinced that every child of God has an equal right to hear his or her Father's voice. Every child of God has an interest, has something invested, in hearing and reading God's Word. And every person under heaven has a duty to read and search the Scriptures.[25]

This sentiment was not shared by the leaders of the Roman Catholic Church who forbid the translation of the Scriptures into languages other than Latin and prohibited people from reading the Scripture in public worship in their own language.[26] It was a sad digression from the use of the Scriptures in the vulgar languages in the

---

23. Ibid., 1.8.
24. The references the Divines use as proof texts are from 1 Corinthians 14:6, 9, 11-12, 24, 27-28.
25. Chad B. Van Dixhoorn, *Confessing the Faith: A Reader's Guide to the Westminster Confession of Faith* (Edinburgh, Scotland: The Banner of Truth Trust, 2014), 24.
26. Martin Chemnitz and Fred Kramer, *Examination of the Council of Trent*. Part 1 (St. Louis, MO: Concordia Pub. House, 1971), 196.

early centuries as McPherson comments, "In the early centuries no restriction was placed on the use of Scripture, but, as ignorance prevailed, it was first neglected by the people themselves, and then prohibited by their rulers."[27] History records great persecution against those who sought to translate the Bible in the language of the people (e.g., John Wycliffe [English], Jan Hus [Czech], Martin Luther [German], William Tyndale [English]). The Roman church only allowed the Bible to be read in Latin which was not understood by most who attended worship services during the Reformation. The Divines shared the concerns of Reformers such as Luther and Calvin who believed the Word of God should be given to the people in their own language so that they could read it and worship God with understanding. Luther was so committed to getting the Word to the people that he risked his own life by translating the Bible into German, the language of his fellow countrymen. Because the Reformers loved God and his Word, they consequently loved the people so much that they were willing to risk persecution to give them God's Word in a language they could understand. Many Reformers were even willing to die for this conviction, a belief fueled by a sincere love for souls. Such sentiments should encourage worship leaders today to make the Word accessible to people in their churches. This may involve providing Bibles in the pews, citing page numbers for Scripture references, using a readable translation, displaying Scripture texts on a projector screen, and explaining the meaning of biblical words. All such activity would be an example of showing a horizontal concern for those attending worship.

The next section that addresses the horizontal is in chapter nineteen and section two on the topic of God's Law. The Confession reaffirms the classic two-fold division of the Ten Commandments when it says, "This law, after his fall, continued to be a perfect rule of righteousness; and, as such, was delivered by God upon Mount Sinai in ten commandments, and written in two tables; the first four commandments containing our duty towards God, and the other six our *duty to man*"[28] (emphasis added). Notice that the Divines believe

---

27. John Macpherson, *The Westminster Confession of Faith: With Introduction and Notes Handbooks for Bible classes and private students*, 2nd ed. (Edinburgh: T. & T. Clark, 1881), 40.
28. WCF 19.2.

that the Law addresses both the vertical and horizontal dimensions. This understanding of God's Law and its application to worship should affect both our practices and thoughts in corporate worship. Identifying the undergirding principle of love one commentary states, "In essence the moral law requires love of God, neighbor, and self (the law-keeper)."[29] It is important to recognize that the Divines believed this two-fold understanding of the moral law's focus on the vertical and horizontal was reinforced by Jesus in the New Testament.[30]

Chapter twenty-one specifically addresses the subject of worship and the Christian Sabbath. Section three comments on a horizontal concern about prayer stating that it should be done "in a known tongue."[31] Not only was the Catholic Church during the Reformation against translating the Bible into a vulgar language due to its promotion of the Latin translation of the Bible, but it also discouraged conducting the Mass in the common language of the people. Commenting on the Divine's requirement that prayers be said in a known tongue Hodge remarks, "This point is aimed at the Romish custom of uttering many of her public prayers in Latin, which to the vast majority of her worshippers is an unknown tongue. This is explicitly forbidden."[32] We discover in this section of the Confession that the Divines were serious about making their services understandable, a view that is not always shared by those who claim to be Protestants today. Some people who are primarily vertical in their perspective on worship have no problem speaking in a way that is obtuse and/or overly pious. The subject of clarity is not that important to them as long as their service focuses upon God. Their prayers come across as confusing and unclear. It would serve them well to listen to the heart of the Divines about this important element in worship. On the subject of prayer, we learn in section four that the Divines are not exclusively vertical in the way they pray. They encourage the horizontal dimension when they say, "Prayer is to be made for things lawful, and *for all sorts of men living, or that shall*

---

29. John H. Gerstner, Douglas F. Kelly, and Philip B. Rollinson, *Guide: The Westminster Confession of Faith* (Signal Mountain, TN: Summertown Texts, 1992), 92.

30. We can deduce this assertion from their citing Matthew 22:37-40 to support their doctrinal position.

31. WCF 21.3

32. Archibald Alexander Hodge, *The Confession of Faith* (London: Banner of Truth Trust. 1992), 277.

live hereafter; but not for the dead, nor for those of whom it may be known that they have sinned the sin unto death"[33] (emphasis added). Notice that the Divines directly tell us that our prayers in worship should include praying for people, a clear horizontal concern, and practice. They provide supporting proof texts from both the Old and New Testaments.[34] We should also acknowledge that they placed some restrictions on horizontal prayers. They speak against praying for the dead which was and continues to be a practice of the Roman Catholic church. They did not believe this was biblical. One Reformed commentary comments on this prohibition, "Once they are dead, people are gone from our world of experience. We have no active communion even with dead saints, not to mention dead sinners. Prayer for the dead, therefore, is dead prayer."[35] The Scriptures teach that there is an impassable gulf between the living and the dead (Luke 16:19-31). There is nothing the living can do to affect the saints who are in heaven nor the wicked who are in hell. The Divines also discourage praying for those who have committed the sin unto death citing 1 John 5:15 as a supporting text. This sin is often viewed as either the blaspheming of the Holy Spirit (Mark 3:29) or the ongoing, unrepentant rebellion of a person against God. This one section of the Confession of Faith clearly illustrates that the Reformers did not believe in the vertical-only view of worship. They were greatly concerned about people since they believed the lives and affairs of people were important enough to God to bring up in prayer during worship. Such concerns likewise should inform our prayers in worship.

In chapter twenty-six, the Confession presents the Reformed understanding of the communion of saints. This chapter reveals doctrinal positions that accord with the horizontal dimension. It addresses the vertical union believers have with Christ but also speaks about the horizontal consequences of such a union. This spiritual union with Christ through grace brings about a union with the body of Christ—the church. Theologians call this union with Christ a "mystical union," meaning believers join Christ in his sufferings, death, resurrection, and glory. This shared union with Christ brings about a

---

33. WCF 21.4.
34. See 1 Timothy 2:1-2; John 27:20; 2 Samuel 7:29; Ruth 4:12.
35. Gerstner, Kelly, and Rollinson, *Guide*, 103.

union between Christians who have placed their faith in Jesus as their Savior and Lord. Williamson remarks, "The union and communion that believers have with each other is explained by and is an outgrowth of their union with Christ."[36] In section one the Confession says the following about the communion of the saints: "And being united to one another in love, they have communion in each other's gifts and graces; and are obliged to the performance of such duties, public and private, as do conduce to their mutual good, both in the inward and outward man."[37] This section clearly points to the horizontal. The communion that believers have in Christ joins them in biblical love for one another. That love, which they have experienced in Christ, should flow over into how they think about and treat one another. The ramifications of this communion are myriad. This doctrinal view should greatly affect the way Christians worship God with one another. Notice that the goal of this union is unto "their mutual good, both in the inward and outward man." This statement speaks to the loving concerns Christians should have for each other's spiritual, mental, and physical needs. If this doctrine is truly embraced by believers, they will express their concern for one another in daily living and in corporate worship. They will think about ways to demonstrate their love and show concern for the good of others. Dixhoorn comments, "Christian communion is not simply occupied with the inner man. It also cares about the outer man. In fact, the sharing of physical, in addition to spiritual, goods is one indication that we know the love that comes from union with Christ."[38] Embracing such teaching should affect the practical things believers do in worship and the way they worship so that their fellow worshippers will be blessed.

Section two talks explicitly about how Christians should treat one another in worship. It says,

> Saints, by profession, are bound to maintain a holy fellowship and communion in the worship of God, and in performing such other spiritual services as tend to their *mutual edification*; as

---

36. G I. Williamson, *The Westminster Confession of Faith: For Study Classes* (Philadelphia, Pa.: Presbyterian and Reformed Publishing, 1964), 196.
37. WCF 26.1.
38. Van Dixhoorn, *Confessing the Faith*, 351.

also in relieving each other in outward things, according to their several abilities and necessities. Which communion, as God offereth opportunity, is to be extended unto all those who in every place call upon the name of the Lord Jesus[39] (emphasis added).

Upon examination of this section, we discover that the thrust of the horizontal concerns is for the "mutual edification" among believers and in "relieving each other." In response to the Confession's teaching Sproul states, "It is our duty to be in church and in fellowship with other Christians, engaged in the worship of God for the mutual edification of the saints."[40] The reference to a "holy fellowship and communion in the worship of God" means that the Word of the church's holy God should direct the people of God in their interactions with one another. The Confession cites Hebrews chapter ten as a proof text which says to the saints: "And let us consider how to stir up one another to love and good works" (Heb. 10:24). Many things can take place in worship that stir up believers to show love and demonstrate good works. Embracing the Confession's teaching that we should relieve each other may lead to meeting a physical need of a fellow believer. Such an action would require that the believer get to know his brother/sister, contemplate what needs they have, pray about that need, and consider how best to help meet the need in question. It could involve giving money, physical assistance, or material resources to aide one's brother or sister. This section is a serious corrective to the common attitude today among many professing Christians who attend church and worship with a selfish and self-serving attitude. It is far removed from the entertainment model of worship that is so prevalent in churches. Countless people attend church with little to no thought about the spiritual and physical needs of their brothers and sisters in Christ. Those who go to church just to observe the worship service for personal reasons are encouraged by the Confession to look beyond

---

39. WCF 26.2
40. R. C. Sproul, *Truths We Confess: a Layman's Guide to the Westminster Confession of Faith*, vol. 3 (Phillipsburg, NJ: P & R Publishing, 2007), 71.

themselves and consider the communion they share with fellow believers. The truths of this section should encourage a visible expression of love and mutual concern for others in the worship service. It should inspire singing songs from the heart with the desire to edify others who may be listening. The Confession should inform our prayers for the salvation and edification of fellow worshippers. The doctrine of the communion of the saints ought to motivate Christians to show a hospitable and inviting attitude to visitors and regular attendees. It speaks indirectly against isolationism and elitism in our worship. In short, this section of the Confession should encourage worshiping believers to seek to edify their fellow worshippers as they strive to worship their holy God.

It is interesting to note that the confession encourages concern not only for those in the local church but also for believers everywhere. It says, "Which communion, as God offers opportunity, is to be extended unto all those who, in every place, call upon the name of the Lord Jesus."[41] How might believers express their horizontal concerns? By setting an example to others in listening carefully to the Word, by joyfully praising God in song with the intent to minister to people near them, by demonstrating a hospitable attitude, and by praying with reverence to the Lord for other believers both locally and abroad.

Chapter twenty-seven addresses the topic of the sacraments. Section one first points to the vertical purposes of the sacraments, and then it states that they "put a visible difference between those that belong unto the church and the rest of the world; and solemnly to engage them to the service of God in Christ, according to his word."[42] There is an important horizontal concern addressed in this statement. It involves the fact that the sacraments draw a line between the types of people who are present in a worship service. The sacraments help to distinguish between Christians and unbelievers. This is clearly shown in baptism since one of its visible purposes is to set apart a believer from the unbelieving world as a member of Christ and his church. The sacrament of the Lord's Supper, which is offered only to believers, likewise demonstrates a similar line of separation between

---

41. WCF 26.3.
42. WCF 27.1

believers and nonbelievers. When the sacraments are rightly administered, they can be a powerful witness to non-Christians that they need to be saved through faith in Jesus Christ which the sacraments declare. They also encourage believers to walk in the ways of the Lord and to share the gospel with the world.

Let's consider the Confession's horizontal comments regarding the sacraments. In chapter twenty-seven the Confession says that "Baptism is a sacrament of the new testament, ordained by Jesus Christ, not only for the solemn admission of the party baptized into the visible Church..."[43] One should not miss the importance of baptism in visibly demonstrating that a new believer has been admitted into the Church of Christ, a significant horizontal truth. The believer who is baptized and the believers who are watching the baptism should ponder and appreciate their spiritual union with one another in this sacred institution. Not only have they joined Christ through faith, but they have left the family of the devil to join the family of God. They have left the world and have entered the church. New horizontal relationships with members of the church are solidified in this holy sacrament.

Chapter twenty-nine covers the topic of the Lord's Supper. It deals with many aspects of the sacrament but also draws attention to its horizontal implications. Section one says that Jesus "... called the Lord's Supper ... to be a bond and pledge of their communion with Him, and with each other, as members of His mystical body."[44] In this statement, the Confession addresses both the vertical and horizontal aspects of the sacrament. When Christians partake of the Supper, they must think about their union with Christ and union with one another in the body of Christ. The Supper is not some individual mystical ritual that is meant only for the one eating and drinking the elements. It is a sacrament that represents the communion of the saints through their common faith in Christ and membership in the family of God. Williamson says it well, "Thus through this sacrament, we receive testimony and assurance of the fact that we have become members of a new race in Christ. We are strengthened in our realization and

---

43. WCF 28.1.
44. WCF 29.1.

assurance of this blessed fellowship and communion with Christ and his people which is ours by virtue of our union with him."[45] The Christian who righty takes communion should contemplate both the vertical and horizontal dimensions lest he forget to properly discern the body (1 Cor. 10:16-17, 12:13). As he sits down to thoughtfully partake of the elements, the Christian must not only consider his relationship with Christ and blessings provided in union with the Savior but he should also rejoice in his blessings and relationship with others. Another horizontal concern for corporate worship is expressed in section four in the Confession's comments against private Masses. It states, "Private masses, or receiving this sacrament by a priest, or any other alone ... are all contrary to the nature of this sacrament, and to the institution of Christ."[46] The Reformers were adamantly against the notion that the priest had some special power to convey grace which was frequently attached to the administration of private Masses typically understood to be "a kind of life-line to grace."[47] Engaging in the practice of private Masses also would be a contradiction of the belief that the Lord's Supper was a sacrament that demonstrated the reality of the communion of believers "with each other."[48] So, the Divines prohibited this practice based upon their commitment to the communion and community of the saints.

Section eight of chapter twenty-nine refers to a principle that is rarely practiced in many churches today typically due to the fear of offending those present. This horizontal concern in the Confession warns those present not to come to the Table in an unworthy manner. This practice is referred to as "Fencing the Table" and is based on Paul's instruction to the church in Corinth (see 1 Corinthians 11:27-28). The closing statement of section eight says, "Wherefore, all ignorant and ungodly persons, as they are unfit to enjoy communion with Him, so are they unworthy of the Lord's table; and *cannot*, without great sin against Christ, while they remain such, partake of these holy mysteries, or *be admitted thereunto*"[49] (emphasis added). It cannot be

---

45. Williamson, *The Westminster Confession of Faith: For Study Classes*, 219.
46. WCF 29.4.
47. Van Dixhoorn, *Confessing the Faith*, 391.
48. WCF 29.1.
49. WCF 29.8.

denied that this position on the Supper says that ignorant and ungodly people "cannot . . . be admitted" to the Supper. Although there are various ways in which churches have practiced "Fencing the Table," it is important to recognize that the leaders of the church are called here by the Divines to prohibit and warn ungodly people not to partake of the Lord's Supper. This would especially apply to those caught in known sin, those under church discipline,[50] and unbelievers. This type of language may seem harsh in our present church climate of political correctness and views of tolerance, but it is biblical. Such horizontal considerations and practices should be happening in churches that claim to respect God, Christ, the body of Christ, the Scriptures, and the holy sacrament of communion. When church leaders ignore "Fencing the Table," they lack biblical love for those under their care since they are allowing people to eat judgment unto themselves without warning them. It is loving to properly instruct those present on how to take communion in a manner that pleases God and gives due respect to this sacrament instituted by Christ. Churches which ignore this critical aspect of their horizontal responsibility simply are sinning against God and the souls who join them for worship. When ministers correctly fence the Table, they encourage contemplation of God's commands, mutual accountability, self-examination, repentance for sin, faith in Christ, love for the brethren, reconciliation between foes, forgiveness, love for the Gospel, compassion for the lost, reasons for witness, and thankful praise to God.

We have covered some of the teachings of the Confession that apply to the horizontal dimension of worship. The truths we have learned are likewise conveyed further in the Westminster Catechisms since those documents serve as catechetical tools to better understand and appreciate the doctrines of the Confession. Due to limited space and time, we cannot provide additional commentary on the Shorter and Larger Westminster Catechisms and their doctrinal statements related to the horizontal dimension. We simply encourage a new perspective in reading through those documents in light of what has been discussed in the Confession regarding the horizontal aspects of worship. One will find much on the topic of the horizontal dimension

---

50. WCF 30.4.

Reformed Creeds & Catechisms

where the catechisms address the Law of God,[51] the reading of the Word,[52] the preaching of the Word,[53] the sacraments,[54] and prayer.[55] We have discovered that the Westminster Confession is not a doctrinal statement that is vertical only in its perspective about Christianity and the subject of worship. The Confession presents a great deal of support for the horizontal dimension of worship. Embracing the many biblical teachings noted in this section should encourage Christians to better appreciate their horizontal responsibilities in public worship. Let us now consider additional support for the horizontal dimension in the statements on worship provided by the Divines in the Westminster Directory of Worship.

---

51. WLC Q. 93, 98, 99, 115, 118, 122-132, 134-148, 151, 167-168; WSC Q. 42, 57, 61 [n. 37], 65, 71, 75, 77-78, 79-80.
52. WLC Q. 156-157.
53. WLC Q. 159.
54. WLC Q. 167-168, 171, 173-174; WSC Q. 97.
55. WLC Q. 183-184, 185 [n. 93], 189, 191-196; WSC Q. 100-106.

9

Westminster Directory of Worship

Before we look at the content of the Westminster Directory of Worship, let us consider the setting, purpose, and influence of this Reformed document. As many historians will attest, the Westminster Assembly was significantly influenced by the theology of John Calvin and mainly by a Presbyterian understanding of the Reformed faith. Of the one hundred and twenty-one ministers who were commissioners at the Assembly, six were Scottish Presbyterians who provided considerable influence. One of the key controversies of the day in Great Britain was whether the church's liturgy should be fixed or free. Those in the camp of promoting a fixed liturgy, primarily the English, sought to force upon the church the Book of Common Prayer (1559/1604) which was mandated by law.[1] The Presbyterians, and more importantly, the Scottish Presbyterians were inclined primarily toward a free liturgy, especially having practiced the worship principles according to the 1564 Book of Common Order "derived from the 1556 Book of Prayers used by Knox and others in Geneva."[2] The Book of Common Order provided a generally fixed outline for worship but gave provisions for free prayer. On December 2, 1643, the Westminster Assembly formed a subcommittee of nine men to draft the Directory for the public worship of God. Of the members of this committee, four were Scotts (Robert Baillie, George Gillespie, Alexander Henderson, and Samuel Rutherford). Among the five other members, Thomas Young was the son of a Scottish minister. So, the Scottish Presbyterian influence was significant. Consequently, the

---

1. Richard A. Muller and Rowland S. Ward, *Scripture and Worship: Biblical Interpretation and the Directory for Public Worship* (Phillipsburg, NJ: P & R Publishing, 2007), 87.
2. Ibid., 87.

Directory would follow a very similar structure and approach to the Scottish Book of Common Order of 1564.

In just over a year, the committee and Assembly would complete its work by December 27, 1644. The House of Commons would vote to approve of the Directory on January 3, 1645. The Directory of Worship would become the first finished work of Westminster Assembly. In many ways, the Directory was a compromise between those who advocated a purely fixed liturgy and those who desired a solely free form of worship. The work provided a rubric to help guide the Reformed churches of England, Ireland, and Scotland. Its principles and teachings would come to provide much-needed wisdom on how to approach biblical worship, albeit subsequently adapted to other settings and foreign lands. In many ways, the Directory reflects the culmination of years of study on the topic of worship among the Reformers beginning in the 1500s. It provides an adaptable rubric for worship which has influenced the Reformed church up till our present day. Although very few churches today lay claim to the Directory precisely as it was originally adopted, many denominations and churches still rely upon its fundamental principles to guide them in their pursuit of Reformed worship. Because of its historical significance and practical influence upon Reformed believers, we will consider some of its statements that address the horizontal dimension of worship. Proof will be provided that the horizontal aspects of worship were supported and promoted by the Divines of the Westminster Assembly as they presented their views on worship in the Directory. Our brief analysis should encourage Christians today, who wish to worship in a way that is both biblical and historically Reformed, to acknowledge the horizontal dimension in their worship of the Lord.

Before we look at the specific sections of the Directory, we need to recognize horizontal comments in the remarks of "The Preface" of the Directory. We discover that the Divines affirm the historical practice of the Reformers who removed Latin as the required language in their worship services and replaced it with the language of the people. The Directory states that "the publick worship was celebrated in our own tongue: many of the common people also receive benefit by hearing the scriptures read in their own language, which formerly were unto them as a book that is sealed."³ This reaffirmation points to the solidarity between the Divines and their Reformed predecessors that worship not only addresses God properly but also ensures that the people are edified and given access to God in a way they can understand. Their sentiment about worshiping in the language of the people should inform our attitudes and practice in our worship today.

In the section entitled "Of the Assembling of the Congregation, and their Behavior in the Publick Worship of God," we are presented with some horizontal concerns. For the sake of reverence to God the Divines say:

> The public worship being begun, the people are wholly to attend upon it, forbearing to read anything, except what the minister is then reading or citing; and abstaining much more from all private whisperings, conferences, salutations, or doing reverence to any person present, or coming in; as also from all gazing, sleeping, and other indecent behaviour, which may disturb the minister or people, or hinder themselves or others in the service of God.⁴

The above comments convey a concern that nothing be done within the worship service that would hinder others from worshiping God. It addresses horizontal concerns that encourage each member present to consider the effects of their actions upon others present in worship. It discourages an individual mindset that dismisses other worshippers and reinforces the acceptance of the corporate nature of worship. These practical instructions would inform many worshippers today who tend to enter corporate worship oblivious to how others may be affected by them in the service. The Divines clearly understand that biblical worship involves careful consideration of others and how our actions in worship might hinder the peace required for the minister and the people to meet with God.

The Divines continue to provide instruction on how to correctly enter a worship service in a way that acknowledges that worship is not

---

3. Mark Dever and Sinclair Ferguson, ed., *Westminster Directory of Public Worship* (Fearn, Ross-shire: Christian Heritage, 2008), 79.

4. Ibid., 83.

about engaging in one's private devotional experience (i.e., vertical only). They communicate that it is a corporate experience that involves the whole congregation (i.e., the horizontal). They instruct us that, "If any, through necessity, be hindered from being present at the beginning, they ought not, when they come into the congregation, to betake themselves to their private devotions, but reverently to compose themselves to join with the assembly in that ordinance of God which is then in hand."[5] It is important to note that "This provision does not prohibit private devotions before the public service begins, but was intended to forbid occupying oneself with private devotions during the public service."[6] This guidance would instruct both those who are either self-focused introverts or extroverts. It encourages the worshipper to see themselves as part of the broader community and body of Christ.

In the section "Of Publick Reading of the Holy Scriptures," the Divines provide several encouraging horizontal comments. The opening paragraph notes that the reading of the word in the congregation is to be done "for the edifying of his [God's] people."[7] The word "edifying" speaks to a horizontal concern. It reminds us that the reading of Scripture should be done in a way that edifies or builds up the people who are listening. Such a consideration calls the pastor or teacher who reads the Word to think about those who are listening and how they might receive the Word. This perspective might affect the tone, intonation, and volume of the reader. This section also states that the Word should be "publickly read in the vulgar tongue, out of the best allowed translation, distinctly, that all may hear and understand."[8] Again, we hear the Divines upholding the Reformation principle of conducting services in the common language of the hearers. The comment that we should use the "best ... translation" reminds us that the Divines are very concerned that church leaders provide the best available translation of the Bible for the people to properly worship God. One cannot translate the original languages without careful consideration of the culture, linguistic nuances, and

---

5. Ibid., 84.
6. Muller and Ward, *Scripture and Worship*, 121.
7. Dever and Ferguson, *Westminster Directory of Public Worship*, 85.
8. Ibid.

education of the people (all very horizontal concerns). This section additionally instructs the church on how much to read of Scripture and how long expositional comments are to be made so that "regard is always to be had unto the time, that neither preaching, nor other ordinances be straitened, or rendered tedious."[9] This instruction shows that the Divines call the reader to consider the sensibilities of the hearers when worship is conducted thus safeguarding other essential elements of the service such as preaching the Word and the proper administration of the ordinances. The Divines were very familiar with the abuses of the Roman church which often filled its services with elements that minimized the preaching of the Word. This admonition provides helpful instruction for the long-winded and insensitive worship leader who leads God's people in worship and inadvertently undermines the preaching of the Word.

Next, we come to the section labeled as "Of Publick Prayer Before the Sermon." A good deal of attention is given to the subject of prayer before and after the sermon in the Directory. Muller states, "a little over 25 percent of the words in the directory are devoted to suggested content of the prayers, half of this in the prayer before the sermon."[10] This instruction on prayer incorporates the horizontal by recommending the confession of sins including "by reason of original sin …" and "by reason of actual sins, our own sins, the sins of magistrates, of ministers, and of the whole nation…".[11] Various types of sins are confessed and provide informative wisdom on how to confess our personal and corporate sins. Acknowledgment of our hope, forgiveness, and intercessory blessings in Christ are presented which grounds the confession in the vertical grace and work of Jesus.[12] Prayer is offered for the growth and blessings of God upon fellow believers. The Divines encourage the minister to focus his prayer on the Great Commission and apply it to the nations. They also are encouraged to request God's protection for his church.[13] Special attention is given to the Reformed churches of "the kingdoms of

---

9. Dever and Ferguson, *Westminster Directory of Public Worship*, 86.
10. Muller and Ward, *Scripture and Worship*, 122.
11. Dever and Ferguson, *Westminster Directory of Public Worship*, 87.
12. Ibid., 88.
13. Ibid., 89.

Scotland, England, and Ireland … united in the Solemn National League and Covenant."[14] Prayer is uttered for the authorities such as the king and his government for the sake of the "propagation of the gospel, for the encouragement and protection of them that do well, the terror of all that do evil, and the great good of the whole church, and of all his kingdoms …"[15] Prayer is offered for the household of the king and authorities (e.g., parliament, nobility, subordinate judges and magistrates, the gentry, pastors, teachers of God, etc.). In their closing remarks, the Divines encourage the minister to pray that:

> he may divide the word of God aright, to every one his portion, in evidence and demonstration of the Spirit and power; and that the Lord would circumcise the ears and hearts of the hearers, to hear, love, and receive with meekness the ingrafted word, which is able to save their souls; make them as good ground to receive in the good seed of the word, and strengthen them against the temptations of Satan, the cares of the world, the hardness of their own hearts, and whatsoever else may hinder their profitable and saving hearing; that so Christ may be so formed in them, and live in them, that all their thoughts may be brought into captivity to the obedience of Christ, and their hearts established in every good word and work for ever.[16]

This largely horizontal prayer for the people should inform the heartfelt prayers of God's people today as they join the minister in praying for themselves as well as their fellow worshippers to correctly receive God's Holy Word.

The section entitled "Of the Preaching of the Word" also gives attention to the horizontal. The minister is instructed, "That he chiefly insist upon those doctrines which are principally intended, and make most for the edification of the hearers."[17] We are reminded again of the importance of edification of the congregation. Being mindful of his hearers, the preacher is called to use "plain terms," solid

---

14. Ibid.
15. Dever and Ferguson, *Westminster Directory of Public Worship*, 90.
16. Ibid., 91.
17. Ibid., 94.

"arguments or reasons," "illustrations ... such as may convey the truth into the hearer's heart with spiritual delight."[18] It is advised that the preachers not "rest in general doctrine ... but to bring it home to special use, by application to his hearers."[19] Such instruction conveys the importance of ministering to the congregation rather than just exhibiting erudition, eloquence, or theoretical concepts. Great effort should be made to deliver and apply God's Word to the hearts and minds of the people. The minister is called to instruct the people on the means that can help them perform the duties God calls them to pursue. He is told to not only help the people discover the "nature and greatness of the sin" they struggle with but to teach them the "remedies and best way to avoid it."[20] The preacher is encouraged to know his flock and to focus on doctrines in the text that "may most draw their souls to Christ, the fountain of light, holiness, and comfort."[21] Such preaching demands careful horizontal considerations of the hearers. To help the hearers understand the message the pastor is told to preach:

> Plainly, that the meanest may understand; delivering the truth not in the enticing words of man's wisdom, but in demonstration of the Spirit and of power, lest the cross of Christ should be made of none effect; abstaining also from an unprofitable use of unknown tongues, strange phrases, and cadences of sounds and words; sparingly citing sentences of ecclesiastical or other human writers, ancient or modern, be they never so elegant.[22]

Such advice on preaching would serve many ministers well today in communicating God's Word more effectively instead of causing confusion and distraction. This sort of preaching is intentional and demonstrates great concern for the salvation and edification of the congregation. The Divines convey the purpose of such preaching by

---

18. Ibid.
19. Ibid., 95.
20. Ibid., 95-96.
21. Ibid., 96.
22. Ibid., 97.

encouraging the minister to preach "Faithfully, looking at the honour of Christ, the conversion, edification, and salvation of the people, not at his own gain or glory."[23] This instruction is indisputably horizontal with a verticle respect for God.

Preachers are also called to show "all due respect to each man's person and place" with "loving affection, that the people may see all coming from his godly zeal, and hearty desire to do them good."[24] If applied in the church, these beautiful words would breathe new life into much of the preaching we hear today that has either drifted into cold indifference or casual entertainment-driven discourse. The Divines, in short, tell preachers to love their neighbor in the way they preach with a heart that deeply loves God.

After the section on preaching, the Divines address the topic "Of Prayer After Sermon." They are not satisfied with preaching that entertains or simply increases the knowledge of the hearers. They encourage the preacher to pray that the message "abide in the heart, and bring forth fruit." The very mention of this sort of prayer would encourage the congregation to join in with similar requests for themselves and others in the worship service. The pastor is directed to "pray for a blessing upon the Assembly of Divines, the armies by sea and land, for the defence of the King, Parliament, and Kingdom."[25] One cannot dismiss the evident horizontal concerns that the Divines echo in their directions on how to pray before and after the sermon with a focus on the application of God's Word in the lives of the hearers.

Further encouragement on the horizontal dimension is provided in the sections dealing with petitions recommended for prayer during special services (e.g., Public Fastings & Days of Public Thanksgiving). Attention is also given to the poor and good deeds. On the day of Thanksgiving at "one or both of the publick meetings that day, a collection is to be made for the poor," and the people should be exhorted at the end of the meeting to exhibit "Christian love and charity one towards another, and of rejoicing more and more in the

---

23. Ibid.
24. Ibid.
25. Ibid., 100.

Lord; as becometh those who make the joy of the Lord their strength."[26]

The Westminster Directory of Worship proves that the Divines were greatly concerned that the church not only love God with all their heart in their worship but also love their neighbor. Having discovered that they gave so much attention in the Directory of Worship to horizontal concerns, we should be moved to conclude that the Divines were highly committed to the horizontal dimension in their views and practices of corporate worship.

---

26. Ibid., 125. It should be noted that the practice of taking collections as they are often done today were not necessary during the time of the Divines due to the assistance typically provided by the state to the church. Collections were not generally done at this time for taking care of buildings, funding the ministries, and paying the minister. Such an arrangement would become more necessary when the state ceased from supporting the church.

10

Summary

We have learned through our survey of some key Reformed representatives, confessions, catechisms, and worship guidelines that the horizontal dimension of worship is deeply rooted in the Reformed tradition. One cannot say that the Reformers were only concerned about the vertical dimension of worship or that they were primarily concerned about the vertical dimension giving little attention to the horizontal. It should not be surprising to find that the Reformers embraced both the vertical and the horizontal aspects of worship because they sought to be thoroughly biblical in their doctrine and practice. They also addressed the abuses they witnessed in the Roman Catholic Church which drifted away from biblical worship. The Reformers and Divines teach us to bring both the vertical and horizontal dimensions into our understanding of corporate worship.

In summary, they teach us to strive to edify the hearers, evangelize the lost, communicate clearly God's Word with humility, to think about the listeners, love our fellow worshippers, pray for those in the local church, the wider body of Christ, and those in authority. Prayer is given no small part in the horizontal concerns they bring before their sovereign God. Their prayers inform the way we should think and feel about our neighbors. The church today could especially use this rich heritage of prayer in the way it worships. The Reformers give us a wonderful tradition of reading, preaching, and teaching the Word that is thoroughly mindful of their hearers. They call church leaders today to apply the Bible to the lives of their hearers and indirectly encourage the listener to apply the Word in their own life in the way they treat their neighbor. A Christ-centered spirit and God-glorifying purpose pervade their understanding of the Word and its application in the church in the context of biblical love. One should conclude from this survey of their teaching and example that believers are called to worship God with love for their neighbor. Upon close examination of the Reformed creeds and catechisms we cannot walk away with the notion that the protestant reformers were cold theologians who cared little for those in the pews. Their biblical-centered perspective pervades their deep love of the Lord wedded with a wise understanding and application of the horizontal dimension of worship.

Part 3

CONTEMPORARY LITERATURE REVIEW

Let us consider some influential contemporary writers and literature to better understand the place of the horizontal dimension of worship within the conservative and Reformed community. We will discover in our examination of several contemporary writings various supporting claims for the horizontal dimension. The authors we will consider will at times provide practical ideas about how to implement the horizontal dimension in worship while maintaining an appreciation of the vertical direction of worship. We will examine these particular writers due to their influence in the Reformed and evangelical community. These authors have also been chosen because of their thoughtful comments about the horizontal dimension and thus lend credibility to the thesis of this project.

It is important to glean wisdom not only from the past but also from modern day scholars, theologians, and pastors who have sought to carefully understand and apply the rich theological history of the Reformation to the worship of the church. The first writer we will examine is an influential Presbyterian theologian and churchman—Robert Rayburn.

11

Robert G. Rayburn

During the late twentieth century Robert Rayburn gave the church a wonderful gift when he wrote *O Come, Let Us Worship*. Rayburn also provides the evangelical community with various academic journal articles about worship. He served as professor of practical theology at Covenant Theological Seminary in St. Louis, Missouri. He pastored five churches providing him insight on liturgical practices and theory. As the contemporary liturgy movement made its way into the church, Rayburn offered wise counsel on how to incorporate modern music without sacrificing the heritage of his Reformed and Presbyterian traditions. Although many authors appeal to Rayburn as an advocate of the traditional model for worship, he also provides helpful ideas on integrating the horizontal dimension.

Rayburn has great respect for God in his treatment of worship. He possesses a keen appreciation of the vertical direction of worship and offers a thoughtful criticism of the entertainment mentality he noticed entering the church. As to the subject of worship, he states, "We must never forget that worship is to be the worship of God! As He is the object of worship our principal concern should be that He is glorified in our worship service. Our primary concern must not be that we ourselves have been entertained or stirred."[1] Although Rayburn does not necessarily use the phrase "horizontal dimension" in his treatment of worship, it becomes clear when we examine his remarks that he is very supportive of the horizontal aspects of worship. We will find that he understands we must always maintain a balance between the vertical and horizontal in our worship. Rayburn could never be accused of being seeker-driven due to his God-centered understanding of biblical

---

1. Robert Gibson Rayburn, "The Relevance of Worship," *Presbyterion* 13, no. 1 (1987): 4.

worship. For Rayburn, worship must also be Christ-centered and offered from hearts that have been converted through the work of the Holy Spirit. He says, "The cross of Christ is at the very center of all truly Christian worship."[2] This perspective must be kept in mind when we consider his statements in support of the horizontal.

Rayburn acknowledges that there is something special about God's people meeting together for worship rather than individual devotion. He believes that there is a stronger intensity when God's people gather together than what we experience in individual worship. Touching upon the horizontal experiences of meeting with God's people, Rayburn says,

> As we bless and encourage one another in personal fellowship, so we are strengthened and uplifted by being together in common worship. To unite one's heart and one's voice with believers all around him as songs of praise are sung, prayers are offered up, confession is made, and the Scriptures are read, is indeed an experience which carries the soul beyond the reaches of individual worship and unites it with the Son of God who Himself leads the worship of those who gather in His name. He promised that 'where two or three are gathered together [unto] my name, there am I in the midst of them' (Matt. 18:20)."[3]

In discussing the biblical elements of worship, Rayburn recognizes that fellowship (*koinonia*) as noted in Acts 2:42, is essential, especially regarding the sacraments. He comments,

> I would insist that fellowship is a particularly important element in corporate worship, and especially in the observance of the sacraments if one is to experience all the fullness of true Christian worship. There is no substitute to the Christian for the realization of the spiritual bond which unites him with other believers and with the Lord Jesus Christ. It is a lack of a sense

---

2. Robert Rayburn, *O Come Let Us Worship: Corporate Worship in the Evangelical Church* (Scarsdale, New York: Westminster Publishing House, 1980), 25.

3. Rayburn, *O Come Let Us* Worship, 25.

of true fellowship with other believers that mars the worship experiences of many today.[4]

Rayburn understands that it can be challenging to develop fellowship in larger congregations where one often runs into strangers, but fellowship should never be ignored or dismissed. Rayburn remarks, "The Christian faith is first an individual matter, but it never remains that. Jesus Christ first brings a soul to Himself, but then He always unites that soul to other believers in His body, the church. The unattached Christian is an impossibility. Thus, fellowship in worship must be expressed and experienced."[5] The importance of fellowship for Rayburn is dear to his heart. He says, "The warmth of sweet fellowship is one important safeguard against spiritual coldness. Perhaps Christians today should restore the greeting of one another with a holy kiss, which was a practice of apostolic times. It might give us a sweeter sense of fellowship."[6] Rayburn's comments encourage a return to the warmth and love expressed in the early church with such greetings. He is not afraid to address what he considers deficiencies in his own more traditional church culture.

Rayburn addresses the topic of singing in worship services in the early church and draws attention to Paul's instruction to the Ephesian Christians that "they were to speak to one another in psalms, hymns, and spiritual songs."[7] Although Rayburn does not emphasize or elaborate on the horizontal aspects of Paul's teaching he does, however, point out verses that clearly address the horizontal expectations in singing during worship. He references Paul's admonition to the Colossian believers (Col. 3:16) "that they were to teach and admonish one another with 'psalms and hymns and spiritual songs, singing with thankfulness in [their] hearts to God (NASB)."[8] Regarding the Lord's Supper, Rayburn reflects upon the phrase "for we are to partake of the one loaf" (1 Cor. 10:17 [NIV]). Speaking about the vertical and horizontal aspects of this admonition, Rayburn notes,

---

4. Ibid., 91.
5. Rayburn, *O Come Let Us Worship*, 91.
6. Ibid., 92.
7. Ibid., 93.
8. Ibid., 94.

"The devout participant in the communion is thus united with Christ and with other true believers in a real though mystical way."[9] It is important to recognize that Rayburn understands the importance of the doctrine of double union in worship and thus supports the vertical and horizontal connections believers experience as a consequence of their union with Christ and one another.

Following the Reformers in their concern that worship be done in the vernacular and also involve the people jointly in the service, Rayburn comments,

> Luther not only gave to the people the Bible in their own language so that God could speak to them clearly, but he also gave them beautiful hymns in the vernacular with which they could unitedly respond to the grace of God in praise and adoration. Luther and Calvin, as well as the lesser Reformers, returned to the people their active participation in the worship of God.[10]

Rayburn understands that biblical participation corporately, or "unitedly" as he puts it, is essential to biblical worship. His support of the Reformation principle of joint participation lays the groundwork for the experience of the horizontal and vertical since God's people are called to participate with both God and one another in their worship. Recognizing the importance of dialogue in worship between God and his people Rayburn bemoans some historical trends that he believes have hindered an appreciation of the importance of that dialogue. Rayburn argues that the centuries following the Reformation indicate there was "a very serious distortion of the dialogue in public worship, a distortion which has continued down to our own day."[11] He believes that there was a strong Calvinistic emphasis upon the sovereignty of God and a large segment of the Reformation that overly stressed a downward focus in their liturgy. He says, "there was a marked tendency to lay an excessive stress on the downward, divine

---

9. Rayburn, *O Come Let Us Worship*, 99.
10. Ibid., 125.
11. Ibid.

side of the dialogue and to neglect the upward human response."[12] Rayburn believes this emphasis occurred among the Puritans who emphasized hearing the Word read and preached, listening to long prayers, and singing the Psalms which were entirely God's Word to his people.[13] He does admit that there may have been some significant exceptions to this general rule among the Puritans and their successors but still states that "Any sense of corporate response to a loving God of infinite compassion and mercy was largely lost and again people became spectators."[14] Rayburn fundamentally argues that this perspective resulted in their neglecting the upward human response in worshiping God. He attributes this liturgical shift to their stress upon "the Word of God, not upon the response of the people."[15] He also criticizes the Anglicans and the American Episcopalians for distorting the dialogue between God and man by overemphasizing the corporate response of the people rather than focusing upon the Word of God. Rayburn encourages the church to engage in both an upward and downward dialogue with God. In so doing, he promotes participation in both listening to the Word and corporately responding to God in worship.

To correct the shift to entertainment in modern churches, he encourages Christian participation in worship with the intent to give praise to God. Rayburn believes Americans have developed a spectator mentality by spending countless hours watching cartoons (while they were young), the dramas, the movies, and sports events. He warns that this mentality has come into the church and threatens historic principles of worship handed down by the Reformers.[16] Believing his ideas are grounded in Reformation practices and theology he writes,

> It was the Reformation which restored the biblical doctrine of the priesthood of all believers and gave to every member of the worshiping congregation full participation in the worship, especially in the offering of praise to God in psalms, hymns,

---

12. Rayburn, *O Come Let Us Worship*, 125.
13. Ibid., 125-6.
14. Ibid., 126.
15. Ibid.
16. Rayburn, *O Come Let Us Worship*, 127.

and spiritual songs. It is unthinkable that churches which sprang from the Reformation should now encourage the use of music which seems designed primarily to please and even entertain the members of the congregation.[17]

It is interesting to note that his concerns in the 1980s are still a significant concern for many Christians in the church today. Rayburn is right to be disturbed by the church's drift toward entertainment and spectating. Such attitudes and practices not only hinder people from listening to God vertically but they also cause believers to dismiss their calling to minister to one another. Such trends turn worship into a selfish, self-serving and self-absorbed experience. They set the church back centuries to the days before the Reformation in which the people were merely spectators rather than worshippers called to engage with God and their fellow worshippers. In a sense, Rayburn warns us today that the contemporary church is returning to Rome.

One of the key elements of worship that has horizontal ramifications is preaching. Rayburn is aware that preaching is not meant just to convey ideas from the Bible but also should be done in consideration of the listeners. He addresses the horizontal dimension in the way the preacher should prepare his sermon and deliver his message. Rayburn states, "The faithful preacher who proclaims the Word of God will always be directing that Word to the needs of men, for that is how God Himself has focused His message in the Scriptures."[18] Rayburn acknowledges the horizontal purpose of the Word which convicts of sin, produces true conversion, edifies, comforts, instructs, and calls men to obedience to God. Understanding the vertical source of real and lasting change through the preached Word, he expresses that it is ultimately the work of God's Spirit who moves people to respond. As he contemplates the hearers, Rayburn teaches that if the preacher primarily seeks the glory of God in his preaching, "we can expect that there will be notable subjective results in the lives of the worshipers."[19]

---

17. Rayburn, "The Relevance of Worship," 5.
18. Rayburn, *O Come Let Us Worship*, 131.
19. Ibid., 132.

Rayburn provides us with many helpful ideas that support the horizontal dimension. He addresses the importance of maintaining a balance between the vertical and horizontal. He points out the significance of biblical corporate participation and fellowship in worship. Rayburn acknowledges the mutual ministry of singing to one another and recognizes the horizontal nature of communion. He defends the corporate nature of worship and speaks about the problems of individualistic worship. He encourages corporate dialogue in worship which supports the horizontal. He warns against the dangers of the spectator and entertainment mentality that has infiltrated the church and has hindered both the vertical and horizontal dimensions. Finally, Rayburn reminds us of the necessity of the horizontal in preaching the Word by encouraging ministers to carefully consider how to apply the text in the lives of their hearers.

In addition to Robert Rayburn's insights into the horizontal dimension, we discover thoughtful views on the subject from David Peterson, a highly respected New Testament Biblical scholar.

12

David Peterson

Dr. David Peterson provides the church with an influential book entitled *Engaging with God*. His book conveys a scholarly but accessible presentation of a biblical theology of worship. Peterson has also written numerous academic articles on the topic of worship and is frequently cited as an authority by many modern authors. He is a noted New Testament scholar and ordained minister of the Anglican Church of Australia. Although Peterson deals with various topics on worship, he does give some attention to the horizontal dimension.

Peterson is aware that worship involves the attitude and act of service. He believes the vertical and the horizontal are interconnected throughout the Bible and sees the call to service as addressing both dimensions. Studying the Scriptures, he remarks, "The Old Testament indicates in several ways that service to God and service to his people are interrelated."[1] Peterson believes that service to others is an outflow of the Christian's service to God. It finds its expression in ministry to others when Christians worship God. The forgiveness they experience in Christ and the outpouring of the Holy Spirit means that "God's people are liberated to serve him in a new way."[2] This is the vertical relationship believers have with God and express to God with thanksgiving. He notes that "Such worship finds particular expression when Christians gather to minister to one another in word or deed, to pray, and to sound forth God's praises in teaching or singing, but it is not to be restricted in our thinking to these activities."[3] For Peterson, service to God finds its manifestation in the ministry of God's people

---

1. David Peterson, *Engaging with God: A Biblical Theology of Worship*, First North American ed. (Grand Rapids, MI: W.B. Eerdmans, 1993), 70.
2. Ibid., 159.
3. Peterson, *Engaging with God,* 159.

to one another as they worship God. It is a product of their relationship with the Lord and a responsibility. In one of his articles on worship, he remarks, "Christians ought to meet together to fulfill the responsibility of ministering to one another in the body of Christ but also to express that unique relationship which they share together with Christ."[4]

Peterson also probes the subject of edification. He understands that edification is a significant theme addressed in the New Testament when the topic of worship is at hand. He reveals that the terminology of edification is used instead of "the language of worship, to indicate the purpose and function of Christian gatherings (e.g., 1 Cor. 14:3, 4, 5, 12, 17, 26; 1 Thess. 5:11; Eph. 4:11-16)."[5] He believes the horizontal is indispensable to the vertical and that the two dimensions must go together. He comments, "The important concept of interacting with one another is not to be divorced from the notion that we come together to engage with God."[6] Peterson observes in the New Testament that edification happens when Christians minister to one another as they worship God. This occurs in the form of word and deed as they seek "to express and encourage a Christ-centered faith, hope, and love."[7] He notes that New Testament worship is not so much an individual enterprise but more an endeavor to contribute "to the life and development of the believing community as a whole."[8]

Peterson observes in 1 Corinthians 14 that worship ministry that edifies involves helping both believers and strangers understand what is said during the service. He determines that in 1 Corinthians 14 "The first issue in the chapter is intelligibility."[9] He points out that "the tongues-speaker 'edifies himself' (v. 4), but the person who prophecies 'edifies the church.'"[10] This observation identifies the importance of the horizontal in the worship service in the sense that the worshipper should not be so concerned with his private communion or personal

---

4. David Peterson, "Further Reflections on Worship in the New Testament," *The Reformed Theological Review* 44, no. 2 (May 1985): 40.
5. Peterson, *Engaging with God*, 206.
6. Ibid., 209.
7. Peterson, *Engaging with God*, 209.
8. Ibid.
9. Ibid., 211.
10. Ibid., 212.

vertical experience with God to the exclusion of his call to minister to others in the service. Peterson teaches that ministry to others in worship should be an exercise of love as they minister the truth to one another.[11] Drawing on Paul's teaching in 1 Corinthians 14, Peterson qualifies the ministry of edification in worship. He recalls that it will encourage others to exercise their gifts. Such worship will also include listening in silence and with discernment, weighing what is said. He notes that disorder is discouraged to enable people to learn and be encouraged. He understands that Paul is discouraging an individualistic attitude in favor of edifying the whole body.[12] Following such Pauline guidelines allows the church to advance in God's way. Peterson concludes that "The balance of Paul's teaching suggests that we view mutual ministry as the context in which to engage with God. Edification and worship are different sides of the same coin."[13]

Peterson also considers Paul's teaching in 1 Corinthians 11 on the Lord's Supper. He views the practice of communion not just as an individual or vertical experience. He comments that throughout church history the Supper has often been understood as deepening the believer's private communion with God but remarks that such a view is a misunderstanding of what Paul is teaching. Peterson states that "We do not simply meet to have fellowship with God but to minister to one another as we express our common participation in Christ as our Saviour and Lord."[14] Understanding that the modern church has often missed this point in its contemporary practice, Peterson calls the church to reassess the way it celebrates the Supper. Believing he understands Paul's instructions on administering communion, he expresses the serious error and danger involved in dismissing the apostle's teaching. He says, "According to Paul, those who disregard their responsibility to welcome and care for fellow believers in this context cannot be worshipping or serving God acceptably!"[15] Given the exegesis of 1 Corinthians 11 provided in chapter two of this project, we must agree with Peterson's assessment.

---

11. Ibid., 213.
12. Peterson, *Engaging with God*, 213.
13. Ibid., 215.
14. Ibid., 218.
15. Ibid.

One of the critical reasons Peterson considers edification so crucial in worship is the view that "ministry to others is an aspect of our service or self-giving to God" and that edification "is really God's work in our midst."[16] If Peterson is correct, then the absence of edification in our corporate worship would mean that we are not worshiping God vertically in the biblical sense. When we accept the importance of edification in our worship, it will affect everything we do. It will mean that we pray or praise God for the purpose of edifying others. Peterson cautions that we should not artificially separate the 'vertical' from the 'horizontal dimension.' He tells us that Paul views both dimensions as necessary. Peterson concludes that the "God-directed ministry of prayer or praise and the notion of edification are intimately linked in the New Testament (e.g., Col. 3:16; Eph. 5:19)."[17] He further recognizes that "in Colossians 3:16 and Ephesians 5:19, speaking or singing to God and ministry to one another are intimately linked."[18] To avoid being misunderstood, he also says that "This does not mean that prayer or praise is a means to an end, namely edification. We worship God because of who he is and because of his grace towards us. Participating in the edification of the church, however, is an important expression of our devotion and service to God."[19] We discover with Peterson that the horizontal dimension will always accompany a biblical understanding of the vertical dimension.

In summary, Peterson has provided helpful insights in support of the horizontal. He reveals that worship involves the attitude and act of service. He points out that service to God and others is interconnected and thus expressed in both the vertical and horizontal dimensions. He notes that service to God finds its manifestation in the ministry of God's people to one another as they worship God. Peterson also presents the importance of edification in corporate worship. He tells us that Paul in 1 Corinthians 14 speaks against an individualistic attitude in worship and encourages believers to make sure the service is intelligible even for the stranger. This perspective reminds the church today to carefully consider the needs of both believers and

---

16. Peterson, *Engaging with God*, 219.
17. Ibid., 221.
18. Peterson, "Further Reflections on Worship in the New Testament," 37.
19. Peterson, *Engaging with God*, 221.

unbelievers in the service. Peterson explains that edification of others is an expression of our devotion to God, not a means to an end. He notes that Paul encourages such attitudes for the sake of the edification of the whole church body instead of taking an individualistic perspective. He also addresses Paul's views on communion in 1 Corinthians 11 and argues that the horizontal is vital to a biblical understanding of the sacrament.

Another notable scholar who provides us with insights into the horizontal dimension is Marva Dawn.

13

Marva Dawn

Dawn has a made her mark on the evangelical community through her numerous books and articles on worship. Her perspective comes primarily from the Lutheran church. Many within the conservative Reformed church have resonated with her critiques about contemporary worship where she offers a correction to what is perceived as a movement away from biblical worship toward a contemporary entertainment model. Dawn is not a fan of the seeker-driven movement. She encourages the church to strive to glorify God as a prime motive for worship which demonstrates an appreciation for the vertical direction of worship. In writings on the matter of worship in recent years, those who emphasize the vertical dimension often appeal to Marva Dawn as a proponent of the vertical perspective. We must, however, acknowledge that upon carefully reading Dawn's diverse comments on worship that she is often taken out of context to promote an over-emphasis on the vertical dimension. Dawn, in fact, has much to say in support of the horizontal dimension, seeing the horizontal aspects of worship as an essential outflow of being biblically vertical.

In her book *Reaching Out Without Dumbing Down,* she expresses great concern over the individualistic mindset of secular culture and believes it has crept into the church. She notes that "advances in technology bring us many advantages, but the advantages are always coupled with profound losses—primarily the loss of community."[1] Dawn understands how important community is to vibrant and biblical worship. She believes that the societal and cultural drive toward individualism has greatly affected the attitude of people regarding

---

1. Marva J. Dawn, *Reaching Out Without Dumbing Down: A Theology of Worship for This Urgent Time* (Grand Rapids, MI: W.B. Eerdmans, 1995), 27.

worship. She bemoans this trend which is dismantling families through an addiction to technological gadgets "because a parent or child is always drawn away to play, work, or experiment on the computer."[2] Dawn believes this unhealthy form of individualism has entered the church and has diminished its commitment to biblical community and has turned many "congregations into mega-businesses instead of Christian communities."[3] One could argue that Dawn does not agree with those who would advocate a purely vertical perspective of worship but rather sees the importance of the horizontal dimension which finds its realization in community. Dawn believes that many people feel that they are lacking in community but have difficulty understanding how to create it. She recognizes that countless churches have recreated the way they run the church to fit the surrounding narcissistic culture by catering to consumeristic desires. Dawn notes that shaping the church to cater to such tendencies will create serious problems. She says, "Since consumption can never keep its promises to fill the aching void in people's lives, to create congregational members who treat religion as another consumer item is to train them not to appreciate the way in which God really does fill our emptiness."[4]

Understanding the important connection between the vertical and the horizontal Dawn states,

> The Church brings truth and love together best if it genuinely praises God and consequently nurtures the character formation of people. In worship, we celebrate the truths of faith in ways that embrace participants in the love of God. The love of the worshipping community, moreover, reaches out to welcome strangers and to instill in them habits of cherishing truth.[5]

Dawn believes that the truth of God's Word will affect the way believers treat others as they worship God with genuine praise. Love will flow out of such a community toward God and others. Dawn is quite aware of the importance of presenting God in the right way

---

2. Dawn, *Reaching Out Without Dumbing Down*, 27.
3. Ibid., 29.
4. Ibid., 65.
5. Dawn, *Reaching Out Without Dumbing Down*, 67.

realizing that if this is done incorrectly that worship can descend into unbiblical directions. She provides wisdom for a balanced understanding of the vertical stating, "Holiness without love incites terror; love without holiness invites libertinism. Worship that focuses on God's transcendence without God's immanence becomes austere and inaccessible; worship that stresses God's immanence without God's transcendence leads to irreverent coziness."[6] Such a perspective of God in our worship will greatly inform and affect the way we view and treat others in our worship services. Dawn criticizes the self-centeredness of the modern world noting that our "technological society increasingly isolates us from one another, with a resulting focus on individual selves and needs, not the good of the community."[7] Notice that she identifies the importance of the horizontal with a focus upon "the good of the community." Her horizontal concern for the community, which is present in corporate worship, exemplifies a perspective that views the horizontal dimension as inseparable from the vertical.

One of the ways Dawn believes the church can encourage a sense of community is to "think in terms of 'we' instead of 'I.'"[8] She says the overemphasis upon the individual within the church and its worship can hinder the call to community. She suggests that the church stress its community by using language that connects the body as a community but also reflects upon the contemporary church's connection with the church of the past. Dawn feels that this approach will help combat the narcissistic tendencies in the church. It is important to recognize that Dawn's insights offer a correction to those who might smugly feel they have worshipped God with their vertical perspective but have actually engaged in a type of narcissism. She challenges those who neglect their calling to think horizontally about the immediate and larger Christian community that worships with them.

Dawn also addresses the area of music as a place to encourage community in worship. She recognizes that various styles of music should be appreciated. She says, "we must also do a much better job

---

6. Ibid., 96.
7. Ibid., 107.
8. Ibid., 131.

of educating worship participants to value a wider variety of styles."[9] She understands that catering to just one type of music that is culturally and demographically preferred (e.g., music appealing to baby boomers) can hinder the formation of a biblical community. She is mindful of the importance of intentionally worshiping with a variety of styles that identify with different cultures and traditions. In this sense, Dawn is keenly aware of the horizontal dynamics involved in helping the church to worship God in a way that reflects truth and demonstrates love for one's neighbor. She believes that when the church exhibits sensitivity on musical styles, it greatly reflects the gospel and "will ultimately prove subversive to the wider culture" that is frequently exclusionary.[10]

A classically-trained musician, Dawn has learned to appreciate musical variety while worshiping in an inner-city church. She does so out of love for others and a desire to demonstrate an appreciation of musical expressions that minister to her diverse brothers and sisters in Christ. She seeks to put others before herself in the spirit of Christian love. Her attitude is commendable and in accord with the calling for Christians to bear with one another in love (Eph. 4:2).

With regard to her appreciation of the vertical, Dawn encourages the usage of the best music that reflects the truth of the Word and demonstrates respect for the glory of God. Her love for others does not jeopardize her view that we should ultimately seek the glory of God in our worship. Dawn writes, "The Bible makes it clear that worship's sole end is to glorify God: we worship because God deserves it."[11] She is mindful that the vertical and horizontal must be present in her decisions about the lyrics that are sung regardless of musical style. She guards against the common attitude of mushy sentimentalism in choosing what to sing or play in worship. In thinking about horizontal concerns, Dawn acknowledges that style can at times be a problem. She says, "Style can be best evaluated by asking whether it disrupts worship."[12] Dawn encourages choosing music that is

---

9. Dawn, *Reaching Out Without Dumbing Down*, 177.
10. Ibid., 178.
11. Marva J Dawn, "Worship and Reconciliation," *Vision* 8, no. 1 (2007): 18.
12. Dawn, *Reaching Out Without Dumbing Down*, 190.

"edifying to the worshipers."[13] Her instruction to think about how the music will affect the worshippers provides helpful advice for worship leaders who desire to plan their weekly services in a way that aides people in worshiping God in an acceptable manner.

Dawn encourages a new appreciation for ritual gestures and postures within worship without reducing it to mindless habits. She notes that thoughtful gestures and postures over time can help to shape character which can affect our daily lives. She gives an example of how our gestures and postures might shape our vertical and horizontal perspectives. She says,

> Our bowing at the altar can influence us to bow to God's will in our daily choices; our telling the creed to each other in worship invites us to share our faith more easily with our neighbors and work colleagues and family. Those who discard ritual as outmoded tradition do not understand the profound effects on character formation of body language and sensory experience.[14]

In Dawn's article "Worship and Reconciliation" she addresses the importance of reconciling with others before we seek to worship God. She highlights both the vertical and horizontal aspects of worship. For the vertical, she notes that confession to God is essential, stating, "in our worship services, as part of our adoration of God, we both confess our sins which separate us from God, and declare God's work of reconciliation, which has entirely overcome those very sins."[15] She is acutely aware that the church in its first centuries began their services with a rite of confession. Regarding the horizontal, Dawn points to the importance of reconciling with others if we wish to meet with God. She notes that churches that acknowledge the peace they have with God are also called to extend that peace to others. She says,

> The goal is that the triune God who has reconciled us all to Himself will be glorified by the complete reconciliation of all

---

13. Ibid., 192.
14. Dawn, *Reaching Out Without Dumbing Down*, 268.
15. Dawn, "Worship and Reconciliation," 19.

those who are gathered to praise Him. It is blasphemy, rather than worship, if those of us who revel in God's restoration of our relationship with Him are at odds with one another. It is also a desecration of the Lord's Supper (which in many churches follows the offering) if we come to Christ's table of reconciliation without the unity that He has made possible.[16]

If churches practiced Dawn's approach to reconciliation— understanding how vertical reconciliation affects our horizontal reconciliation— it would greatly bless the body of Christ today with peace and love. How often do people come to worship God expecting a blessing while holding a grudge or harboring unforgiveness in their hearts? Many make a mockery of the gospel they claim to believe. Dawn's comments about reconciliation should move all Christians to seek peace and unity with their fellow worshippers.

In her book *A Royal Waste of Time* Dawn presents some practical suggestions on how to develop community in Christian worship. She warns against a shallow understanding of community where "too often the concept of community is perceived merely in terms of a feeling of coziness with God or compatibility with other members of the congregation."[17] She notes that this way of thinking is dangerous and "often the result is the formation of an elitist 'in' group or a narcissism that takes the focus off God."[18] To encourage the formation of community, she promotes thinking beyond just the "greeter" ministry to encouraging the whole congregation to participate in welcoming the stranger. She also reflects on Molly T. Marshall's thought about describing the church as a family versus a community stating, "for that can inhibit our ability to welcome strangers or cause us to squeeze out people with whom we cannot attain intimacy."[19] She states the community is:

---

16. Dawn, "Worship and Reconciliation," 22.
17. Marva J. Dawn, *A Royal Waste of Time: The Splendor of Worshiping God and Being Church for the World* (Grand Rapids, MI: W.B. Eerdmans, 1999), 179.
18. Ibid., 179.
19. Dawn, *A Royal Waste of* Time, 179.

> ... more open to the realities of differences, more openly gracious to all, more deliberate, an act of will. It does not depend upon feelings of affection. God seems to put us in a community together with people whom we don't like so that we learn the real meaning of *agape*—that intelligent, purposeful love directed toward another's need which comes first from God and then flows through us to our neighbor.[20]

Dawn encourages the removal of barriers that hinder community. She acknowledges that many congregations use overhead projectors but notes that they can be hard for the elderly to see. She recommends making available plenty of songbooks, bulletins, large print worship materials for the visually impaired, and interpreters or earphones for the hearing impaired. She expresses concern that there be "no impediments to wheelchairs."[21] Dawn encourages training the congregation to be hospitable to strangers and one another. She tells us in our worship services to "welcome those who sit beside us, make sure they know how to follow our order of service, point them to pages or instructions, and, with specific education, explain to them why we do what we do."[22] Regarding the selection of music, Dawn recommends guarding against choosing songs that are "self-centered, that fail to convey the we-ness (and wee-ness) of the Church.[23] She further comments, "We want to avoid music that focuses only on our personal feelings of happiness, instead of equipping us to be a missional community that reaches out beyond ourselves with the good news of grace in Christ and cares for the world around us with peacemaking and justice building."[24]

Regarding communal prayer during the service, Dawn recommends praying through the list of members and lifting up the members' ministries and occupations. She believes that if we regularly offer such prayers members will be encouraged to minister to one another outside the service by doing things like sending cards, taking

---

20. Ibid., 180.
21. Ibid.
22. Ibid., 181.
23. Ibid., 182.
24. Dawn, *A Royal Waste of* Time, 182.

flowers, preparing meals, doing housework, caring for children, offering rides, etc. She also mentions that some congregations encourage concern for the larger global church by praying for sister congregations, missionaries, churches hit by natural disasters, and for persecuted Christians.[25]

Preaching is one of the chief means Dawn believes community is built. She recommends using simple language and speaking with the third person plural "we" to move people beyond the individualism of our culture. She encourages saying the creeds using the plural "we" and at times looking at one another to reinforce a "sense of communal faith."[26] She recommends dealing with horizontal themes in preaching by addressing foundational doctrines such as our creation command to care for each other, the doctrine of the incarnation and its implications for embodying grace, and the spiritual gifts given for the unity of the church. She believes sermons that promote community provide specific instructions to be hospitable, put the corporate prayers into practice in daily life, encourage reaching out to neighbors, and apply the Scriptures to members' daily occupations.

Dawn, although committed to honoring God in worship, encourages us to balance the promotion of God's glory (the vertical) with a gracious consideration of the community (the horizontal) that comes together for worship. Her insights inspire worship leaders to think carefully about how their worship practices and theology affect the promotion of the Christian community.

Reviewing Dawn's key thoughts on the horizontal dimension: She provides a thoughtful critique of the problems with an individualistic mentality and regrets that it has been brought into the church and its worship. She then calls the church to recognize the value of community to its worship. Dawn addresses the importance of character formation in worship and how Christians should pursue this goal by praising God and showing love to others in worship. She believes that when the truth of God's Word fills the worship service that very truth will become visible with Christians loving both God and their neighbors. Dawn discourages self-centeredness in worship

---

25. Ibid., 184.
26. Ibid.

and promotes the idea that believers should pursue the good of the community. Her emphasis upon the church community is a unique contribution among the contemporary authors we examine in this chapter. She provides practical suggestions on how the church and individuals can welcome the stranger. In her attempt to encourage community through music Dawn talks about the importance of an attitude of love for one's brothers and sisters in Christ. She presents various thoughts on how to think about this issue by graciously acknowledging different musical styles and appreciating their effect on the congregation. Ultimately, she is concerned about honoring God and edifying the people. She demonstrates a sensitive and caring attitude that is frequently missing among other writers on music in worship. Dawn speaks about the need for appreciating ritual gestures and postures within worship. She believes that such actions can encourage people to appreciate God vertically and love one another horizontally even after they leave the worship service. She reminds believers that their vertical relationship with God entails a great blessing since they are reconciled to God through Christ. She then, in light of that reconciliation, encourages believers to pursue horizontal reconciliation with others. Dawn gives practical advice on how to pray during the service to encourage the congregation to minister to others during the week. Finally, she writes about the importance of preaching in calling the congregation to build community through reaching out and living the Christian life in their daily vocations. She encourages the use of the pronoun "we" versus "you" in preaching to accentuate the idea that the body of Christ is a community rather than just a collection of individuals.

In short, Dawn is thoughtful and loving in her perspective about worship with a clear focus on honoring God in all that she does. Many of her ideas on worship are worthy of consideration and encourage a biblical understanding of the horizontal dimension in light of the vertical calling to praise and honor the Lord. Let us now consider the views of another modern Reformed writer—Bob Kauflin.

14

Bob Kauflin

Bob Kauflin is a minister with Sovereign Grace Ministries. He traveled with the Christian group GLAD for eight years as a songwriter and arranger before becoming a pastor. He has written a few influential books on worship. In his book entitled *Worship Matters*, he devotes a chapter to the topic of the vertical and horizontal aspects of worship. Kauflin's theological understanding of God's sovereignty moves him to fully embrace the idea that the direction of worship is vertical in that God is the primary focus of our worship. He is committed to the view that "biblical worship is God-focused (God is clearly seen), God-centered (God is clearly the priority), and God-exalting (God is clearly honored)."[1] Committed to Reformed theology, he remarks, "God's glory is the end of our worship, and not simply a means to something else."[2] Nevertheless, Kauflin recognizes the importance of the horizontal.

He understands that one's perspective on the vertical can become warped. Commenting on this possibility, he says, "But this all-encompassing, God-saturated emphasis can produce unbiblical distortions."[3] Kauflin knows that some people can falsely conclude that any emphasis upon the horizontal will lead to man-centered worship or the view that ministering to each other is not worship.

Kauflin believes that a "significant way we worship God is through building one another up through encouragement and blessing."[4] He sees this activity as a method of proclaiming God's glory and works.

---

1. Bob Kauflin, *Worship Matters: Leading Others to Encounter the Greatness of God* (Wheaton, IL: Crossway, 2008), 177.
2. Ibid., 177.
3. Ibid.
4. Ibid., 178.

Kauflin states, "Worship and edification are two sides of the same coin. When we serve others for their good, we're bringing glory to God. And when we exalt God through our expressions of praise, prayer, and thanks, we're building up those around us. At least, that's the way God intends it to work."[5] He quotes Hebrews 10:24-25 to support the concept of mutual encouragement in worship. He also mentions 1 Corinthians 14:26, "Let all thing be done for building up," noting that "Everything in our time together has that same purpose—'building up.'"[6] Kauflin identifies the importance of both the vertical and horizontal and supports this view by pointing to Paul's teaching in Ephesians 5:19. He notes that the apostle says that we should be "addressing one another in psalms, hymns and spiritual songs," while at the same time "singing and making melody to the Lord."[7] Kaulfin's holds to the view that worship is not just an individual experience as some vertical proponents contend. He adopts the perspective of Donald Whitney who said, "The thought that the Church at worship is an accidental convergence in one place of a number of isolated individuals who practice, in hermetically sealed compartments, their own private devotional exercises, is foreign to the New Testament."[8]

Commenting on singing, Kauflin reminds us of Paul's words to the Colossians where the apostle encourages Christians to engage in "teaching and admonishing one another (Col. 3:16)." Reflecting upon this passage Kauflin says, "While we make melody to the Lord in our hearts, we also address one another in song."[9] Speaking about his own personal experience, he states that he often opens his eyes when singing to look out at the congregation to remind himself and others "that we're affirming truth together."[10] His application of Colossians 3:16 is a corrective for many who engage in singing just for their own pleasure and personal edification. Kauflin tells worship leaders to think about the horizontal when choosing music for the worship service. In

---

5. Bob Kauflin, *True Worshipers: Seeking What Matters to God* (Wheaton, Illinois: Crossway, 2015), 86.
6. Kauflin, *Worship Matters*, 178.
7. Ibid.
8. Donald Whitney, *Spiritual Disciplines of the Christian Life* (Colorado Springs: NavPress, 1977), 77.
9. Kauflin, *Worship Matters*, 105.
10. Kauflin, *True Worshipers*, 178.

planning services, he says, "We don't simply plan for meetings; we plan for people. Ask God for songs that will serve those you're leading rather than one you like or one that will make you look good."[11] He believes it is vital to consider the people who are present in worship and advises leaders to plan their services contextually. Kauflin further states, "The context for choosing your songs includes background details such as the sermons that have been preached, your congregation's demographic mix and level of spiritual maturity, plus weekly variables such as special occasions or events."[12] He is acutely aware of the fact that the music sung or played in worship has a powerful effect upon the hearers and needs to connect to them in a way that is understandable and edifying. Kauflin's comments provide sensible insight into the importance of the horizontal dimension in worship preparation and ministry. Those who wish to ignore his perspective might choose music or songs that hinder the ability of worshippers to praise God. For example, one might choose to play a sophisticated classical piece in a jungle tribe, a culture that may have little musical training, just because he feels its style is culturally superior. But in making that choice, the worshippers may find the music incomprehensible and thus become distracted by the experience. Kauflin would not be against ever playing such music, but he may in that context choose a different musical selection that might better communicate in a way the hearers can understand. For him, the horizontal context is very important.

Another crucial horizontal consideration for Kauflin is intelligibility. Basing his thinking upon Paul's instruction in 1 Corinthians 14:6-11, Kauflin expresses concern that leaders conduct the worship service in a manner that is understood by attendees. He says, "I've been in contexts where a church had grown so used to certain expressions, forms, or patterns that newcomers had little chance of understanding what was happening. Guests shouldn't feel that if they don't know the code words, they'll be lost."[13] Kauflin encourages the church to use words that are understandable and to be aware of things that can become a stumbling block to those who may

---

11. Ibid., 111.
12. Ibid., 113.
13. Kauflin, *True Worshipers*, 93.

visit our worship services. Regarding the importance of making our time of worship intelligible, he remarks, "As we seek to be clearly understood, God can use us to build up others for his glory."[14] Again, we see Kauflin's concern for the horizontal in light of the vertical focus to honor God.

Let us consider some of the practical ways in which Kauflin encourages the horizontal dimension. He speaks about praying for others who are dealing with life-threatening diseases. The congregation "might honor an individual or specific group in the church for their faithful service or godly example."[15] He cautions against pursuing the honor of others and edification for their own sake. Kauflin connects honoring and edifying others to the ultimate purpose of glorifying God when he states, "If we pursue honor and edification for their own sake, we quickly lose sight of the One we're seeking to please. Meetings become all about what we're doing for each other, meeting people's needs, and making sure everyone is happy."[16] He encourages honoring and edifying people "in a way that draws attention to God's grace" and fulfilling the scriptural command to give "honor to whom honor is owed" (Rom. 13:7).[17] Kauflin commends keeping the vertical and horizontal in healthy tension "so that God will be worshipped and his people will be built up, all for his glory."[18]

Let us consider Kauflin's key points in summary. He sees worship as including both the vertical and horizontal. He understands that when we praise God and pray to him, we are serving others and building them up as they observe us. He writes that when we serve others, we are glorifying God. Therefore, he points out that the vertical and horizontal are two sides of the same coin. He draws our attention to passages like Hebrews 10:24-25 to promote the idea of encouraging others in worship and points to 1 Corinthians 14:26 as support for the view that worship needs to build up others. He reflects upon Ephesians 5:19 and Colossians 3:16 arguing that singing in worship should not only praise God but also build up other believers. Kauflin

---

14. Ibid.
15. Kauflin, *Worship Matters*, 178.
16. Kauflin, *Worship Matters*, 179.
17. Ibid.
18. Ibid.

speaks against the individualistic mindset and affirms that worship is a community event. To confirm the horizontal dimension, he mentions that he often opens his eyes to look out at the congregation singing together. With reference to song selections, Kauflin tells leaders to think about the horizontal and consider songs that will serve those being led. He believes we should think about things like the demographic mix and level of maturity of the people. He encourages worship leaders to choose music that the hearers can understand. Kauflin takes Paul's teaching seriously in 1 Corinthians 14 about making sure the service is intelligible. He instructs leaders to use words that are understandable and asks them to be mindful of those things that might hinder visitors from grasping what is happening. He believes God can use such efforts to build up others for his glory. Kauflin gives various practical suggestions about how to encourage the horizontal dimension. He cautions the church that the horizontal should never be pursued for its own sake but for the ultimate purpose of glorifying God and drawing attention to his grace.

We now turn to another Reformed writer and theologian who has impacted many church leaders on the subject of the horizontal dimension—John Frame.

15

John Frame

Professor Frame is a widely influential Reformed theologian. He served the Reformed and evangelical church as a professor of systematic theology for many years.[1] As a skilled musician, Frame has faithfully ministered to the local church as a director of worship. His writings have had an extensive impact upon many issues in the church, especially on the topic of worship. Frame holds to the view that worship should be governed by Scripture as he states, "In biblical worship, we seek God's glory, not our own pleasure. And we have no sure way of determining what pleases God in worship except God's own revelation of Himself in scripture."[2]

Frame fully embraces the Reformed view that worship should be God-centered and Christ-centered. He states:

> God-centered worship, following the richness of the New Testament revelation, is always worship in the name of Christ and by the Holy Spirit. The only name by which we may be saved is that of Christ (Acts 4:12), and we can come to know him only by the sovereign working of the Holy Spirit (John 3:3; Rom. 8:14-15; 1 Cor. 2:12). God-centered worship is Trinitarian worship. Our worship should be clearly directed to God as Father, Son, and Holy Spirit.[3]

---

[1]. John Frame has served as a professor of systematic theology at Westminster Theological Seminary in Philadelphia, PA and Escondido, CA. He also taught at Reformed Theological Seminary in Orlando, FL.

[2]. John M. Frame, "A Fresh Look at the Regulative Principle: A Broader View," *Frame-Poythress.org*, June 4, 2012, accessed September 16, 2016, http://frame-poythress.org/a-fresh-look-at-the-regulative-principle-a-broader-view/.

[3]. John M. Frame, *Worship in Spirit and Truth* (Phillipsburg, NJ: P & R, 1996), 7.

Frame also defines worship as "acknowledging the greatness of our covenant Lord."[4] Although Frame believes that worship should be God-centered, and therefore the vertical direction of worship must take precedence, he recognizes that it also should have a horizontal dimension. He cautions that as we seek to maintain a horizontal perspective, we do so without creating man-centered worship. He warns against "catering to their wants" and says "Worship is not, therefore, a program to provide entertainment, or to enhance self-esteem, or to encourage self-righteousness."[5] Frame understands that some who focus on the vertical believe that "we should not pay any attention to human needs in worship," but he also argues that the Scriptures do not teach that point of view.[6] Taking the position that God-centered worship requires the horizontal he says, "It is to be God-centered, but it is also to be both edifying and evangelistic. Worship that is unedifying or unevangelistic may not properly claim to be God-centered."[7] Frame addresses various topics related to the horizontal dimension in worship.

He draws attention to the fact that "worshippers should not ignore the needs of the poor (Isa. 1:10-17; compare 1 Cor. 11:17-34; James 2:1-7)."[8] Frame says that it is important to make sure our worship is edifying to believers. Worship, as described by the apostle Paul in 1 Corinthians 14, emphasizes the necessity of intelligibility when we worship. Frame believes that Paul teaches that it is essential that everyone in the service, both believers and unbelievers, understand what is happening so that they might fall down and worship God (1 Cor. 14:25). Frame remarks, "Paul places a high priority on the clarity, the intelligibility, of the language used in worship. Similarly, the Protestant Reformers insisted that worship be conducted in the vernacular languages rather than in Latin."[9] Frame summarizes Paul's

---

4. John M. Frame, "Worship and the Reformation Gospel," *Frame-Poythress.org*, May 30, 2012, accessed January 4, 2017, http://frame-poythress.org/worship-and-the-reformation-gospel/.

5. Frame, *Worship in Spirit and Truth*, 8.

6. Ibid.

7. Frame, *Worship in Spirit and Truth*, 8.

8. Ibid.

9. John M. Frame, *Contemporary Worship Music: A Biblical Defense* (Phillipsburg, NJ: P & R Publishing, 1997), 18.

emphasis, "So, worship has a horizontal dimension as well as a vertical focus."[10]

Frame believes that worship should demonstrate not only our love for God but also our love for others. He writes that "worship leaders should be like Jesus in the way they relate to the congregation, showing love to church members and visitors alike."[11] He believes that seeking to edify others is a significant way to show Christian love. Frame thinks "Worship is a time to care for one another, to build up the unity of our fellowship in Christ (Heb. 10:24-25)."[12] Part of edifying the congregation involves making sure the service is intelligible according to Paul's teaching in 1 Corinthians 14. Commenting on Paul's instruction about intelligibility, Frame notes that "When churches use archaic language and follow practices that are little understood today, they compromise that biblical principle."[13] He recommends giving attention to the matter of communication to make the things of God clear. He says that this is in keeping with the principles that Jesus sets forth in the Great Commission to disciple, baptize, and teach all the nations (Matt. 28:18-20).[14] Frame draws attention to the Greek word *latreia* which is translated in the Bible as "worship," and he notes that it focuses upon labor and service. Applying the meaning of this Greek word for worship, he points out that Christians are called to participate in worship and carry out their priestly service. Addressing believers directly he then states, "we should go to church to do something: to bring praise to God and to minister to one another."[15] This attitude of service should encourage us who profess faith in Christ to be less concerned about what we get out of worship versus what "we contribute to God and to our brothers and sisters."[16] For Frame, a servant attitude is key to biblical worship since it exemplifies the same attitude exhibited by Christ (Luke 22:24). He says, "worship is not a

---

10. Frame, *Worship in Spirit and Truth*, 8.
11. John M. Frame, "Worship and the Reformation Gospel," *Frame-Poythress.org*, May 30, 2012, accessed January 4, 2017, http://frame-poythress.org/worship-and-the-reformation-gospel/.
12. Frame, *Worship in Spirit and Truth*, 8.
13. Ibid., 66.
14. Ibid.
15. Ibid., 80.
16. Frame, *Worship in Spirit and Truth*, 80.

time for us to cut ourselves off from one another in order to meditate on God as individuals. At worship, as everywhere else, God calls us to serve him by serving one another."[17] Frame views love for both God and one another as a key virtue for biblical worship. He argues that it fulfills God's law.[18] In serving those who worship with us, we demonstrate our love for God and those he has called us to love.

Frame provides tangible examples of how to serve others in our time of corporate worship. He says, "It is a time to pray for one another's needs. It is a time to look around and see that everybody has a seat, has the bread and wine. It is a time to welcome strangers and explain to them what is going on, to help them find bulletins, bathrooms, nursery facilities."[19] For Frame, love for others is expressed with concrete actions of service and therefore demonstrates our love for and respect for Christ, the chief servant.

Frame also encourages the horizontal in addressing the importance of fellowship in worship. He includes some biblical expressions of fellowship that happen in Christian worship. He says, "… horizontal focus can be seen in our prayers for one another, in our exhorting of one another through preaching and teaching (Heb. 10:24-25), in the greetings and benedictions, in confessions and vows, in church discipline, in the sacrament (see 1 Cor. 10:14-17; 11:17-34), and in the collection of gifts."[20] Fellowship in worship inherently encourages the horizontal connections between believers and fosters biblical unity in the church.

Correcting the individualism that is prevalent today, Frame challenges believers to look beyond focusing on their personal preferences and comfort to pleasing God and considering the needs of their neighbors in worship. He comments,

> Worship is not merely for ourselves as individuals, but for God, for our fellow Christians, and for the unbelieving visitors (1 Cor. 14:22-25). We must distinguish between what God

---

17. John Frame, "Serving One Another in Worship," *Frame-Poythress.org*, May 28, 2012, accessed March 29, 2018, https://frame-poythress.org/serving-one-another-in-worship/.
18. Frame, *Worship in Spirit and Truth*, 81.
19. John Frame, "Serving One Another in Worship."
20. Frame, *Worship in Spirit and Truth*, 59.

requires and what we are comfortable with, between scriptural standards and mere individual preferences. And in matters of individual preferences, we must be willing to consider others ahead of ourselves."[21]

Many people have an aversion to the horizontal because they are more interested in pursuing their own personal preferences rather than considering others better than themselves as Paul teaches in Philippians 2:3. Dismissing the biblical principle of considering others better than ourselves leads to much division in the church on the matter of worship. Such division can be resolved if believers are willing to be gracious and considerate of one another. Frame clearly grasps the importance of this principle in our understanding of the vertical and horizontal dimensions. Music is one of the areas of worship that has been especially controversial in recent years. Frame believes that divisive camps about worship music are often caused by insensitive and dismissive attitudes regarding the preferences of others. Divisions in the church have frequently revolved around those who prefer either traditional or contemporary music.

Having dealt extensively with the topic of contemporary worship, Frame states that musical styles are not the issue at hand in the worship wars. He recognizes that the issue is not between traditional or contemporary music. It has more to do with whether Christians will show the love of Christ toward one another's stylistic musical preferences. He says,

> Those who find high art or traditional liturgy to be their natural language of worship should accept contemporary forms of music, if not for themselves, as a service to other members of the body. Those who find real worship only in the contemporary style should likewise defer to those on the other side. That is the way it should be in the body of Christ: people washing one another's feet, serving one another rather than themselves.[22]

---

21. Ibid., 84.
22. John M. Frame, *The Doctrine of the Christian Life*, A Theology of Lordship.

For Frame, it is essential to reflect a gracious spirit on such topics as musical selections in worship because that is the attitude demanded in the Bible. This all reflects a knowledge and appreciation of the horizontal dimension in that worshippers are called to consider the spiritual needs of others rather than focusing only on their own desires. Frame sees music as a type of language just like English is a language for English speakers and Spanish is a language for Spanish speakers. He believes it is important to consider the musical language of the people we wish to lead in worship. He says,

> It is true that some music is more effective at edifying immature Christians than mature Christians, and some vice versa. So some have argued that music should be geared to the mature, to communicate with them and to challenge the immature to grow up. But that is to misunderstand the nature of education/edification. The way to teach mathematics to a child is not to put him in a college calculus course. It is, rather, to bring him along step-by-step, through addition, subtraction, and so on. Similarly, in worship, there should be words, and songs, that communicate with people at every level: child, adolescent, adult, unbeliever, new convert, growing believer, mature Christian. And these should also be words and songs that challenge people of each level to grow to the next level of maturity.[23]

Frame is deeply concerned that we obey Paul's instruction in 1 Corinthians 14 that our worship edifies and communicates in a way that is intelligible. Frame advises us to construct our worship services in the spirit of 1 Corinthians 9 where Paul says, "… I have become all things to all people, that by all means I might save some" (1 Cor. 9:22). He believes these Pauline principles help Christians move toward maturity and unbelievers toward salvation. He acknowledges that when the church makes the things that happen in the service more accessible and understandable (without compromising the gospel), the church is following the spirit of Paul's teaching. He says, "It is not a

---

(Phillipsburg, NJ: P&R Publishing, 2008), 905.
    23. Frame, *The Doctrine of the Christian Life*, 907-8.

compromise of the gospel, but it is rather a way of removing unnecessary offense so that the offense of the cross itself may be heard all the more vividly, all the more offensively."[24] This perspective calls us to consider the maturity and needs of others in worship. Considering others in this way requires humility and deference for the sake of building up the body of Christ in the spirit of Christian love (1 Cor. 13). Concerned for all involved in worship, Frame wisely counsels the church,

> We should not selfishly insist on using music only for our own favorite tradition. Rather, in the spirit of Christ the servant, we must be willing to sacrifice our own preferences in order to reach others with the truth. The Great Commission turns us outward, rather than inward: it calls us even in worship to reach out to those who are ignorant of Christ and of our musical traditions. It is a good idea, then, for all of us to learn to appreciate music that doesn't immediately appeal to us. In that way we serve one another, and we also grow by learning to praise God in new ways.[25]

Whether one agrees or not with all of Frame's conclusions on worship, there should be universal agreement with the sentiment he expresses in the above quote. It demonstrates a true love for God and his precious church. If we could simply agree on this point, much unity could be achieved amid our disagreements about what music we choose and approve of in our worship services. Frame encourages us all to demonstrate a more gracious and loving servant attitude as we think about worship. He speaks about the horizontal dimension always with great respect for God's Word and glory.

In summarizing Frame's comments on the horizontal dimension, we note a key principle that Frame repeatedly emphasizes—a firm commitment to following what the scriptures teach on worship. He notes that worship is focused upon God as Trinity and therefore is God-centered, but he also acknowledges the significance of the horizontal dimension throughout the Bible. He warns that worship

---

24. Frame, *Contemporary Worship Music*, 96.
25. Frame, *Worship in Spirit and Truth*, 141.

which eliminates the importance of edification and evangelism (which are horizontal ideas) cannot claim to be God-centered. He calls attention to considering the poor when we worship citing various verses to support his concern. Frame focuses upon Paul's instruction in 1 Corinthians 14 and acknowledges the need for intelligibility and edification in worship. Noting that Christians are commanded to love both God and others, he upholds the vital place of love in worship. Frame says the practice of edifying others is one of the main ways to demonstrate Christian love to the congregation. To pursue intelligibility in worship, he encourages communicating with clear language and advocates using worship practices that people can understand. He believes the principle of clearly communicating to congregants is in keeping with Christ's Great Commission in which he calls his disciples to teach all the nations. Frame focuses upon the importance of serving others in worship viewing service as an act of worship. He defends this point stating that believers are called to serve God and others as priests of God. He argues that this attitude of service is demonstrated when Christians minister to one another as they worship. Emphasizing the servant role of believers, Frame corrects those who attend worship to be served rather than to serve. He writes that serving God involves serving others. Frame offers tangible ways to serve others in worship such as praying for their needs, making sure everyone has a seat, and helping people find bulletins, bathrooms, and nursery facilities. He calls believers to follow in the footsteps of Jesus who is the chief servant. Frame also mentions the necessity of fellowship in worship. Dealing with the issue of individualism that is widespread today, Frame calls believers to look beyond pleasing themselves to worshiping God and considering the needs of others in worship. Instead of focusing on their personal preferences Frame asks Christians to consider others ahead of themselves as the apostle Paul teaches in Philippians 2:3. Frame applies this principle especially to the subject of music and believes that embracing Paul's teaching on considering others ahead of ourselves would resolve many divisions that have occurred in the church. He argues that the love of Christ is needed to help people demonstrate a gracious attitude about musical preferences in worship. Frame challenges all believers to love one another as they worship God with the same love they have received from their Father through faith in Christ. In short, he calls Christians to worship God with love for their neighbor.

Another Reformed theologian that addresses the horizontal dimension of worship is R.C. Sproul.

16

R.C. Sproul

Sproul was a widely respected Reformed theologian, author, and the founder of Ligonier Ministries. This ministry promotes the Reformed faith through various written and media-related resources. Sproul served as a seminary professor at Reformed seminaries and pastored Saint Andrews Church in Sanford, Florida. He wrote a book on worship called *A Taste of Heaven* that has ministered to thousands. Although Sproul primarily gives attention to the vertical side of worship, he makes some comments in support of the horizontal dimension.

In his chapter on prayer, Sproul focuses on corporate prayer. He draws attention to the priest Zacharias (Greek name) who was chosen to serve the Lord in the temple by representing the people of Israel before God in prayer (cf. Luke 1:6-10). Zacharias was of the division of Abijah and the husband of Elizabeth, a cousin of Mary, the mother of Jesus. A multitude of people was praying outside at the hour of incense. Sproul notes that Zacharias "wasn't going into the Holy of Holies and he wasn't going to offer the Paschal lamb, but he was going to the altar of incense to pray the pastoral prayer for the nation."[1] Intercessory prayer was one of his horizontal responsibilities as a priest of God. As Zacharias was praying and serving the Lord in the temple, Luke records, "And the whole multitude of the people were praying outside at the hour of incense" (Luke 1:10). Sproul remarks,

> There was a scheduled hour for the assembling together of the saints as a corporate congregation. The priest represented the believers, the congregation, to God. He went to the altar of

---

1. R C. Sproul, *A Taste of Heaven: Worship in the Light of Eternity* (Orlando, FL: Reformation Trust Publishing, 2006), 53.

incense not to pray for himself but to deliver the prayers of the people. While he prayed for the people, they were gathered as a large body, and they also prayed. This was the assembling together of the whole corporation for corporate prayer.[2]

At this time, the angel of the Lord appeared to Zacharias and told him that God had heard his prayer and that his wife would bear a son named John (Luke 1:11-13). Sproul draws our attention to the importance that God placed on corporate prayer in the ministry of Zacharias to remind us that prayer was vital to biblical worship. Including both the vertical and horizontal in his understanding of prayer Sproul says, "It is appropriate when we come before God to make our requests, to give our intercession, to offer the sacrifice of praise, and to bespeak our thanksgiving…"[3]

Sproul acknowledges that many churches will have the minister lead in prayer similarly to the way Zacharias prayed but he also notes that the people prayed as well. He concludes that "It would seem to me that it is pleasing to God when His people participate with the pastor in the corporate prayer."[4] Such prayer would mean that not only would the minister be thinking about the people in his prayers but so would the members who join him in praying to God. In other words, the joint participation between the minister and the people in corporate prayer means that they both will engage in vertical and horizontal topics as they pray together. Further commenting on the horizontal nature of corporate prayer, Sproul states,

> This involves directed prayer. The pastor directs the congregation to pray by name for those who are ill, then by name for those who are burdened, then those who are at the house of mourning. Individuals in the congregation don't give 15-minute orations in prayer, but are able to say aloud the names of the people about whom they are concerned at the moment. It also helps us to know what's on other people's hearts, so that when we're outside of the church we can carry that person with us.[5]

---

2. Sproul, *A Taste of Heaven*, 53.
3. Sproul, *A Taste of Heaven*, 57.
4. Ibid., 58.
5. Ibid.

Given the minimalization of prayer in many churches today, Sproul provides wise counsel to congregations to make corporate prayer an essential part of their worship services. He understands that prayer played a major role in the lives of the Reformers and most importantly to the Lord. Sproul reminds us that Jesus considered prayer vital to temple worship when he said, ". . . My house shall be called a house of prayer . . ." (Matt. 21:13; Isa. 56:7). Sproul strongly believes that "In ancient Israel, the primary function of worship was the offering of praise, the offering of prayer. And so it should be in our churches today. Our sanctuaries should be houses of prayer."

17

Conclusion

We have discovered that some important contemporary Reformed theologians and pastors have given the church helpful and insightful confirmation that the horizontal dimension is vital to biblical worship. The concept of the horizontal dimension cannot be ignored if we are to carefully prescribe the principles of biblical and Reformed worship. Many of the authors reviewed above have noted similar concepts that promote the horizontal, such as love for our neighbor, edification, intelligibility, service, community, and spiritual union with one another in the Lord's Supper. Some authors also recognize that the Reformers were intent on encouraging God's people to participate in worship serving one another as a priesthood of believers rather than engaging in worship as mere spectators seeking to be entertained. The writers recognize that worship in the church is not an individualistic experience but rather a corporate practice of the body of Christ involving concern and love for others. In fact, they argue that a corporate view of worship was clearly promoted by the Reformers and thus encourage the church today to return to this biblical and Reformed emphasis upon caring, corporate participation. The authors we have reviewed understand the importance of considering both the physical and spiritual needs of unbelievers and believers in worship. They believe that the vertical and horizontal dimensions are intertwined rather than at odds. These worship experts correct those who wish to turn worship solely into a vertical experience or primarily horizontal. They recognize that both the vertical and horizontal are required for our worship to be pleasing to God. They encourage an attitude of grace and sensitivity when dealing with subjects as sensitive as music. In summary, they ask all believers to engage in worship with love for both God and their neighbor.

Having covered in previous chapters the biblical, historical and now contemporary support for the horizontal dimension, we now turn to the practical implications and practical considerations for the church.

Part 4

MINISTRY MODEL

In this chapter we will offer tools to aide church leaders in educating their congregations in understanding and applying the biblical truths of the horizontal dimension of worship. Attention will be given to sample worship services that implement the horizontal in light of the Reformed tradition. There is also provided a visual diagram that explains the relationship of the vertical to the horizontal, a series of Sunday school lessons that cover Bible verses dealing with the horizontal, and a sermon series that addresses key texts in support of the horizontal dimension. The corresponding Sunday lessons may be used for Sunday evening studies, a two-day workshop on worship, a weekend retreat, or a midweek service. The lessons and sermons target texts that are addressed in chapter two of this project. Chapter two provides additional exegetical research to enhance one's teaching and preaching of the selected texts in this chapter. The Vertical/Horizontal Dimension diagram provides a visual aide for teachers to clearly communicate the complementary but necessary aspects involved with the vertical and horizontal dimensions of biblical worship. It is my prayer that the tools in this chapter will strengthen and enrich believers' worship, fully engaging them with love for God and their neighbor. I hope that souls will be saved, saints will be sanctified, God will be honored, Scripture will be upheld, and the church will be edified.

18

The Vertical/Horizontal Dimension Dynamic

The diagram below provides a visual to aid in instructing others regarding the importance of the vertical and horizontal dimensions of worship.[1] Notice that the primary direction of worship is to God.

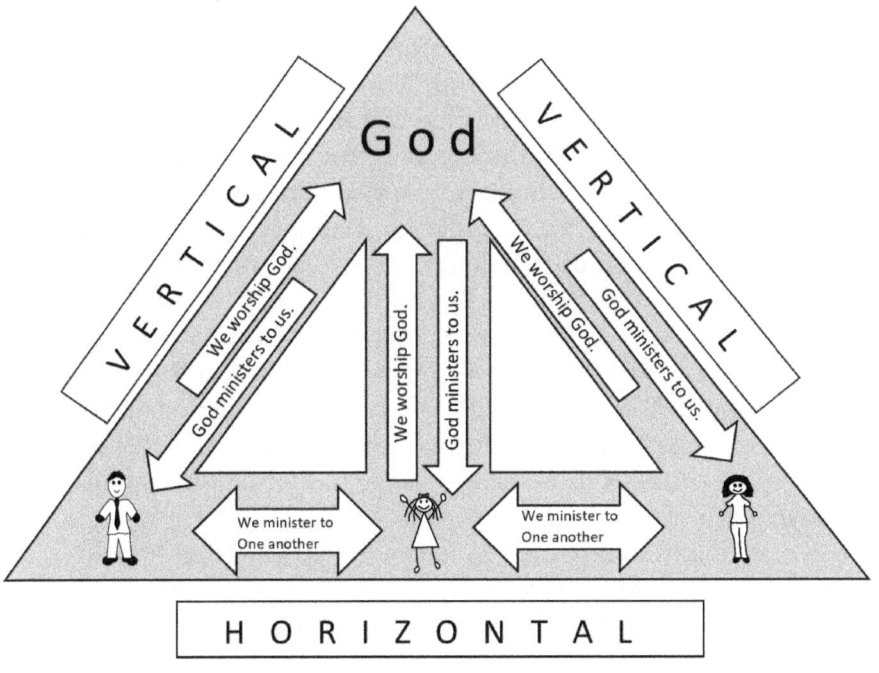

---

1. David Peterson, *Engaging with God: A Biblical Theology of Worship* (Grand Rapids, MI: W.B. Eerdmans, 1993), 221. This visual was inspired by a diagram created by Peterson to help illustrate the importance of God-directed prayer or praise and the notion of edification.

The vertical direction of worship reminds us that only God is worthy of worship. Christians should only worship the God of the Bible as he has commanded since to do otherwise is to engage in idolatry which the Scriptures forbid (Exod. 20:3-6; Deut. 5:7-10). This vertical direction is upward and downward (or bi-directional) with blessings provided for the worshipper. The upward vertical direction includes praise, prayer, confession, reverence, singing, listening and applying God's Word, and participating in the sacraments. The upward is motivated by love for and thanks to God. The downward aspect of the vertical involves God ministering to the souls of the worshippers by transforming them, convicting them, saving them, blessing them with the fulness of the Spirit, filling them with his Word, enriching them with his presence, and encouraging their souls. The downward work of God toward people is motivated by his love, compassion, care, and desire that he be glorified.

The horizontal dimension involves each worshiper ministering to one another as they worship God. Their ministry to one another is motivated by Christian love for God and their neighbor. Worshippers minister to one another through prayer, responsive readings, singing, encouragement, smiles, helping people find a seat, explaining the order of service, and setting an example of attentiveness to the preached word. God has given each believer a spiritual gift that aids them in ministering to one another. Notice that worshippers are interconnected with one another as they are connected to God. When unbelievers come to worship, Christians minister to them with the hope that they will convert to faith in Christ and begin to truly worship God from thankful hearts. Through the ministry of believers God works in the hearts of those he is drawing to himself through his Spirit (John 6:44; 1 Cor. 14:23-25).

Notice that for Christians to fully worship God they should experience the vertical and horizontal. These two dimensions should never be separated. Now let us consider some practical ways to instruct the church in the implementation of the horizontal and vertical dimensions of worship.

19

Worship Samples that Incorporate the Horizontal

Worship Sample 1 (Liturgy of the Word):

Welcome (horizontal):

Suggested Welcome:

"Good morning everyone. It is a joy to join with you this Lord's Day for the praise and honor of our Savior and Lord. We especially welcome all our guests and are thankful that God has brought you to Faith Community Church. It is our hope that you and your family will be richly blessed as we worship together. Please let us know if we can serve you in any way. Let us now hear God's call to worship him."

Call to Worship (vertical):

Suggested Introduction:

"As we prepare our hearts to worship the Lord this morning, hear this Psalm's call to make known the character of God to all generations. This means it is a call for us this morning to declare to one another in our worship the character and actions of God. Psalm 89:1-2 states…"

1) I will sing of the steadfast love of the Lord, forever;
with my mouth I will make known your faithfulness to all generations.
2) For I said, "Steadfast love will be built up forever;
in the heavens you will establish your faithfulness."

Suggested prayer:

"O Lord our God, the rock of our salvation. Receive our worship and praise through your Son Jesus. Come and help us to worship you in spirit and in truth. You are faithful in keeping your covenants with your people to all generations. Enable us in our worship to declare to one another and our generation your steadfast love. In the name of the Father, the Son, and the Holy Spirit. Amen."[1]

Songs of Praise: Include an antiphonal song: One such song is entitled "Antiphonal Praise (We Worship You)" by Steve Green. It is often sung with the women starting and the men echoing the same verse sung by the women. Both then join on the chorus. It involves the horizontal engagement between the men and women in praise to God. This song encourages both parties to minister to one another through singing.

To encourage men and women to minister to one another consider this transitional statement:

"As we prepare to sing the song *We Worship You* let us minister to one another with the women singing a verse and the men repeating the phrase that the women sang. Then we will join together on the chorus to reflect our unity in Christ. Let us encourage one another to worship our great God in song."

---

1. See Hughes Oliphant Old, *Leading in Prayer: A Workbook for Ministers* (Grand Rapids, MI: Eerdmans, 1995), 11-17. This prayer conforms to the pattern of invocations provided by Old. He also provides samples of various invocations he has used in worship (see pages 18-54).

Greet Your Neighbor (horizontal):

Encourage the congregation to take a moment to greet people near them with a friendly greeting. Note to the worshippers this is a brief opportunity to show their love and hospitality. Some refer to this as the "Passing of the Peace." "Passing of the Peace" is an ancient Christian practice that is found in some church traditions. It involves an attender saying to another "Peace be with you." The respondent generally says, "And also with you." This practice was based upon the words of Jesus to his disciples (Luke 24:36; John 20:19, 26) and the greetings of Paul (Rom 1:7; 1 Cor 1:3; 2 Cor 1:2). This greeting fits with the Christian's calling to be a peacemaker (Matt. 5:9; 2 Cor. 5:20).

Scripture Reading (vertical & horizontal): Pick a verse or passage from chapter two of this thesis that will encourage the church to think about the horizontal. Comment on how the text encourages both the vertical and the horizontal.

Matthew 22:34-40:

34) But when the Pharisees heard that he had silenced the Sadducees, they gathered together.
35) And one of them, a lawyer, asked him a question to test him.
36) "Teacher, which is the great commandment in the Law?"
37) And he said to him, "You shall love the Lord your God with all your heart and with all your soul and with all your mind.
38) This is the great and first commandment.
39) And a second is like it: You shall love your neighbor as yourself.
40) On these two commandments depend all the Law and the Prophets."

Confession of Sin (vertical & horizontal): [2]

---

2. Often church leaders view confession of sin as limited to the vertical seeing their offense only against God (Ps. 51:4) but forget to note that our corporate confessions also address the need to confess our sins against one another. By confessing our sins against

Suggested Transition:

"As we prepare our hearts to confess our sins, notice in our confession today that it involves both an individual confession and a collective confession. It reflects not only our personal, vertical relationship with God but also our horizontal, covenantal relationship with one another. It is biblical to confess our personal and corporate sins against God and our neighbor."

Psalm 106:3-6
3) Blessed are they who observe justice,
    who do righteousness at all times!
4) Remember me, O LORD, when you show favor to your people;
    help me when you save them,
5) that I may look upon the prosperity of your chosen ones,
    that I may rejoice in the gladness of your nation,
    that I may glory with your inheritance.
6) Both we and our fathers have sinned;
    we have committed iniquity; we have done wickedness.

Assurance of Pardon (vertical): Psalm 103:8-12.

Suggested introduction to reading Psalm 103:8-12:

"As we hear God's pardon in Psalm 103, realize that his pardon is not just for individuals, but it is communal and provided for the people of God. It reflects our communal blessings as a communion of saints. Be encouraged by God's example to forgive one another as Paul declares in Ephesians 5:32, "Be kind to one another, tenderhearted, forgiving one another, as God in Christ forgave you." God's example and promise of pardon encourages us to forgive one another when we hear the plural pronouns "us" and "our" in the prayer of the psalmist. Let us read Psalm 103:8-12."

God and each other, we reflect the gracious nature of God, minister in His name, and humbly express a spirit of forgiveness in the congregation (James 5:16).

Psalm 103:8-12:

8) The LORD is merciful and gracious, slow to anger and abounding in steadfast love.
9) He will not always chide, nor will he keep his anger forever.
10) He does not deal with **us** according to **our** sins, nor repay **us** according to **our** iniquities.
11) For as high as the heavens are above the earth, so great is his steadfast love toward those who fear him;
12) as far as the east is from the west, so far does he remove **our** transgressions from **us**.

Hymn of Praise (vertical and horizontal): Encourage the congregation to minister to one another in song as they sing praise to God.[3]

Suggested introduction to the hymn:

"Let us join together in song to our God. Paul declares in Ephesians 5:18-20, '... be filled with the Spirit, addressing one another in psalms and hymns and spiritual songs, singing and making melody to the Lord with your heart.' Let us minister to one another declaring to each other the virtues and character of our Lord."

Congregational Prayer (vertical and horizontal): Each week during the congregational prayer, pray to God making reference to specific individuals, ministries, groups in the church, activities, and even other churches to reflect God's concern for the horizontal.

This Sunday, include prayers for some of the sick of the church by name and lift up one of the ministries that the church supports (e.g., Evangelism Visitation, Crisis Pregnancy Center).

---

3. Two helpful texts that may be briefly mentioned to encourage people to minister to one another in song are Ephesians 5:19 and Colossians 3:16.

Announcements (horizontal and vertical):

Suggested introduction:

"We want to welcome our guests today. We are so blessed to have you join us. As the ushers pass out the welcome books, we encourage everyone to sign them and share any prayer requests or praises. If you desire your request to be confidential for the church officers, please write confidential beside your request. For all our activities, we wish to extend an invitation to you and your family. God has called us to praise his name in worship, but he also wants us to minister to one another. One of the ways we do that for God's glory is to encourage one another to attend our events and activities. We want you to be involved in the ministry and the life of the church. This builds up the body of Christ, the church, and pleases God. Let us keep this in mind as we consider the announcements today."

Worship in Giving (horizontal and vertical):

This is an opportunity to encourage the church to give to the Lord's work with enthusiasm. Before you read the Scripture, encourage the people as they prepare to give to God's work to consider the enthusiasm and joy of the Magi who gave their gifts to Christ.

Suggested introduction to the Scripture:

"Giving to God's Kingdom work is a privilege, joy, and blessing. Consider the magi as they came to give gifts to Jesus. Ponder their attitude in giving."

Matthew 2:11:

11) And going into the house, they saw the child with Mary his mother, and they fell down and worshiped him. Then, opening

their treasures, they offered him gifts, gold and frankincense and myrrh.

Suggested prayer:

"O Lord God, we eagerly come like the magi to bring our tithes and offerings to you. We bow in our hearts, acknowledging it is a privilege and joy to give to build the kingdom of Jesus. Please use these gifts to carry on the ministry of the gospel, bring souls to Christ, and encourage others with your Word. In Jesus' name we pray. Amen."

Special Music (horizontal considerations): If the music is instrumental, encourage the congregation to use this time to meditate on God and to pray for his blessings upon other worshippers. Encourage people to pray for people by name and for their specific needs, even those who are shut-ins or sick.

Dismiss the children to children's church.

Prayer of Illumination (vertical and horizontal):

"O Lord, bless us today with wisdom and insight from your Word that we might understand it, apply it in our lives, and love our neighbors as you have loved us in Christ. Move us through your Holy Spirit to treat others in accord with your character and truth. In Jesus name. Amen."

Sermon (vertical and horizontal): Make sure you explain, illustrate, and apply the text in the lives of the people. The sermon is vertical in the sense that its message is from God's Word to the people through the preacher. The preacher's careful handling and interpretation of God's Word entails his vertical respect for God and God's vertical ministry in and through the preacher. The sermon also involves the vertical for the people hearing the Word in that God ministers to them by his Spirit through the preached Word and they respond to God. Preaching also includes the horizontal. The preacher horizontally relates to the people. He must consider the best Bible translation and style that most communicates at a level the people can understand. He needs to deliver his message with Biblical love and care for all those listening to his sermon. The horizontal dimension is involved in the choice of illustrations and applications informed by the preacher's knowledge of and relationship with the people. He must think about them to truly communicate God's Word to them. The message also has horizontal implications for the life of the body of Christ. As they hear the Word, they should be encouraged to think about how to apply God's truth in the way they treat one another in the congregation and the world at large. Jesus tells us to be doers of the Word and not hearers only (Matt. 7:24-27).

Hymn of Response (vertical and horizontal): Pick a song to reinforce the sermon. Call everyone to give praise to God and minister to one another in song.

Benediction (vertical):

2 Corinthians 13:14:

"The grace of the Lord Jesus Christ and the love of God and the fellowship of the Holy Spirit be with you all."

Worship Sample 2 (Liturgy of the Word):

Prelude

Welcome (horizontal):

Suggested greeting:

"Good morning. It is a blessing to be in the house of the Lord. We welcome you today to Faith Community Church. We also extend special greetings if you are visiting the church for the first time and hope you will be encouraged with God's Word and the praise of his people. With glad hearts let us turn now to the Bible to hear God's call to worship.

Call to the Worship (vertical):

Suggested Introduction:

"As you hear the psalmist call the church to worship today, listen for his concern for his fellow worshippers to praise the Lord. Notice that he is personally concerned to praise God but extends his concern to the covenant community. This is Psalm 34:1-3 …"[4]

Psalm 34:1-3:
1) I will bless the Lord at all times; his praise shall continually be in my mouth.
2) My soul makes its boast in the LORD; let the humble hear and be glad.
3) Oh, magnify the LORD with me, and let us exalt his name together!

Suggested Prayer:

---

[4]. Additional passages that include the horizontal and vertical include Psalms 22:22-26; 40:6-10.

"Lord our God, give us the heart of the psalmist today who desires to praise you in his soul but also wishes to encourage others in his praise to join him in worshiping you. Amen"

Songs of Praise (vertical and horizontal): Use praise songs that sing about God versus just to God. Such songs allow for the horizontal as the saints minister to one another in song and encourage one another to consider truth claims about God. Encourage the congregation to minister to one another.

Suggested introduction:

"As we prepare to praise our God in song, let us minister to one another by declaring with joy and faith who God is and what he has done for us."

In Christ Alone
Amazing Grace

Scripture Reading (vertical and horizontal): Pick a verse from chapter two of this thesis that will encourage the church to think about the horizontal. Comment on how the text encourages the horizontal.

Confession of Sin (vertical): Extrabiblical confession.[5]

Almighty God, we acknowledge and confess that we have sinned against you in thought, word, and deed;
we have not loved you with all of our heart, soul, mind, and strength;
we have not loved our neighbor as ourselves.

---

5. Based upon a confession of sin in the Presbyterian Church (U.S.A.), Presbyterian Church (U.S.A.), and Cumberland Presbyterian Church, eds., *Book of Common Worship* (Louisville, Ky: Westminster/John Knox Press, 1993), 53.

Deepen within us our sorrow for the wrong we have done, and the good we have left undone. Lord, you are full of compassion and gracious, slow to anger, and plenteous in mercy;
there is always forgiveness with you!
Restore to us the joy of your salvation;
bind up that which is broken,
give light to our minds, strength to our wills, and rest to our souls.
Speak to each of us, and let your Word abide with us until it has wrought in us love for you and our neighbor. Amen.

Assurance of Pardon (vertical):

Suggested introduction to the Scripture:

"Listen to God's Word to his people about his assurance of pardon. Isaiah 53:4-5 says…"

Isaiah 53:4-5:

4) Surely he has borne our griefs and carried our sorrows; yet we esteemed him stricken, smitten by God, and afflicted.
5) But he was pierced for our transgressions; he was crushed for our iniquities; upon him was the chastisement that brought us peace, and with his wounds we are healed.

Hymn (vertical and horizontal): Holy, Holy, Holy – Ask the congregation to encourage one another by declaring in song God's holiness, reminding us all that it is his holiness that makes us holy.

Congregational Prayer (vertical and horizontal): Pray for God to give the congregation his affections for others. Include praying for those who struggle in their faith and need God's help. Encourage the congregation to take time in silent prayer to pray for someone in the church today. Encourage the congregants to pray for specific blessings upon their neighbor in worship. Ask them to pray for blessings upon their enemies just as God shows them mercy in Christ even when they were his enemies.

Fellowship Books & Prayer Concerns (vertical and horizontal):

Note: Ask the ushers to pass out the Fellowship Book/Visitor Pad. Welcome new visitors and ask them to fill out the church Fellowship Book. Ask people to also submit their prayer requests so we can pray for them and others.

Suggested wording to introduce the Welcome Book and Offering:

"Would the ushers please pass out the Welcome Books. Please use our Welcome Books to help us get to know you better, especially if you are visiting. We are so glad you have joined us today. We invite you to share any prayer requests and praises you may have. If you wish to keep your requests or praises confidential for the church officers, please make a note to let us know.

Opportunities at Faith (horizontal motivated by the vertical): This is the announcement time in the order of service. The leader could preface the announcements with words like:

Let us consider some of the opportunities provided in the announcement section of our bulletin. It is important to realize that it pleases God in worship when we encourage one another to be involved in his church. Activities and ministries provide opportunities for us to fellowship and build one another up. Consider getting involved and attending these upcoming events and activities. We especially want to invite our guests to attend the opportunities provided by the church."

Worship in Giving (horizontal and vertical): This is an opportunity to encourage the church to give to the Lord's work with enthusiasm. Remind the people that their giving of tithes and offerings will support the ministry of supporting those in need, funding the work of the church, and promoting the spreading of the Word and Gospel of Christ both here and abroad.

"Would the ushers please come forward as we prepare our hearts to give to the Lord's work with our tithes and offerings."

Suggested introduction to the Scripture:

"God's Word calls us to store up our treasures in heaven rather than on earth. One of the ways we get to do this is by cheerfully and prayerfully giving to the work of the church. When you give, you store up heavenly treasures by supporting ministries like teaching our children, youth, and adults with the eternal Word of God for their salvation and spiritual growth. You help us keep the lights on and the air conditioner running to enable people to hear and concentrate on God's Word without distractions. Give with such treasures in mind."

Matthew 6:19-20:

19) Do not lay up for yourselves treasures on earth, where moth and rust destroy and where thieves break in and steal, 20) but lay up for yourselves treasures in heaven, where neither moth nor rust destroys and where thieves do not break in and steal.

Suggested prayer after reading Scripture:

"Let us pray."

"Oh Lord, thank you for the privilege of giving to the work of your kingdom through Faith Community Church. We give with joy and expectation at the good and great things you will do through these gifts to build up treasures in heaven for your glory and praise. Amen."

Note: Each week you can highlight one of the key horizontal aspects of the church's ministries that the people are supporting in their giving.

Special Music (vertical and horizontal):

Song introduction:

"As you listen to the music today, pray in your heart for someone to understand and embrace God according the truth of his word."

Dismiss the children to children's church.

Prayer of Illumination (vertical):

"Heavenly Father, we praise you for your precious Word. It is a gift that shows how much you love us and care for our souls. O Lord, use your Word today to open hearts to receive Christ. Grow us in love for you and in our love for others. Deepen our love for the saints and those who need your saving grace. Enrich us with us with joy to share Jesus with others. In Christ's name, Amen."

Sermon (vertical and horizontal): Make sure you explain, illustrate, and apply the text in the lives of the people. The sermon is vertical in the sense that its message is from God's Word to the people through the preacher. The preacher's careful handling and interpretation of God's Word entails his vertical respect for God and God's vertical ministry in and through the preacher. The sermon also involves the vertical for the people hearing the Word in that God ministers to them by his Spirit through the preached Word and they respond to God. Preaching also includes the horizontal. The preacher horizontally relates to the people. He must consider the best Bible translation and style that most communicates at a level the people can understand. He needs to deliver his message with Biblical love and care for all those listening to his sermon. The horizontal dimension is involved in the choice of illustrations and applications informed by the preacher's knowledge of and relationship with the people. He must think about them to truly communicate God's Word to them. The message also has horizontal implications for the life of the body of Christ. As they hear the Word, they should be encouraged to think about how to apply God's truth in the way they treat one another in the congregation and the world at large. Jesus tells us to be doers of the Word and not hearers only (Matt. 7:24-27).

Hymn of Response (vertical and horizontal):

Suggested introduction:

"As we respond to God's Word today in song, let us as God's holy priests declare to one another the message that we have heard. Through this coming week let us be encouraged to declare God's person and work in Christ to people in our community and neighborhood."

Benediction (vertical):

Numbers 6:24-26:

24) The Lord bless you and keep you;
25) the Lord make his face to shine upon you and be gracious to you;
26) the Lord lift up his countenance upon you and give you peace. Amen.

Worship Sample 3 (Liturgy of the Lord's Supper):

Introduction to the Lord's Table (vertical and horizontal):

Suggested introduction:

We now join together today to remember and declare the work of Christ and celebrate what he has done for us. This Supper is also called the Lord's Table. Jesus called his disciples together in the upper room to remember what he would do for them through the elements of the bread and the cup. The bread represents the body of Christ and reminds us that he bodily suffered and died upon the cross to save us from our sins. He was our substitute who bore our sins upon himself that we might be delivered from death, sin, and eternal judgment. The bread reminds us that we are spiritually fed and sustained by Christ who is the Bread of Life. It encourages us to feed upon him daily through faith. The cup represents the blood of Christ which is poured out on the cross for the sins of God's people. It was Jesus' perfect and holy blood that was needed as a perfect sacrificial offering to the Father for the cleansing of our sins unto salvation. As we drink the cup, we are reminded through faith in Christ's blood that we are forgiven of our sins by Jesus' once for all sacrifice upon the cross. We are also offered forgiveness for our sanctification when we humbly confess our sins to Christ who is our great high priest. Jesus' body and blood spiritually unites the people of God as one body of Christ.

Fencing of the Table (vertical and horizontal):

Before we partake in the Lord's Table it is important that we examine ourselves. First Corinthians 11 gives us an account of the Lord's Supper where people in the church at Corinth did not properly participate. Some treated it as just another meal, not considering their brethren. Since this is a spiritual ordinance, the Lord judged some in the church for improperly taking elements and some people died. The apostle Paul warned the church that they needed to properly examine themselves and to discern the Lord's body. First, this means that they needed to make sure they were believers in Christ. The Table in that sense is only for Christians. If you are not a believer today, we ask you to allow the elements to pass you by. We say this out of love for you but encourage you also to seek to be right with God through Christ. Let the supper today remind you to repent of your sins, put your faith in Christ alone for your salvation, and join his church. The call to discern the body also calls us to consider the body of Christ. We encourage only those who are members of a local Bible-believing and evangelical church to partake. Such membership reflects the fruit of Christian faith since God's people should seek accountability through membership in the church because Christ has ordained elders to provide oversight and shepherding of his church. Not only do believers need oversight from church elders but they also need the body of Christ for mutual encouragement, aid, and service. These horizontal aspects of the church body represent the immediate context of Paul's teaching on the Lord's Supper in 1 Corinthians 11. Therefore, if you are not a member of a local church please allow the elements to pass you by. Be encouraged, however, to seek membership in Christ's church. Additionally, even as a Christian, if you are living in unrepentant sin and unwilling to pursue new obedience, we ask you to allow the elements to pass by. It is essential that we seek reconciliation with our brothers and sisters in the church. The supper today is a call to you to repent and obey the Lord. For all repentant Christians in Christ's church, the table is open to you to celebrate. Come celebrate the forgiveness you have in Christ through faith and your common faith as his body, the church. Look forward to his future return to redeem his people and bring justice upon the earth. Come to the Table in faith and find nourishment for your soul.

Prayer of Institution (vertical and horizontal):

Let us pray, "Lord thank you for the gift of the Lord's Supper. Please use these elements today to nourish our faith in Christ and encourage us to love others as he loved us in the gospel. In Christ's name we pray. Amen."

Words of Institution (vertical & horizontal): The sacrament of the Lord's Supper is a vertical institution given by Christ, but it is to be administered to the congregation acknowledging both its vertical benefits and blessings as well as its horizontal implications. In considering the "body of Christ" we must include both the person of Christ and his body which is the church. To call the congregation to wait, as suggested below, and to take the elements together directs believers to consider one another. Such instruction involves the horizontal dimension in the words of institution and administration. It calls believers to consider both Christ (i.e., the vertical) and one another (i.e., the horizontal) as they experience the sacrament of the Lord's Supper. The instructions below encourage the congregation to acknowledge their double union with Christ and one another in eating and drinking the elements.

The Bread (Minister takes the bread and breaks it).

<u>Minister says</u>:

On the night in which the Lord was betrayed he took the bread and he broke it and gave it to his disciples. He said, "This is my body which is for you, do this in remembrance of me" (1 Cor. 11:24).

<u>Minister distributes the bread to the congregation</u>: As the minister hands the trays of bread to the elders, he should instruct the people saying,

"I encourage you to wait to take the elements together. Taking them together reminds us of our spiritual union with both Christ and one another. To discern the Lord's body calls us to recognize both the body of Christ himself and his body, the church.

Minister distributes the bread to the elders: As the minister gives the bread to the elders, he should recite some portion of Scripture that refers to the sacrifice of Christ (e.g., Matt. 20:28; Mark 10:45; Eph. 5:2; Titus 2:14; Heb. 9:28).

Words of reception:

When the bread has been distributed, the minister should say,

"Take and eat."

The Cup (The minister takes the cup and speaks about it.)

Minister says:

The Lord Jesus also took the cup, gave thanks and gave it to his disciples, saying, "Drink of it, all of you (Matt 26:27), for this cup that is poured out for you is the new covenant in my blood (Luke 22:20) which is poured out for many for the forgiveness of sins" (Matt. 26:28).

Minister distributes the cup to the congregation: The minister passes to the elders the trays of communion cups.

Minister distributes the cup to the elders: As the minister gives the communion cups to the elders, he should recite some portion of Scripture that refers to the sacrifice of Christ. John 1:29 is an excellent text.

Words of reception:
When the communion cups have been disseminated, the minister should say, "Let us drink."

Communion prayer (vertical and horizontal):

Suggested prayer:

God our redeemer and friend, thank you for this holy communion. We praise you this day for the wonderful and gracious sacrifice of Christ on the cross. Thank you for your forgiveness and mercy. Please use this Supper today to encourage us to see our union as one body. Encourage us to go into the world to joyfully tell others how Jesus has saved us and can save them. Empower us to show the love of Christ to our neighbors. Encourage us to look forward to Jesus' return to redeem the saints and consummate his kingdom. In Christ's name. Amen.

Communion Hymn (vertical and horizontal): *The Church's One Foundation*

Hymn introduction:

Let us together celebrate our common faith in Christ as one body redeemed by the blood of Christ by singing "The Church's One Foundation."

Benediction (vertical):

May the goodness of the Lord, the redeeming power of Christ, and the love of the Holy Spirit bless you and make you a blessing to others, Amen.

20

Sunday School Lesson Outlines

Lesson 1 Outline:

BIBLICAL WORSHIP – LESSON ONE
Seven Fundamentals of Worship

1. **Worship Defined:** The word '*worship*' occurs over 192 times in various forms in the Bible (ESV).

   Latreia (Greek) – The word means "service/worship (of God)."[1] This word is used in Hebrews 9:1, 6; 12:28 and Romans 12:1.
   Hebrews 9:1: Now even the first covenant had regulations for **worship** and an earthly place of holiness.
   Hebrews 12:28: Therefore let us be grateful for receiving a kingdom that cannot be shaken, and thus let us offer to God acceptable **worship**, with reverence and awe.
   Romans 12:1: I appeal to you therefore, brothers, by the mercies of God, to present your bodies as a living sacrifice, holy and acceptable to God, which is your spiritual **worship**.
   The emphasis of worship with the word *latreia* is upon the act of service as one engages in the worship of God. Therefore, worship is about serving God versus serving oneself.
   Proskuneo (Greek) – "to express in attitude or gesture one's complete dependence on or submission to a high authority figure, (fall down and) worship, do obeisance to, prostrate oneself before, do

---

[1]. *A Greek-English Lexicon of the New Testament and Other Early Christian Literature,* 3rd ed. (Chicago: University of Chicago Press, 2000), s.v. "λατρεία."

reverence to, welcome respectfully."[2] Some key passages in which this word appears are:

Matthew 4:10: Then Jesus said to him, "Be gone, Satan! For it is written, 'You shall **worship** the Lord your God and him only shall you serve.'"

John 4:24: God is spirit, and those who **worship** him must **worship** in spirit and truth.

Revelation 4:10: The twenty-four elders fall down before him who is seated on the throne and **worship** him who lives forever and ever. They cast their crowns before the throne…

Dr. Smith, first stated clerk of the PCA, notes that, "The word "worship" in English is derived from the Anglo-Saxon 'woerthscipe' meaning 'worth' 'shape'. It denotes worthiness of an individual to receive special honor in accord with that worth."[3]

2. **Who is called to worship God?** <u>Everyone</u> is called to worship the Lord. This includes believers and unbelievers. Consider…

Psalm 96:9: "Worship the LORD in the splendor of his holiness; tremble before him, **all the earth**."

Psalm 47:1: "Clap your hands, **all peoples!** Shout to God with loud songs of joy!"

Psalm 148:7, 10: "7) Praise the Lord from the earth, you great sea creatures and all deeps, 10) Beasts and all livestock, creeping things and flying birds!"

Psalm 150:6: "Let everything that has breath praise the Lord! Praise the Lord!"

Only true believers can worship God, but every human being is called to worship. The elect will respond positively while the non-elect will rebel and refuse to worship God and trust in his Son Jesus for their salvation (2 Cor. 2:16). It is **the duty** of all Christians **to call** other human beings **by invitation** to worship the true God with the hope that they will respond.

---

2. Ibid., s.v. "προσκυνέω."
3. Morton Smith, *The Regulative Principle of Worship: Is It Biblical?* (Greenville, SC: Greenville Presbyterian Theological Seminary, 1995), 1.

3. **Worship with Love for Your Neighbor (as you express your love for God):**

<u>Worship should be directed to **God alone**</u>. Reformed theologians refer to this as the **vertical dimension** (Exod. 20:1-6). It is **bidirectional**. God is our audience and we are called to praise and honor his name. To direct our worship to any other is idolatry. In the vertical dimension God also ministers to our souls through his Word and Spirit. He convicts, corrects, encourages, empowers, inspires, blesses, strengthens, corrects, teaches, illuminates, rebukes, etc. Worship also includes a **horizontal** dimension. Worship entails loving your neighbor as you express your love for God. This means Christians will do things in the worship service that address or affect those present. It is important to realize that we do not know the hearts of every attendee. We believe that there is a visible and invisible church in our worship services. We must humbly acknowledge that only God knows who is part of the invisible church (WCF 25). As a result, people may need to hear the gospel many times before they respond. This should make Christians concerned about everyone who attends the worship service rather than showing favoritism to certain people (James 2:1-4). In 1 Corinthians 14, Paul reminds the Corinthians that their worship affects people who attend their church services. It has an edifying effect on believers (1 Cor. 14:17) but it also has an effect upon nonbelievers. There were those in the Corinthian church who were practicing uninterpreted tongues in worship services, but Paul tells them that intelligible words need to be spoken in order to edify those present. In 1 Corinthians 14:19 the apostle says, *"Nevertheless, in church I would rather speak five words with my mind in order to instruct others, than ten thousand words in a tongue."* Paul goes on to teach that worship should be done in such a way that it is understood by even the unbeliever in the hope that he will be convicted with the gospel and be converted to the faith. This is why he emphasizes prophecy which would have been the clear teaching of the Word. In 1 Corinthians 14:24-25, he says, " But if all prophesy, and an unbeliever or outsider enters, he is convicted by all, he is called to account by all, the secrets of his heart are disclosed, and so, falling on his face, he will worship God and declare that God is really among you." Therefore, we should

encourage church members to invite family, friends, neighbors, and acquaintances to come and worship God so they can experience God among his people in worship. 1 Corinthians 14 teaches that worship has both an **edifying** and **evangelistic** purpose. With this in mind, it is important for the church to consider the spiritual needs of the listeners during the service in order to make the gospel and its application to life as clear as possible. The horizontal dimension involves loving your neighbor in worship. It includes a call to **respond to the Word of God** (Acts 16:31; 2 Tim. 2:15). It also includes the importance of **fellowship** which takes place among believers during the worship experience (Acts 2:42-47). Christians meet with God but also meet together in order to **encourage** one another (Heb. 10:24-25). Such biblical principles may be used as a reason to **greet** one another, give ministry **reports**, **pray** for one another, and share **announcements** about the life of the church body during a service. Such activity helps to connect God's people and promote Christian love which glorifies God and demonstrates the reality of the gospel (1 Cor. 10:31-33; John 15:8-17). Let us never forget that Christ calls believers to **love God and their neighbor** (Matt. 22:37-40) in every area of life, including our worship services.

4. Worship Is Not Entertainment:

Worship is for God and is not a performance for the congregation. This does not mean there are no entertaining aspects to what we do in how we worship. The way one plays an instrument for God, for example, will have entertaining aspects. But the entertainment value is not why we should come to worship. In secular entertainment the activity is done for the praise of men; Christian worship activities are to be done for the praise of God, edification of his people, and the salvation of the lost—all for the glory of God (1 Cor. 10:31).

5. The Regulative Principle:

We should seek to order (regulate) worship according to the Word of God, not by man-made ideas. The Reformed tradition says, "If it's not supported by the Bible, then we should not do it." This principle comes from the words of Jesus in John 4:24: "God is spirit, and those who worship him must worship in spirit and truth." The place we find truth is in God's Word. The regulative principle is also expressed in the Westminster Confession of Faith, chapter 21, par. 1. This approach is in accord with John Calvin's view. Our Reformed tradition, however, is different than the Lutheran position which says, "if the Scriptures do not speak against a practice, then we can allow it." This idea allowed for many of the rituals practiced in the Lutheran church, which are similar to many Roman Catholic church rituals, and were repudiated in the Reformation.

Please also note that the Reformers differentiated between **elements** and **circumstances**. Circumstances may involve the ways and times one can express the elements. The Westminster Confession of Faith, chapter 1, par. 6 notes that, "there are some **circumstances** concerning the worship of God, and government of the Church, common to human actions and societies, which are to be ordered by the **light of nature**, and **Christian prudence** (good sense), according to the **general rules** of the Word" (WCF 1.6). Examples of this would be the use of chairs or pews, mikes, speakers, pianos, organs, computers, times for worship, podiums, use of hymnals in singing, etc.

6. **Orderly worship:**

Although the New Testament does not give a fixed order of service, it is important to note that worship must still be conducted in an orderly manner (BCO 47-6).[4] Addressing the context of worship, Paul says in 1 Corinthians 14:40, "But all things should be done decently and in order." This speaks against doing worship in a willy-nilly or haphazard way.

7. **The Gospel of Christ:**

The gospel should be at the center of worship because Christ, the

---

4. All references to the abbreviation BCO refer to the Book of Church Order for the Presbyterian Church in America.

Lamb of God is at the front and center of worship. In Revelation 5, we are given a picture of worship in heaven which focuses on Christ. In Revelation 5:12, the apostle John looks and hears the voice of millions of angels. They encircle God's throne and the living creatures and the elders. John hears the angels "saying with a loud voice, 'Worthy is the Lamb who was slain, to receive power and wealth and wisdom and might and honor and glory and blessing!'" The evangel (good news or gospel) is all about Christ's person and work. Belief in the gospel is necessary for God's people to worship God acceptably (Eph. 2:12-13). Christ and his work on the cross are central to the whole plan of God for the salvation, sanctification, and glorification of mankind (Gen. 3:15; John 3:16; 1 Cor. 1:23, 2:2). The Scriptures testify about Jesus and his work (Luke 24:25-27; John 1:45). The gospel must be a part of Christian worship or it ceases to be Christian. The gospel when properly presented calls for a response. Therefore, it is appropriate to invite people to respond to the gospel during worship services (Acts 2:38; John 6:47). Without the gospel of Christ, worship ceases to be Christian and ceases to please the Father in heaven. Our contemplation of and thanks for the gospel in our worship on earth is practice for our future gospel-centered worship in heaven. Christian worship is therefore distinctively Christ-centered because the gospel is Christ-centered.

As we close, I pray that you personally have come to know Jesus Christ as your Savior and Lord. To properly worship God, you must go through Jesus. Almost two thousand years ago, Jesus, the Messiah came into this world and lived a perfect life you cannot. He paid the penalty for the sins of his people by dying on the cross to satisfy the justice of the heavenly Father. Jesus took the punishment due to us upon the cross. He rose from the dead on the third day and is alive today. He offers you right now the forgiveness of your sins and eternal life. You can receive these gifts if you will truly repent by confessing your sins and turning away from trusting in yourself to trusting in Jesus alone as your Savior and Lord (John 14:6). Will you trust in Jesus alone today for your salvation and eternal life?

Lesson 2 Outline:

BIBLICAL WORSHIP – LESSON TWO
General Principles

Theme Verse: John 4:24 says, "God is spirit, and those who worship him must worship in spirit and truth."

1. **Attitudes for Worship:**

    a. **Joy**.
    Hebrews 12:22 says, "But you have come to Mount Zion and to the city of the living God, the heavenly Jerusalem, and to innumerable angels in **festal** gathering.". The attitudes of **joy** and **praise** are mentioned the most in the Psalms.

    b. **Thanks and Reverence**
    Hebrews 12:28-29 says, "Therefore let us be **grateful** for receiving a kingdom that cannot be shaken, and thus let us offer to God acceptable worship, with **reverence** and **awe**, for our God is a consuming fire."

    c. **Humility** – It is essential that we humble ourselves before the Lord and one another in worship.
    James 4:10 says "Humble yourselves before the Lord, and he will exalt you."

    The Lord will not accept our worship if we enter worship with critical, prideful, arrogant, and judgmental attitudes (Matt. 7:1-5; 9:9-13). We must never forget that it was the humble tax collector who went away forgiven in the temple rather than the arrogant Pharisee (Luke 18:9-14).

    In the chapter on the principles and elements of public worship, the <u>BCO 47-7</u> says, "Nor may any member of the church presume to exalt himself above others as though he were more spiritual, but each shall esteem others better than himself."

2. **Frequency and duration of Worship:**

The Early Church

A. In its beginnings, Christians met every day of the week (Acts 2:46).

B. The church at least met on the first day of the week (Acts 20:7). This is the day Jesus rose.

C. The church had no set time prescribed for worship (e.g., 8-9 A.M.). Some churches today spend 1 ½ hours in worship. Other churches spend around four hours in worship. There are some churches that spend most of the day in worship.

3. The Elements of Biblical Worship

Ordinary Elements:
- Call to Worship (Psalm 100).
- The reading of Scripture (Col. 4:16; WCF 21.5; LC 108; BCO 50).
- Preaching of the Word (2 Tim. 4:2; WCF 21.5; LC 108; BCO 53).
- Singing of psalms, hymns, and spiritual songs from the heart (WCF 21.5; BCO 51-1; Eph. 5:19).
- Prayer & Thanksgiving in the name of Christ (1 Tim. 2:1; WCF 21.3; LC 108; BCO 52 notes that this can include confession of sin). The Westminster Confession of Faith states that "this includes prayer for lawful things, all sorts of men living, not for the dead, or those who have committed the sin unto death" (WCF 21.4).
- Tithes and offerings (LC 108; BCO 47-9; 54; 1 Cor. 16:1-2; 1 Tim. 5:17-18).
- Greetings and Benedictions (2 Cor. 13:12-14; 1 Pet. 5:12-14; Heb. 13:20-21). Holy kisses were encouraged. Greetings and blessings were given.
- Encouragement (Heb. 10:24-25; 1 Thess. 3:2; 5:11) – We might apply this call to encourage others by making announcements and recognizing various ministries for involvement in the

church. It encourages the church when they hear what God is doing in their midst.

Occasional Elements:
- Reporting the work of God (Acts 14:27; 15:4; 21:19; Eph. 6:22; Col. 4:8).
- Confessing the faith (BCO 47-9, 55-1; Rom. 10:9-10).
- Church Government (LC 108).
- Church Discipline (LC 108).
- Religious oaths (WCF 21.5; LC 108).
- Religious vows (WCF 21.5; LC 108).
- Solemn fastings (Joel 2:12; WCF 21.5; LC 108).
- Thanksgivings upon special occasions (WCF 21.5; Esther 9:22).
- Lord's Supper (1 Cor. 11; WCF 21.5).
- Baptism (Matt. 28:19; WCF 21.5).

4. **Expressions in Worship**
   - Clapping of hands (Ps. 47:1). Note that the trees are spoken of metaphorically as clapping their hands to the Lord (Isa. 55:12). This is consistent with God's encouragement for the nations to clap their hands (See also Ps. 98:8).
   - Shouting for joy (Ps. 47:1).
   - Singing praise to God (Ps. 33:1).
   - Using musical instruments (Ps. 150).
   - Lifting hands in prayer (Ps. 28:2).
   - Lifting hands in praise to God (Ps. 134:2; 63:4).
   - Standing (Exod. 3:5).
   - Kneeling before the Lord (Ps. 95:6).
   - Speaking about the wonders of God (Ps. 9:1, 11).
   - Bowing before the Lord (Ps. 22:27).
   - Dancing (Ps. 149:3) – We have examples of worship dancing with Miriam in Exodus 15:20. King David worshipped the

Lord through dance when he brought the Ark of the Covenant into Israel in 2 Sam. 6:15, 16.
- Saying Amen (means "so be it") (Deut. 27:15-26; 1 Chron. 16:36; Neh. 8:6; Ps. 41:13; 72:19; 89:52; 106:48; Rev. 7:19; 19:4).
- Selah (used 75 times in the OT, 71 of which are in the Psalms). Selah is some sort of direction about the singing. It literally means "lift up or exalt."[5]
- Stillness. God says in Psalm 46, "Be still and know that I am God. I will be exalted among the nations, I will be exalted in the earth!"

5. Music in Worship

Style Background:

The Bible does not specify a particular style of music that is appropriate for worship. Traditional church music developed in the Classical Period in Europe (from the middle ages through the eighteenth century). Southern and black gospel styles started in the nineteenth century. More popular styles such as western, rock, country, pop, and jazz music are a twentieth century phenomenon. Praise and contemporary has it roots in the 1960s. Music, itself, is a neutral creation of God that is defined morally by its usage and lyrical content. Music is morally good or bad based on how it is used and what message it conveys (1 Tim. 4:4-5; 1 Cor. 10:23-26).

The apostle Paul's reference to distinctive types of songs in Ephesians 5:19 and Colossians 3:16 (e.g., psalms, hymns and spiritual songs) indicates a distinction in the types of songs used in the New Testament church. Paul uses these terms "to highlight the wide range of musical expression that grateful and heartfelt praise to God calls forth from the body of Christ."[6]

---

5. *Enhanced Brown-Driver-Briggs Hebrew and English Lexicon* (Oxford: Clarendon Press, 1977), s.v. "סלה."

6. R. C. Sproul, ed., "Music in the Church," *The Reformation Study Bible* (Nashville: Thomas Nelson, 1995), 1891.

Sunday School Lesson Outlines

Our Church Practice:

Since there is no specific style of music that is mandated from the Bible, our church is open to different styles of music in our worship service. Being mission-minded we wish to be sensitive to church tradition and musical styles that are familiar to the culture around us. For this reason, we have chosen to conduct a **blended service** which includes both contemporary praise music and traditional hymns. This concept of being sensitive to our cultural musical styles fits well with Paul's missional emphasis in 1 Corinthians 9:19-23 where he seeks to be all things to all people that he may win some. Paul sought to be sensitive to the culture, without compromising the gospel. With this principle in mind, it is essential that the church use musical styles familiar to the people the church is trying to reach. This fits with the principles of our Reformed tradition which has sought to clearly communicate God's Word to the nations in a language they can understand (WCF 1:7; BCO 53-4).

Quality of Music:

God deserves our best (2 Tim. 2:15). Worship is an offering to God and we should seek to help God's people give their very best to the Lord (Rom. 12:1-3).

It is important that musicians and vocalists who lead worship exhibit the musical gifts that will enable us as a church to lead God's people to worship God with quality. This means that our musicians should be able to sing with controlled feeling and on pitch, play with few mistakes, work with a team, and exhibit a humble attitude. This also means that singers and musicians should practice sufficiently to offer their very best to the Lord.

On occasion, children may present a song in worship that is not as professionally prepared as the presentations by adults. Those who lead the children, however, must do their utmost in helping the children to give their best to the Lord. We should remember that such offerings are not meant to please the congregation, but to minister to the people and give praise and glory to God. These are principles we should teach to our children.

Repetition is an ancient teaching tool that is represented in the psalms of the Old Testament. Themes and lines were often repeated within a psalm (Ps. 136; 118). This was not vain repetition which the pagans participated in with their mantras (Matt. 6:7). This repetition included biblical truths and principles. We will be mindful of this in our music selection. Many of the praise songs repeat similar phrases just as the hymns often repeat choruses. It is our hope that when this occurs in our worship people will think about what they are singing and meditate on these repeated truths to the glory of God (cf. Rev. 4:8).

We want the congregation to participate in singing to the Lord with their hearts and minds.

Choice of Music

All music needs to be Biblical and within the scope of our Reformed faith as expressed in the Westminster Confession of Faith, Shorter, and Larger Catechisms. Each song should have a strong melody line and a good instrumental arrangement. This means that we might not sing a traditional hymn or contemporary song if it is musically weak. Also, if a traditional hymn or contemporary song has some theological problems within the lyrics, we will sing it only if the words can be changed to bring the proposed song into conformity with the Bible.

6. Summary on Worship

If we were to summarize a Reformed view of worship we could define it as such: **"Worship is for everyone, by only true believers, unto God alone for his glory and praise."** Since the call to worship is given to all the earth (Ps. 96:9; 100:1), we can say that it is <u>for everyone</u> (Ps. 67:3). It is <u>by only true believers</u> because a person's heart needs to be convicted by the gospel and converted by the Holy Spirit before he or she can acknowledge the true and living God (John 3:3; Eph. 2:1). The apostle Paul reminds us in 1 Corinthians 14 that evangelism takes place in Christian worship. Some unbelievers who attend corporate worship will be converted by the gospel and the truth of God's Word. Paul says, "But if all prophesy, and an unbeliever or outsider enters, he is convicted by all, he is called to account by all, the secrets of his heart are disclosed, and so, falling on his face he will worship God and declare that God is really among you" (1 Cor. 14:24-25). We must also believe that worship is <u>unto God alone</u> who is the God of the Old and New Testaments. Only God deserves our worship.

In application as this definition applies to people, we must not forget that as we worship God in a vertical posture of joy, reverence, and humility that we are called to also love our neighbor (i.e., the horizontal dimension). In loving our neighbor, true Christians should emulate the call of their God to worship by regularly calling everyone (including unbelievers) to come and worship the true and living God, ruler of heaven and earth. In other words, Christians have a significant reason to invite both believers and unbelievers to come worship God with them. Christians have no right to play God or choose whom they will invite since only God knows who are his elect. This reiterates the redemptive thrust of the Scriptures and God's plan to save souls through his Son Jesus from every tribe and language and people and nation (Rev. 5:9). Christians who engage in worship must also consider those people present in worship with a prayerful concern for their souls. Believers should desire to clearly communicate the gospel and convey the full counsel of God's Word to save and build up everyone present in worship. In our communication we should seek to make the Word as clear as possible without the pretense of arrogance or an attitude of superiority. This will affect the type of music we choose, words we speak, and prayers we offer to God in consideration of those present. As we truly seek to love our God in worship, we will strive to also love our neighbor with the hope that he or she will in turn sincerely worship God in Spirit and in truth. John 4:24 says, *"God is spirit, and those who worship him must worship in spirit and truth."*

Let us continually with joy, humility, and compassion invite others to come and worship in the Spirit, God the Father, and God the Son,

Worship God with Love for Your Neighbor

the Lord Jesus. Jesus is the one who died for our sins on the cross and rose from the dead to save our souls. He deserves our hearts and our worship! Amen!

Lesson 3 Outline:

BIBLICAL WORSHIP – LESSON THREE
Justice and Worship

Text: Isaiah 1:10-23

Introduction: Many people today engage in worship with a vertical perspective but treat their neighbors terribly. They think that God finds their worship acceptable because they methodically follow a certain ritual or order of service. They believe their worship is acceptable since they offer it to God with passion and singular focus. They forget, however, that God demands and expects them to live justly. Their worship must include a life that pursues justice in the way they treat others. The issue of justice was frequently a topic that the Old Testament prophets addressed when speaking to Israel. It is so easy to miss this aspect of our lives as it relates to our worship of God. Let us look at what Isaiah the prophet tells Israel about the subject of worship and justice.

Read Isaiah 1:10-23.

1. **What does God say to Israel regarding the way they are treating their neighbors, the oppressed, the fatherless, and the widow (See Isa. 1:17, 21-23b)?**

They have treated them poorly and unjustly. It appears that they have taken advantage of orphans and widows through an abuse or distortion of the laws in Israel. They either literally or metaphorically murdered people through their unjust practices (Isa. 1:21). Considering the wicked examples of the kings and their servants in First and Second Kings and First and Second Chronicles, Isaiah may be addressing literal murder. The people engage in corrupt business and judicial practices (Isa. 1:22-23). They abuse and deceive others.

2. **How does Isaiah address the leaders and people of Israel (see Isa. 1:10)? What does his description remind us about?**

Isaiah compares the leaders and people to Sodom and Gomorrah. It reminds us of the wickedness and corruption of those cities and people. It is also indirectly warns Israel that God will judge such practices if they continue.

3. **What is the attitude of God toward the worship of the Israelites (see Isa. 1:11-15)?**

He considers it to be corrupt because the people are unjust to others. He does not and will not accept worship from such people. He is outraged at their trampling of his courts of justice (1:12). He considers their offerings an abomination (1:13). He cannot endure their unrepentant sin and worship (1:13b). God hates their worship festivals and is weary of them (1:14). He refuses to listen to their many prayers (1:15). John Calvin describes the people well, "It is because they are cruel and bloody, and stained with crimes of every sort, though they come into his presence with hypocritical display."[7] The worship that God finds acceptable is loving one's neighbor through justice'.

4. **How would you describe injustice versus biblical justice (use the text to guide you)?**

Injustice involves treating people with contempt, disrespect, hatred, and abuse. It involves disobedience to God's commands about how to treat others. Biblical justice, on the other hand, involves showing mercy and respect for one's fellow man. It entails respectful and lawful treatment of the vulnerable of society, especially widows and orphans.

5. **Do you think that Christians engage in worship today the way Isaiah describes? Explain.**

---

7. Jean Calvin, *Calvin's* Commentaries, vol. 7, *Commentary on the Book of the Prophet Isaiah* (Grand Rapids, MI: Baker, 1979), 61.

Many people go to worship and take a vertical-only perspective but do not think about their responsibilities to others. Like Israel, they treat other people unjustly but expect God to accept their worship. They do not understand that for their worship to be acceptable to God, God requires them to love their neighbors and treat them with justice. They lie to their neighbors. They deceive them. They steal. They abuse and take advantage of those less fortunate. They show favoritism to those they like in the worship service. They demonstrate little concern or care about others who worship with them.

6. What does God say to Israel about how the people should address his rebukes (Isa. 16-17)?

They are called to repent of their sins. They should specifically stop committing these sins against their neighbors. They are called to learn what God considers good. They are also called to seek justice, especially for orphans and widows.

7. How could Christians apply verses 16-17 today?

They could pay attention to the widows in their church and worship service. They could strive to protect them from people who would seek to take advantage of them. This may mean they check in on them during the week or take them to church. They could help them with their social security responsibilities, medical care, and bills. Christians could adopt orphans and strive to protect babies in the womb. They should encourage mothers to carry their babies to term. They may connect them to crisis pregnancy centers and assist them financially.

8. What hope does God give us in verses 18-19?

If we come to God and repent of our sins of injustice he will cleanse away our sins "as white as snow" and "like wool." He will bless and forgive us.

9. What warning does the Lord provide in verse 20?

God would judge Israel with the sword. Due to her lack of repentance, the Northern Kingdom would be destroyed and exiled by the Assyrians. This should be a lesson to Christians today to take God's demands for justice and the horizontal dimension seriously.

10. Are there any sins you wish to confess to God regarding your unjust attitudes and practices toward other people? If you desire to worship God vertically in an acceptable manner, how could you improve the way you treat others horizontally?

Lesson 4 Outline:

BIBLICAL WORSHIP – LESSON FOUR
Worship and the Old Testament Golden Rule

Text: Micah 6:6-8

Introduction: People often walk into a church with no interest in getting to know anyone. They operate like an undercover spiritual CIA agent who is there for an assignment, but other people are simply a distraction. One lady who was talking about her attitude in going to church said, "I go to church, but I really don't want to talk to anyone. I just want to worship and leave without being noticed." This has become the attitude of many people today who attend corporate worship. They don't realize that they have taken a vertical-only position that the Bible speaks against. The prophet Micah addresses Israel's unbiblical worship and calls it out. He tells the nation about the type of attitude and life he desires and thus lays the ground work for acceptable worship.

Read Micah 6:6-8.

1. Before we go to worship God, what are some things we should think about? What do you think will get us ready for attending worship?

2. According to Micah, what appears to be the focus of the people in their preparation for worship (see 6:6)?

    The people are focused on the types of sacrifices they plan to offer to God in their worship (e.g., burnt offerings, calves, etc.). Their sole focus appears to be on the ritual and outward ceremony of their worship rather than their neighbor or their own hearts.

3. Looking at verse 7a, what is the concern of the people?

    They are wondering if they increase the number of their sacrifices by the thousands will they be acceptable to God. This is a focus on the volume of their sacrifices. The answer to this rhetorical question is that simply increasing the number of their sacrifices will not earn them favor with God. He is not impressed.

4. **Why is this request a problem in verse 7b?**

The people are likely thinking like pagans who often sacrificed their children to please their false gods. God would surely have nothing to do with such sacrifices. The people asking this question reveal their unfamiliarity with the Scriptures which forbid child sacrifice. It reflects hearts that are not seeking to obey God's Word.

5. **Dr. Waltke teaches that justice involves those "who are in a socially superior position and calls them to step in and deliver the weaker and wronged party by punishing the oppressor."[8] What injustices do chapters two and three describe?**

The powerful devise wicked ways to take the property of others and oppress people (2:1-2). They deceive people by gaining their trust (2:8). They take advantage of the widows and their young children (2:9). The leaders of Israel treat the people like they are just a piece of meat (3:2-4). The prophets cry "peace" when they get what they want but "war" against those who do not pay them (3:5). They love money. The rulers "detest justice" and are crooked (3:9). They engage in blood money, bribes, peddling God's Word for money, and divination (3:9-11).

6. **What are some ways that Christians can pursue justice toward their neighbor, especially those in the church?**

Christians can look after the widows in the church and try to protect them from fraud and abuse. If they are mistreated they can fight for them in the court system. Believers can generally fight to help the needy who are unable or ill-equipped to defend themselves.

---

8. Bruce Waltke, *Obadiah, Jonah, Micah* (Downers Grove: InterVarsity Press, 1988), 195.

Christians in the church can help the needy get assistance that they qualify for. They can confront businesses that take advantage of the vulnerable in the church.

7. **God calls Christians to love kindness (v. 8). What might that look like in the congregation?**

   The Hebrew word here for "kindness" is *hesed*. Some scholars translate this as "lovingkindness." This word is best translated as "covenant faithfulness" or "covenant love." It reflects the faithful covenant love God has for his people. Kindness exhibited by God's children reflects God's covenant love to his people. God wants his people to express covenant kindness through compassion for the needy, the helpless, and the lost. This might involve helping visitors with directions, locating bathrooms, and finding classes for their children. Instead of getting annoyed at visitors, church members should kindly educate visitors about the beliefs of the church. They should try to address their needs by assessing their level of maturity. They should make the effort to get to know visitors who come to the church. This involves asking questions and carefully listening.

8. **The Lord calls believers to walk humbly with their God. What might this look like in the worship service?**

   It might involve setting a godly example of being attentive and actively participating in worship. This would involve speaking during responsive readings, joining in prayer, singing the songs, saying amen where appropriate during the service, and paying attention to the sermon. It could involve serving as an usher or greeter. Being humble means, we should seek to serve God and others rather than looking for others to serve us.

9. **Why is humility so important to God?**

   Jesus willingly came into this world as a humble savior to save our souls (see Philippians 2). He came to serve others and give his life as a ransom for many (Matt. 20:28). Jesus told his disciples to be servants willing to wash the feet of other people for the kingdom of God (see John 17:1-13).

10. What is the most challenging thing you have learned in this passage? Take time to pray for God's grace to help you to apply this passage in your life.

Lesson 5 Outline:

BIBLICAL WORSHIP – LESSON FIVE
David and the Horizontal Dimension

Text: Psalm 40

Introduction: I was reading a blog once about the concept of lighting in corporate worship. Many companies today are constantly trying to sell stage lighting to churches to mimic a concert-like feel during church worship services. One man who helped to lead worship in his church expressed that he liked to lead the church with lots of lighting with the lights dimmed down low in the congregation so that he would not have to look at the faces of the people. He did not want to be distracted by looking into faces that were at times gloomy or distressed. He wanted to feel uplifted and focus on God rather than the people. For him it was ideal if the sanctuary lighting was dimmed so low that he did not have to look at the congregation. This attitude about worship and lighting is not uncommon; but the question arises, "Is this the way we should think?" One of the best places to discover the right attitude we should have in corporate worship is found in the Psalms. The most famous psalmist was King David of Israel. He was a man after God's own heart and loved congregational worship (Acts 13:22; Ps. 122:1). Let us take a look at one of his psalms to gain insight about how we should consider the vertical and horizontal dimensions in worship.

1. **Before we look at the text, let us think about our motives when we enter worship. What do you expect out of corporate worship before you enter the sanctuary?**

    Read Psalm 40. Encourage the students to read the text by asking for volunteers. To get people involved you might have one student read verses 1-8 and have another read verses 9-17. Note that scholars debate on whether to call Psalm 40 a thanksgiving or lament psalm, but many recognize it has elements of both types. Verses 1-11 seem to focus on thanksgiving while verses 12-17 present a lament.

2. In reading Psalm 40, would you describe the Psalm as optimistic or pessimistic? Explain.

3. David in his worship of God did have a vertical focus that we cannot deny. Describe the vertical focus of David in verses 1-2, 5, 9-11, and 13-17?

David cannot help but give praise to God for his deliverance (Ps. 40:1-2, 9-10), greatness (Ps. 40:5), his law (Ps. 40:8), and his love and faithfulness (Ps. 40:10b-11). He also calls out to God to deliver and help him as he faces his enemies (Ps. 40:13-17).

4. In verses 1-5 do we see any emphasis on the horizontal dimension?

In verse three David thinks about other people in his singing praise to God. He considers how his singing will affect others. He thinks about them seeing him. He ponders the ministerial effect which will move others in worship to fear God and trust in the Lord. One could argue that he sings with an evangelistic thrust to bring people to faith in God. Christians might consider their singing as a way to bring people who listen to faith in Christ. In verse five, he speaks of God's wonderous deeds but also seeks to proclaim God's works to others. He desires to edify his fellow worshippers and does not just think about himself.

5. When you sing and praise God, do you think about the effect of your singing and praise on others in the worship service? Explain.

6. What does David say about sacrifice in worship (see vv. 6-8)? How does David address the vertical in these verses?

David echoes a familiar Old Testament theme that God is not impressed by ritual and sacrifice (cf. 1 Sam. 15:22-23). He desires the heart of the worshipper in worship. He demonstrates the truth that for vertical worship to be acceptable to God it must be from the heart and a heart that delights in the Law of God. God is not pleased with vertical worship void of an attitude of obedience.

7. How do verses 8-11 address the vertical and horizontal?

David is concerned for the people so much that he tells them of the "glad news" of God's deliverance (v. 9). This "glad news" is a precursor to the horizontal concerns that New Testament believers should have toward others in corporate worship who need to hear the message of redemption provided in the Gospel of Christ. He addresses God vertically in talking directly to the Lord and appealing to God's awareness of his faithful proclamation of God's saving work. He speaks to the congregation about God's faithfulness and salvation. This represents David's concern that his fellow worshippers be saved and acknowledge God's saving work. He is thinking about evangelism and edifying his neighbor. David expresses his vertical confidence in God's mercy, love, and preservation.

8. In what way do verses 12-15 address the vertical and horizontal?

Acknowledging his own sinfulness (v. 12) David directly addresses God and asks him to provide deliverance from his enemies. In addressing God, he is vertical but also horizontal since he is concerned about his enemies.

9. What positive message does David provide in verses 16-17?

He indirectly announces blessing upon those who seek God and love God's salvation. He is concerned about God's reputation. In the last verse, David in vertical fashion expresses his dependence on God and requests the Lord's help and deliverance from his enemies.

10. How has God challenged your attitude today about the vertical and horizontal dimensions of worship?

Lesson 6 Outline:

BIBLICAL WORSHIP – LESSON SIX
Worship and Communion

Texts: 1 Corinthians 10:14-17; 11:22-33

Introduction: One weekend I visited another church. On this particular Sunday, the church was practicing the Lord's Supper. Although the congregation claimed to be a Reformed church their practice of the supper was quite different than my experience in previous Reformed churches. The minister stood in front with a number of elders and told the congregation that we were going to partake in the Lord's Supper but little was said to explain it. Their administration of the table was definitely minimalistic. As the minister prayed the elders held the trays of wine and the bread in front of the sanctuary. Everyone in the congregation was encouraged to walk up front to get in line to take the elements. Nothing was said about contemplating what we were about to do. Music was played to underscore the event and people began getting in line to receive the elements from the minister and elders. I felt disconnected and ill-informed about what communion was all about through this church's tradition. I was given no information about how communion truly related to the body of Christ. I felt we were being herded along rather than being treated as members of Christ's body. Today, a similar story could be recounted in many churches. Little is said about how to properly understand or take communion. The sense of contemplation and biblical community is often minimalized for the sake of ritual or expediency. The question arises, does it really matter?

Let's share. What has been your experience in taking communion when you have visited different churches?

Read 1 Corinthians 10:14-22.

1. **What warning does the apostle Paul give the Corinthians regarding the Lord's Supper?**

Sunday School Lesson Outlines

He warns them against idolatry (v. 14). He refers to the idolatrous sacrifices of the pagans who made offerings to demons and thus warns Christians against participating in such ceremonies and the Lord's Supper (vv. 20-21). He warns believers against provoking the Lord to anger (v. 22).

2. **How does Paul's description of the Lord's Supper convey the idea that it is more than a mere memorial (see vv. 16-17, 20-22)?**

His language that the supper is a "participation" in the blood and body of Christ point to the spiritual nature of the sacrament. His comparison to the participation with demons in the sacrifices of the pagans indicates that Paul sees the Lord's Supper as a spiritual participation in Christ. Thus, John Calvin's *Dynamic View*, otherwise known as a *Spiritual View* of the Supper, is supported by this passage.

3. **How does the Supper join Christians to Jesus?**

Believers participate in both the blood and body of Christ when they are partake of the elements (v. 16). This concept is best explained as a spiritual union with Christ. In other words, Christians participate spiritually with Christ when they partake by faith of the elements which represent his blood and body.

4. **In what way do believers join with fellow Christians in partaking of the Supper?**

When Christians partake of the bread it not only represents the very body of Christ, but it also represents the church which is called the body of Christ (see 1 Cor. 12:12-31). In partaking of the bread, the believer experiences spiritually their double union with both Christ and his body, the church. It is a physical representation of this spiritual union. This experience is both a vertical and horizontal experience.

5. **How does Paul's theology on the Lord's Supper challenge you in this passage?**

I am encouraged to take seriously what is happening when I partake. It encourages me to think about the importance of my covenantal bond and spiritual union with both Christ and my fellow believers. I am challenged to see the spiritual reality and significance of this sacrament and it strengthens my faith in the Lord. In warning me against idolatry, Paul encourages total devotion to Christ and his church.

Read 1 Corinthians 11:17-34.

6. In verses 17-22, what problems in the Corinthian church does the apostle address?

There is a serious lack of horizontal concern about how the members are treating one another. There are divisions and factions among them (vv. 18-19). They are eating a meal (i.e., some theologians call this a "love feast") but are exhibiting gluttony and stinginess rather than unity and a spirit of sharing. The poor are being left hungry (v. 21). The people are getting drunk (v. 22). On the vertical side, they are not treating this feast and ultimately the Lord's Supper with respect for God (v. 20). In their selfishness and arrogance some in the congregation are despising the church of God and humiliating the less fortunate (v. 22). They are acting more like pagans than God's people.

7. What do the elements represent (see vv. 23-26)?

The bread represents the body of Christ and the cup points to the new covenant transacted in Christ's blood spilled on the cross. It all points to Jesus' death until he comes again.

8. How does Paul fence the Table (vv. 27-34)?

He warns believers not to partake in an unworthy manner, which would make them guilty concerning the body and blood of Christ (v. 27).

He calls each person to examine themselves. This calls for spiritual examination and seriousness in taking the Lord's Supper. It should not be taken flippantly or carelessly. It should be consumed thoughtfully.

Christians should discern the Lord's body (v. 29). This addresses both having an understanding of the death of Christ on the cross and the spiritual union that exists between fellow believers through faith in Christ. The call to discern the Lord's body excludes unbelievers from the supper. This warning is both a vertical and horizontal concern. It involves respecting others in the congregation and maintaining biblical peace. It demands pursuing biblical reconciliation in relationships.

Paul warns about the potential of God's judgment, even death in improperly taking the Lord's Supper (vv. 30-32) as well as eternal judgment (v. 32b).

Believers are warned to wait for one another which is clearly a horizontal concern that would demonstrate respect and love for others in the congregation (v. 33b).

The apostle warns the congregation to treat the Supper as unique. Some theologians believe this warning led the church to separate the Lord's Supper from the Love Feast (vv. 33-34).

9. In what way does 1 Corinthians 11:17-34 challenge you regarding the vertical and horizontal dimensions of worship?

I am moved to take seriously the practice of the Lord's Supper and to make sure I am thinking about its spiritual significance. I am challenged to repent of my sins as I examine my heart and relationships with others in the church. I am encouraged to contemplate the covenantal unity I have with Christ and other believers when I partake in the supper and to treat everyone with the respect and love God' demands. Communion encourages me to not only love the people during worship but also to minister to them and love them after communion since my Savior has so loved me in his sacrifice on the cross.

21

Sermon Series Outlines

Sermon 1 Outline:

Worship with Love for Your Neighbor
Exodus 20:1-17; Matthew 22:36-40

Purpose: To demonstrate the necessity of love for God and neighbor in all of life and worship.

I. The OT Law is Bidirectional (Exodus 20:1-17):

God's moral law lays down a blueprint for the vertical and horizontal dimensions to take place in corporate worship. Moses was given the Decalogue or Ten Commandments to teach the Israelites how they should approach God and treat one another in response to God's grace. The Westminster Shorter and Larger catechisms teach us that the Ten Commandments still apply today. They teach the negative and positive application of each commandment. The Ten Commandments reinforce the mutual concepts of loving God and loving our neighbor. This dual structure within the Ten Commandments encourages the church to engage in the pursuit of the vertical and horizontal. We cannot only focus upon the section of the Law that primarily deals with the vertical and leave out the horizontal in our daily lives, especially in our worship. Let us consider the bidirectional structure of the Ten Commandments. We are first called to…

A. Love God (Exod. 20:1-11): The first four commandments are prefaced by the grace God provides in delivering Israel from Egypt.

This reality reminds us that God's people should ultimately be motivated to follow the commands based on God's grace and redemption. The focus of these commands is primarily upon God which is vertical. Not only does the fourth command address the vertical it also references the horizontal (e.g., caring about slaves, servants, and animals). It represents the close correlation between the vertical and the horizontal aspect of the commands.

Secondly, God tells Israel to...

B. Love your Neighbor (Exod. 20:12-17): When we carefully examine the other six commandments, we discover their interdependent relationship with the first four commandments.

Fifth Command (v. 12) – Honoring parents flows from honoring and loving God.

Sixth Command (v. 13) – Respecting the life of others is rooted in loving the giver of life and the God who made human beings in his image.

Seventh Command (v. 14) – Honoring marriage flows from loving God, the one who is joined to his people in a spiritual marriage. The seventh command foreshadows the marriage of Christ to his bride the church and encourages Christian spouses to be faithful to one another and singles to honor their neighbor sexually since they are married to Christ.

Eighth Command (v. 15) – God's people should not steal because they respect what God has given to their neighbors.

Ninth Command (16) – Telling the truth to one's neighbor flows from a love for the true God of truth who tells us the truth in his Word.

Tenth Command (v. 17) – Respecting another person's property should flow from being content with the spiritual and material blessings God has provided to us. It is a call to honor the stewardship responsibilities that God gives to our neighbors. This command encourages us to exercise our God-given responsibility over our possessions.

II. The NT Law requires the Vertical and the Horizontal (Matt. 22:37-40):

Before we directly consider Matthew 22:37-40, it is important to understand that the New Testament moral law is the same as the Old Testament moral law. We see this fact in Jesus' Sermon on the Mount in Matthew 5-7 where he reiterates the Ten Commandments and deepens our understanding and application of it for the New Testament age. He does not do away with the Ten Commandment but rather upholds them. This brings us to Matthew 22:37-40.

A. Loving the Lord is vertical vv. 37-38: Jesus answers the scribe's question about what the most important commandment is by noting that it involves loving God with our whole being. Jesus was fully aware of the Ten Commandments and their vertical and horizontal structure. This awareness surely informed his comments and answer. He knew the first commandment dealt with the vertical dimension and therefore he summarizes its priority and importance calling it "the great and first commandment" (v. 38). He also knew that it could not be separated from the second half of the decalogue. It was complementary rather than mutually exclusive. So, Jesus then addresses the importance of the horizontal in relation to the vertical. He teaches that…

B. Loving your Neighbor is horizontal v. 39: The Savior believes the second commandment is like the first in its importance saying, "And a second is like it." Although the second commandment follows the first commandment in priority, it joins it as vital to understanding the whole Law of God. The horizontal obligations of the second part of the decalogue are represented in the simple phrase, "You shall love your neighbor as yourself." Jesus summarizes the significance of his teaching in verse 40. He tells the lawyer of the Law…

C. The Bible depends on bidirectional love v. 40: Bidirectional love applies to life and worship. Jesus teaches that both the vertical and horizontal laws must go together. He says, "On these two commandments depend all the Law and the Prophets." In other words, you cannot have one without the other. Both laws are needed to uphold all the Law of God and the teachings of the prophets. They actually uphold the teachings of the whole Bible. We cannot choose one to the exclusion of the other. So, how do we apply this passage to life?

Application: God's calling to love him and our neighbor extends to all of life even to our times of worship. We cannot come into God's sanctuary to worship him and forget the commands that call us to love our neighbor. The vertical and horizontal commands should affect our attitudes and motivations in worship. Our love for God should flow over into our love for one another. Our love for one another should spring from our love of and for God. Such love should be exhibited not only in our times of worship but also before and after worship. Our daily lives should demonstrate love for God and our neighbor. This attitude of love for others must begin with a love for Jesus Christ who showed us love in dying for our sins on the cross. Do you know the love of Christ in the gospel? Have you received the forgiveness of sins Christ offers by repenting of your sins and trusting in him as your Savior and Lord? Are you striving to love your neighbor like Jesus loved you on the cross?

Sermon 2 Outline:

A Call to Mercy
Mt. 9:9-12

Purpose: To encourage believers to show mercy to others in their worship and daily living.

I. Show Mercy because of Christ's <u>calling</u> (vv. 9, 13):

   A. What was Christ's call?

   Follow me (v. 9) - This in fact was not a suggestion but a command. In obedience Matthew immediately left his job and followed Christ. Matthew surely knew that his life would now be controlled by his Master and that his past life of selfishness would now have to be a life of service and mercy.

   B. Who does he call?

   1. <u>**Tax collectors**</u> **(v. 10):** Tax collectors were considered traitors of the Jewish people and nation. The Pharisees considered them ceremonially unclean because of their contact with Gentile Romans. But Christ in his mercy called even a tax collector to follow him.

   2. <u>**Sinners**</u> **(v. 10):** Sinners were those whom the Pharisees also considered unclean because they did not keep the ceremonial law. They included prostitutes, thieves, and basically anyone who did not keep the rules of the Pharisees.

Illustration: Bob had committed armed robbery and had been in jail most of his life. His life gravitated around drugs and violence. But one day he heard Christ calling "follow me." In his need for the mercy of Christ he decided to give his life to Christ and follow him. Now he is totally a different person. He's always sharing how he is thankful for Christ's mercy in saving him. He now tries to be merciful to others whereas before he became a Christian, his life was driven by selfish desires. Christ calls us to also follow him by showing mercy to others.

Application: 1. Christ commands us to follow him by showing mercy to those around us. Our calling is a life of mercy. 2. Give over your selfish tendencies to Christ and ask him to help you to be merciful to others.

II. Show mercy because of Christ's <u>example</u> (v. 10):

A. Christ <u>ate</u> with sinners (v. 10): The Pharisees were utterly amazed that Jesus would eat with sinners and tax collectors. In Jesus' culture to eat with someone was understood as a sign of an intimate or close relationship with that person. Jesus showed his love and mercy toward sinners in eating with them.

B. Christ <u>healed</u> sinners (v. 12) Christ healed sinners both physically and spiritually. His mercy was physically demonstrable as with the paralytic (9:6,7) and spiritually redeeming (9:2). The sick were sinners in need of mercy and Christ gladly provided such mercy to them. Jesus always focused on the physically and spiritually needy.

Illustration: Years ago, when I was in high school, I had a friend named Andretta. She had one of highest grade point averages in the school. She was president of the Student Council Association and seemed to have everything going for her. Many of the other students that were similarly talented tended to separate themselves from the other students and stayed in their elite cliques. Not so with Andretta. Whenever there was a new student who came to school and needed a friend and someone to show them around, Andretta would be there. No matter how odd the visitor seemed, she would befriend them. In a similar manner, Christ calls us by his example to show mercy to the unlovely, unpopular, and needy.

Application: 1.If someone new moves to your community you could go out and visit them and bring them a plate of cookies. 2. Perhaps there is a widow in the church who needs her house cleaned or leaves raked. You might be able to help out. 3. Maybe you could serve as a volunteer at the Christian Helping Hands ministry here in Pearland. They can always use help.

III. Show mercy because of Christ's <u>desire</u> (vv. 13):

A. He did not desire <u>sacrifice</u> (v. 13): Jesus tells the Pharisees to go back to the Old Testament and discover the meaning of the phrase "I desire mercy, and not sacrifice." He was quoting Hosea 6:6. The Pharisees in their cold ritualistic practices in worship had forgotten what God desired. God would never accept mere outward ceremonial rituals and traditions. Ancient Israel engaged in all types of rituals in her worship to God, but later people just went through the motions without the involvement of the heart. They were not treating people with mercy but still went to worship expecting God to bless them. So Jesus is saying that just as Israel's ritualistic and heartless sacrifices were unacceptable in Hosea's day, God likewise finds unacceptable the empty ceremonies and heartless worship of the Pharisees.

B. He desires <u>mercy</u> (v. 13): God desires acts of compassion for the lowly and needy rather than mere religious ceremony. God is not telling us that he does not want us to participate in Christian ceremonies, but he does not want us to do so without the motive and attitude of mercy in relation to our neighbors. He would not accept their vertical offerings of worship without their horizontal acts and attitudes of mercy. How we deal with others provides proof of our relationship with Christ and our sincere love of God. Jesus has shown us tremendous mercy by dying on the cross for our sins and he desires that we willingly and eagerly show that same mercy to others as we emulate his character and presence in the world. If we expect to worship God in an acceptable manner, we must show mercy to our neighbors, even those who are despised by the culture.

Illustration: Often churches tend to get engrossed in tradition. They get more attached to denominationalism than sharing the simple gospel and love of Christ. Sometimes the church becomes a social club to meet people and to go through our religious ceremonies. The church's purpose of ministering mercy in the world becomes secondary and Christianity becomes cold and ritualistic. We must realign our priorities with those of Christ. When our sacrifices of praise, study, and worship are warmed by lives of mercy, then and only then will our sacrifices be acceptable to God.

Application: Jesus challenges you to change your attitude about others in worship. He calls you to show them mercy, not just the ritual of your worship. He is calling you to really care about other people. He is calling you to love your neighbor, even the one that others don't like or despise. He is calling you to show mercy to sinners. This would entail praying for their salvation and treating them with kindness and grace. It involves treating them with respect and sharing the gospel and truths of the Word with them. His example calls you to reach out to others in the community to show them such mercy as well. Ask God to give you opportunities to show the mercy of Christ.

Conclusion: So, we have seen three reasons why we should show mercy to others in our worship and daily lives. It's because of Christ's calling, example, and desire for mercy. When Ted entered the Men's Club program at Sunshine Mission (a Christian rehab ministry) he was beginning to grow in Christ. Months passed as he grew in the Word and learned to appreciate the mercy God had given him. He began showing mercy to others as they entered the program. He'd take time to talk to the new guys and hear their problems. He even gave them some of the few clothes he had to help them get on their feet. After he graduated, he became a supervisor in the program and had the opportunity to daily show mercy to the Men's Club participants. He experienced joy as he served others. May we all learn to grow to appreciate the mercy of Christ and learn to be merciful to those God puts in our way. **Let us pray.**

Sermon 3 Outline:

Singing to God with Love for Your Neighbor
Ephesians 5:19; Colossians 3:16

Purpose: To encourage God's people to praise God in song and to edify those who join them in worship.

Introduction: Years ago, I began to investigate the way churches did their music during their worship services. I called a worship leader in a mega church in Houston to get some ideas about how to lead our church in song. He was very gracious, and we had an honest conversation about the idea of participation. He noted that he agreed that people should participate in singing during worship services because that appeared to be the biblical model, but he bemoaned the fact that his congregation had become so used to having professionals do all the singing that the people simply would not sing. He remarked that they had become accustomed being entertained. He said he was working on how to move them away from an entertainment to a participatory model in which the congregation and those leading in song would join together in worshiping God. I commended him for trying to shift the church back toward a biblical pattern of worship. In his pastoral epistles to the churches in Ephesus and Colossae, the apostle Paul encourages those congregations to engage in singing to the Lord. Entertainment or passive attendance is the furthest thing from his mind. He calls Christians to thoughtfully engage in singing during their corporate worship. He addresses both the vertical direction of praise and the horizontal dimension in singing. Let us consider some of his instruction on the way we should sing in our times of worship.

I. Address one another (Eph. 5:19):

Paul uses the participial phrase "addressing one another" to indicate that the time of singing in worship is not just a vertical experience. In fact, he emphasizes that it involves the horizontal. He tells the Ephesians to address one another. They need to sing with the intent to sing to one another. This is a product of being "filled with the Spirit" that Paul speaks about in verse 18. Being filled with the Spirit indicates that the Holy Spirit will move them beyond a self-serving and self-edifying experience to serving and edifying others in the congregation. They have an obligation to minister to those around them and those who join them in worshiping God. Paul is highlighting the horizontal dimension in their worship. How does he describe it?

A. Sing with variety: Notice that verse 19 mentions three types of songs. Some theologians believe these all represent the psalms only and thus see the different words as representing the same type of song. Other scholars, however, see Paul providing different terms to represent different styles of songs. One scholar helps us with this debate. Writing on worship, Ralph Martin states,

> It is hard to draw any hard-and-fast distinction between these terms; and modern scholars are agreed that the various terms are used loosely to cover the various forms of musical composition. 'Psalms' may refer to Christian odes patterned on the Old Testament Psalter. 'Hymns' would be longer compositions and there is evidence that some actual specimens of these hymns may be in the New Testament itself. 'Spiritual songs' refer to snatches of spontaneous praise which the inspiring Spirit placed on the lips of the enraptured worshipper, as 1 Corinthians 14:5 implies. These 'inspired odes' would no doubt be of little value, and their contents would be quickly forgotten.[1]

One of the things we learn from the variety of music Paul mentions is that we should show a gracious spirit toward the variety of songs that people unlike ourselves may sing. To be considerate of the different types of songs others may appreciate is a horizontal aspect of our worship in song.

B. Turn others to the Lord: The apostle addresses both the vertical and horizontal. He tells believers what they should be singing

---

14. Ralph P. Martin, *Worship in the Early Church*, rev. ed. (Grand Rapids, MI: Eerdmans, 1975), 47.

about as they address one another in song. They are called to make a "melody to the Lord" meaning they are to direct their fellow worshippers to think about and honor the Lord. In verse 20 Paul speaks about some of the things Christians should do when singing. They should give thanks to God the Father in Jesus' name. This means they should thank God in song for his many blessings. They are not singing in a concert or man-centered event. They are called to minister to their fellow worshippers by encouraging them to praise and give thanks to God.

C. Sing from the heart: Drawing upon the Old Testament themes of heartfelt worship, Paul tells the Ephesians to sing with their "heart." This addresses the right vertical attitude they should have in worship. Their singing should not be mindless empty ritual or mere tradition. It must come from their hearts. It must come from hearts that love God and their neighbor (see Eph. 5:1).

II. Teach and admonish one another (Col. 3:16-17).

Dr. Douglass Moo in his commentary on Colossians states, "This verse is one of the very few that provide us with any window at all into the worship of the earliest Christians."[2]

Those who wish to reduce worship to a vertical-only experience are corrected by the apostle. Those who limit their time of praise to a personal and individual experience have missed a horizontal aspect in their singing. Paul clearly includes both the vertical and horizontal in corporate music/singing. He tells Christians to teach one another, meaning to instruct those around them through their act of singing in worship. He calls believers to admonish, meaning to correct and direct their fellow worshippers. Worship, for Paul, is not just a personal thing but a corporate activity. It is an act of service and ministry to others. In this sense it is inherently horizontal. So, the question arises, "How should believers teach and admonish one another?"

---

2. Douglas J. Moo, *The Letters to the Colossians and to Philemon* (Grand Rapids, MI: William B. Eerdmans, 2008), 290.

First, they should…

A. Sing with knowledge v. 16. The apostle tells them to "Let the word of Christ dwell in you richly." This means they should be a people who constantly store up and apply the Word of God in their lives, especially the word about Christ. This would include the message of the gospel, the gospel accounts, and the doctrines of Scripture. The word "richly" conveys the notion that the believer should take this calling seriously and engage in it faithfully. This encourages the careful and diligent study and application of the Word. They should love the Word of God. They should love sermons and Bible lessons taught by the teachers of the Word. They should hold in high esteem the apostolic teaching of the apostles. Storing up richly the Word of God in their hearts will equip them to teach and admonish others according to the Word.

B. Sing with wisdom v. 16. Singing with wisdom entails singing the Word of God from life experience. The idea of wisdom reminds Christians that they need to apply the Word of God, which dwells in them, by thinking, living, and speaking according to the Word. To sing with wisdom implies that they will sing the Word with thoughtfulness and careful consideration about how it applies to the lives of other worshippers.

C. Sing with thankfulness v. 16-17. Like Paul's message to the Ephesians (Eph. 5:20), he repeats his encouragement to Colossian believers to sing "with thankfulness … to God." They should praise God with an attitude of thanks for the salvation, grace, mercy, love, and providence God has provided. Paul notes in verse 17 that they should give "thanks to God the Father through him." The word "him" refers to Christ. Such thankfulness authenticates the genuine nature of their praise and models for others how they should live for and sing to God.

D. Sing with heart v. 16. Lastly, Paul mentions that their thankful singing should come from their hearts "to God." Again, Paul mixes the vertical with the horizontal. The two always go together in his understanding of biblical worship. He repeats what he has told the Ephesians and thus reminds the church that God desires worship from the heart. Likewise, he calls for instructive singing that ministers to others from hearts devoted to God. All admonishment and instruction should come from hearts that are thankful to God through Christ. Empty ritual and tradition will not please God. Only heartfelt praise will do.

Conclusion: So, how should you apply Paul's instruction on singing in your worship to God? Let the Word of God richly dwell in you through serious study, contemplation, and application of the Word. Scripture should inform your understanding of the music and lyrics you sing. God is calling you to sing your praises to him but also to seek to minister to others with what you believe about him. Sing what you believe God has done and what he will do in Christ. Sing from your heart with thankfulness to God. Avoid a spectator mentality when you sing. Be a participant. Admonish and teach one another through the songs you sing that are in accord with Scripture. Sing as if you are preaching a sermon to those around you. Sing to bring others to Christ. Sing to bring people back to Christ. Sing to grow them in the Christian faith. Sing to bless them through Jesus Christ. Let us pray.

Sermon 4 Outline:

Build Up Your Neighbor in Worship
1 Corinthians 14:1-25

Purpose: To encourage churches to make sure their worship services edify those who attend, whether they are believers or unbelievers.

Introduction: I had just become a Christian and I was sixteen years old. I had heard the gospel from a missionary who had returned to America from serving in Africa. Christ changed my heart, giving me a hunger for the Word and a desire to worship. Since I lived in a trailer court out in the country and had no means of transportation or understanding of what to look for in a church, I asked my neighbor and friend Mark if I could attend his church. One Sunday morning I caught a ride to his Catholic church. I was excited about going to worship God. When everyone sat down for the service the priest began the ceremony. As he stood in the front of the sanctuary, he tilted back his head looking into the air to avoid eye contact with the people. He led the service in a foreign tongue I had never heard before. I simply did not understand anything that was done that Sunday morning and wondered, "Is this really worship?" I would later discover that the priest was speaking in Latin, which explained why I could not understand the liturgy or his comments. To tell you the truth, I don't believe my friend Mark and his family understood anything that was said any better than I did. One of the things that happened in the Protestant Reformation regarding worship was that the protestant leaders decided to conduct their services in the language of the people. Like me, people generally could not understand the Roman Catholic liturgy which was spoken in Latin. The people in Protestant churches were glad, once the changes took effect, to worship God in a language they could understand. In 1 Corinthians 14 the apostle Paul is disturbed hearing that the Corinthians are confusing people in their worship services with an over-emphasis on the gift of tongues. He believes it keeps people from being edified. This leads him to provide instruction on how to build up those who come to worship. Today, let us consider the principles for biblical worship Paul provides.

I. Biblical worship minimizes confusion vv. 1-2, 9-12.

Paul compares the gift of tongues with prophecy (Read v. 1). There are people in the church who are emphasizing speaking in tongues, but they have no consideration of whether others understand what they are saying. We cannot be sure whether the tongues in 1 Corinthians 14 are the same type as the tongues Luke speaks about in Acts 2. In Acts 2, people are able to hear in their own language foreigners praising God, even though the hearers do not know the language of the foreigners. That miracle is either a gift of speaking or hearing. It appears that the tongues in 1 Corinthians 14 are induced by the Spirit and are revelatory since the utterances are "mysteries in the Spirit" (Read v. 2). It is possible that these tongues are of a different type than the tongues we see in Acts 2. The tongues in 1 Corinthians 14 may be ecstatic utterances since the Corinthians need an interpreter, and the tongues they speak are only helpful to the tongues speakers themselves. The Acts 2 type of tongues need no interpreter. Nevertheless, Paul in 1 Corinthians 14 notes that speaking in tongues creates confusion in the church since people do not understand what is being said. He rather prefers prophecy, a gift that conveys God's truth through words that we can understand. What is prophecy? Prophecy is a gift of speaking forth revelation from God in the language of the listeners. This gift drastically reduces confusion in the church over against the gift of tongues. Paul is thinking beyond the self-serving attitude of the Corinthians and encouraging them to consider how their worship is affecting others. When we think about other people in our services such thoughts represent the horizontal dimension of worship. Paul wishes to reduce confusion in the church by promoting prophecy over tongues because it minimizes confusion.

II. Biblical worship builds up the body vv. 3-5.

The apostle Paul goes on to further speak about the horizontal dimension in relation to prophecy and tongues. He understands that there is a vertical dimension to worship in which believers personally benefit when they speak in tongues (vv. 2, 15, 17-18, 39) but he also notes that it is much more important to consider the effect of our worship upon the whole church. He prioritizes the horizontal aspect of corporate edification over the vertical desire for personal edification (Read vv. 3-4). He even says that prophecy is more important to the church than tongues since it builds up the church (Read v. 5). This would definitely deal a blow to the arrogant attitudes of those in the church who prioritize speaking in tongues in worship. Calvin grasps Paul's emphasis on the horizontal dimension in verse four stating "anything that is done in the Church ought to be for the good of all."[3]

III. Biblical worship communicates with clarity vv. 6-19.

Building upon Paul's argument that worship should edify the congregation and that prophecy is better than tongues for edification, the apostle supports this claim by talking about intelligibility. In other words, clarity in worship is essential in building up the body of Christ. Paul speaks about musical instruments to build his case. He says that "distinct notes" must be played with a flute or harp otherwise the people will not know the melody of the song being played (Read v. 7). He points out that if a bugle provides an "indistinct sound" no one will get ready for battle (Read v. 8). So, he then argues that speaking in tongues is a practice that is unintelligible and therefore a problem. No one will understand anything if people are using unintelligible words, and it will be as useless as "speaking into the air" (Read 9b). Paul compares listening to people speaking in tongues to the barriers that exist between foreigners who cannot understand one another because they speak different languages (Read vv. 10-11). The apostle says we should strive for gifts that "build up the church" (Read v. 12). The apostle then speaks about the vertical nature of tongues and its uselessness to others in the congregation. It may benefit the speaker, but it is worthless to the listeners (Read vv. 13-17). Then Paul drives home the importance of intelligibility (Read vv. 18-19). The principle is this: worship that is biblical and useful for the church must communicate with clarity the will of God.

---

17. Calvin, *Calvin's New Testament Commentaries*, 9:287.

Application: This teaching reminds us all how important it was in the Reformation for the Protestants to worship in the language of the people versus the dead language of Latin which the Roman Catholic Church clung to for the sake of tradition. Likewise, the church today needs to consider the people they are ministering to and do its best to communicate clearly the Word of God. The practical implications of Paul's teaching mean that we need to do our best to make sure our liturgy and communication of the Bible is clear. This might mean defining our terms (e.g., justification, sanctification, etc.). We might need to explain our confessional and credal responsive readings to help people understand the historical and doctrinal importance of such worship elements. This can be done orally or in written form in our bulletins. We may need to explain why we order our liturgy a certain way. These concerns are especially applicable to Reformed churches which tend to use at times unfamiliar terms, insider language, and references to Reformed history unfamiliar to many in our culture. Paul is serious about clearly instructing others in our worship services in order to build up the body of the Christ.

IV. Biblical worship considers the lost vv. 20-25.

Many today dismiss the importance of thinking about unbelievers in corporate worship. They say things like, "Worship is only for believers, not unbelievers." This sort of thinking has nothing to do with the teaching of Scripture. It is true that only believers can worship God, but that does not mean that our worship services should not consider unbelievers. In fact, Paul in 1 Corinthians 14:20-25 calls the church to consider them. He says his view is a mature way of thinking (Read v. 20). Then he goes on to describe how tongues are a sign of judgment to encourage the church not to use them in worship (Read vv. 21-22). If Christians speak in tongues, unbelievers will not understand what is happening and will think they are crazy (Read v. 23). But if they prophesy, meaning they communicate God's gospel and Word with clarity, then unbelievers may be convicted of their sins, trust in Christ, and worship God (Read v. 24-25). The puritan commentator Matthew Henry says it well: "Religious exercises in Christian assemblies should be such as are fit to edify the faithful, and convince, affect, and convert unbelievers. The ministry was not instituted to make ostentation of gifts and parts, but to save souls."[4]

Application: God is calling us to make his gospel and Word clear to unbelievers when they join us for worship so that they might be saved. This passage should encourage us to make sure we sing, pray, and preach the gospel of Christ clearly in each service. We also should be mindful to preach the whole counsel of God so the Lord can do the convicting needed in their hearts and souls with the Word. There is no room for being politically correct or seeking to please men. We must sing, pray, and proclaim the truth of God's Word. We should also be encouraged to pray for the Lord to convict hearts with his Word.

Conclusion: Years ago, I was talking to someone about a previous pastor they had. As they talked about him, they ranted about how he often used fifty-dollar words and seemed so intelligent. They noted that he was such an educated man who often said new things. Talking further, I found that this person frequently did not understand what the pastor was saying. But he sounded impressive. Several other members exclaimed that they too could not understand what the minister was preaching about. They simply did not get the point. To be honest, many churches and church leaders pride themselves on being so obtuse when they communicate to others that they forget what Paul called the church to do. Such communication is no different than speaking in tongues, which Paul corrected in 1 Corinthians 14. If people do not understand what we are saying even though we might sound educated or smart, we have helped no one come to Christ or spiritually grow in the faith. To operate like that demonstrates the same arrogant attitude we see in the Corinthian church about the subject of tongues. It is an attitude of selfishness when we do not try to clearly communicate the gospel and God's Word to others. Paul encourages us to do our best to communicate God's Word with love and concern for those he brings to our church and worship services. Each Sunday service, remember the horizontal dimension in your calling to

---

4. Matthew Henry, *Matthew Henry's Commentary on the Whole Bible: Complete and Unabridged in One Volume* (Peabody: Hendrickson, 1994), 2271.

evangelize, minister to, and build up others in the worship of God. This attitude should also affect the way we minister to others during the week. In summary, always seek to build up your neighbor in worship. Let us pray.

22

CONCLUSION

As we conclude our discussion of the horizontal dimension let us consider the path we have traveled and the things we have learned. We discovered at the outset of this project that a study on the horizontal dimension was greatly needed in the church today. We found that some in the body of Christ have so over emphasized the vertical dimension that they have either negated or diminished the importance of the horizontal dimension in corporate worship. Few resources provide one location for scholarly guidance for understanding the place of the horizontal in relation to the vertical in worship. Consequently, the need for a careful defense of the horizontal dimension was established.

It has been argued from numerous scriptural passages that the horizontal dimension of worship must be conjoined with a biblical understanding of the vertical direction of worship. We have learned that the horizontal dimension includes the attitude of Christian love for God and our fellow worshippers. We have discovered that the horizontal involves maintaining a pattern of justice toward our neighbors before, during, and after worship. In dealing with passages that specifically address the topic of worship and the horizontal, a case has been made that the horizontal dimension is required for worship to be acceptable to God. By good and necessary inference from holy Scripture. we deduced that worship which honors the Lord must always include both the vertical and the horizontal dimensions.

In studying the Reformed tradition by considering Luther's and Calvin's writings, creedal statements, catechisms, and the Westminster Directory for the Public Worship of God we have learned that it is indeed theologically and historically Reformed to include the horizontal dimension when we lead and participate in corporate worship. Although Reformers such as Luther and Calvin did not necessarily use the phrase "horizontal dimension" in their comments on Reformed worship, we can conclude from their statements that the horizontal was essential in their understanding of it. They often encouraged the church to consider those present in worship as they provided guidance on how to construct Reformed worship services. Even though we have considered the ideas and practices of Luther and Calvin, further study of other major Reformers and their Puritan progeny might offer more insight on what the Reformers' thought about the horizontal dimension. Such research may uncover additional wisdom that the Reformation tradition offers for the church on the place of the horizontal in corporate worship.

Conservative and contemporary theologians and pastors have been consulted for their insights and applications of the horizontal dimension to the church. They teach believers in their corporate worship to appreciate the importance of edifying one another, encouraging the body, conducting services with clarity, praying for people, and ministering to fellow worshippers. The importance of ministering to others in worship through singing was also presented. It was argued that it is essential to view the horizontal and the vertical dimensions as aspects of worship that are necessary and interdependent rather than mutually exclusive of one another. For corporate worship to be biblical, we learned that the vertical and the horizontal dimensions must occur together. Every contemporary author reviewed would agree that Christians must worship with biblical love for their neighbors. With further study on the importance of the horizontal in worship, additional contemporary authors may provide more insight on how to promote the horizontal dimension in the church today. It is my hope that this project inspires future writers on worship to add scholarly and practical advice on the topic of the horizontal dimension and its interrelationship with the vertical. Such research is greatly needed in the church today due to an over-emphasis by some upon the vertical often to the minimizing of the horizontal. The church and its mission to reach the world for Christ would greatly benefit from continued study on this subject of the horizontal dimension and God would be glorified even more as a result.

A fifth and practical chapter was provided to present some guidance on the application of the horizontal in the church. It is hoped that the suggested services, lessons, visual graphic, and sermons will give worship leaders helpful tools to further educate and build up the local church in its practice of corporate worship.

A "Worship Checklist for Developing the Horizontal Dimension" is provided in Appendix B to offer additional assistance on how to implement the horizontal in corporate worship. This checklist is by no means exhaustive but is a helpful place to begin assessing ways to implement the horizontal.

In summary, it is the desire of this project to equip the body of Christ to worship God from the heart and glorify his name combined with a biblical love that leads others to trust in Christ alone for salvation and fall on their face declaring, "… God is really among you" (1 Cor. 14:25).

APPENDIX A

Luther's German Mass (Annotated)[1]

- **Hymn** (Luther replaces the Introit with singing by the congregation of a hymn or a German Psalm.)
- **Kyrie** (It is sung three times. The Gloria is absent.)
- **Collect** (This prayer is evangelically based.)
- **Epistle Reading** (the traditional Roman practice of reading the Old Testament is removed)
- **Hymn** (The Gradual (a chant) is replaced with a German hymn such as Luther's "Now Let Us Pray to the Holy Ghost" or any other. The hymn is sung with the whole choir. Notice that Luther makes sure the people participate with the choir in singing.)
- **Gospel Reading**
- **Apostle's Creed** (The whole congregation sings the Creed in German which is Luther's text: "We All Believe in One True God.")
- **Sermon**
- **Paraphrase of the Lord's Prayer** (Here we have Luther's making the intercessory prayer by the preacher more personal. This adds a horizontal dimension to a once very ritualistic prayer.)
- **Admonition before Holy Communion**
- **Liturgy of the Sacrament with Words of Institution** (Verba)
- **Distribution of the bread** (After the words in the Verba concerning the bread.)
- **Sanctus** (Luther's composition: "Isaiah in a Vision Did of Old.")

---

1. Martin Luther, *Luther's Works*, vol. 53, *Liturgy and Hymns*, ed. Ulrich S. Leupold (Philadelphia: Fortress Press, 1965), 61-90. This mass was written by Luther in 1526. It reflects Luther's strong emphasis upon involving the congregation in the language of the people particularly in congregational singing.

- **Distribution of the cup of wine** (After the words in the Verba concerning the cup.)
- **Agnus Dei** ("O Christ Lamb of God" is sung.)
- **Hymns**
- **Collect** (Post-communion Prayer.)
- **Benediction**

APPENDIX B

Checklist for Developing the Horizontal Dimension

- **Educate the congregation at times during the service about God's concern for community.** We cannot disconnect our worship of God from our concern and love for others. Marva Dawn highlights the importance of community when she says, "Before we consider some practical ways to build community, we must note this obvious, but often overlooked, truth: the Triune God wants our churches to be genuine communities."[1]
- **Make sure the service is intelligible.** Paul defends this point in 1 Corinthians 14. The Reformers were concerned that people understood what was happening in worship and that the Word was clearly communicated in the language of the people. It is also essential to realize that the things of the Spirit are spiritually discerned (1 Cor. 2:14), but this fact should not be used as an excuse to make things obscure and more difficult for people.
- **Make all the presentations of the written word clear without distractions.** Be mindful of doing projection slides well. Use properly spaced wording, a large font (at least 36 point text), and smooth transitions between slides. Make sure words in the slides and the bulletin are spelled correctly. Ensure that the information provided is up to date and accurate and that the lyrics of songs projected match the words the music leaders are singing.
- **Make sure the space for corporate worship is well maintained in order to avoid distractions, providing a place to clearly**

---

1. Marva J. Dawn, "Body Building: Worship That Develops Strong Community," *Reformed Worship* 45 (September 1997): 26–29, accessed March 21, 2019, http://search.ebscohost.com.rts.idm.oclc.org/login.aspx?direct=true&db=rfh&AN=ATLA 0001029668&site=ehost-live.

hear God's Word and engage in worship. Make sure lights are working, and the room is lit well so that people can see what is happening and can minister to one another. Make sure seats are comfortable and clean. Ensure the sound system is functioning well. You may need to provide an ear monitoring system through your sound board for those who have trouble hearing the service. All such preparations reflect love and care for the worshippers. They also demonstrate that you are serious about helping people worship and glorify the Lord without hindrances, confusion, and distractions.

- **Make sure the worship facility is accessible to the handicapped and disabled**. This entails making your place of worship wheelchair accessible.
- **Be hospitable**. Be friendly and kind to everyone, especially visitors. The word "hospitable" derives from the idea of love of strangers. Train your greeters, ushers, and congregation on how to show hospitality. Volunteers often give more attention to those they know rather than being attentive to newcomers. Encourage volunteers to be mindful of this tendency and train them to pay special attention to visitors.
- **Provide pew Bibles and announce the pages for Scripture readings**. Put the page numbers in the bulletins. Understand that some people know little about the Bible and need help learning it and finding passages. Many people will not return to a church service if they cannot find passages referenced during worship. It is loving to help people discover and learn the Bible.
- **Help people understand terms and what is happening in worship by explaining the liturgy**. This encourages intelligibility and expresses love for those in attendance.
- **Make bulletins clear by properly spacing sections and words**. Group topics to make them clearly identifiable (e.g., announcements, calendar, order of service, memory verse, sermon notes, etc.).

Appendix B

- **Provide sermon outlines.** Include them in bulletins and projection slides to help people understand the message from God's Word. This enhances intelligibility for edification.
- **Order the service in the bulletin with understandable terms.** Avoid using cryptic and odd phrasing without explanation so that people can see clearly what you are doing and understand what you are saying.
- **Speak in the language of the people to which you are ministering.** This involves getting to know the people, their level of education, and their unique colloquialisms.
- **Announce what is happening.** Announcements are quite appropriate during the worship service since they inform the body of Christ about the work of God among his people. Announcements offer encouragement to the people of God. They demonstrate to unbelievers that God is alive in practical ways through church ministries, meals, fellowship times, classes, etc. (1 Cor. 14; Heb. 10:23-26).
- **Help others who are having trouble with any part of the service.** This is especially beneficial when parents or other adults help the little children understand what is happening in the service. For example, an adult can show the child where in the Bible to find the passage or what song to turn to in the hymnal. Some need guidance to understand the liturgy.
- **Offer a translator.** This service may be needed for people who wish to attend worship but do not speak English.
- **Offer sign-language assistance.** For the hearing impaired, have someone provide sign-language to communicate the words of the service.
- **Offer an assisted listening system.** This is especially helpful for some elderly people who have trouble hearing.
- **Greet one another** (e.g., handshakes, hugs, kisses on the cheek in some cultures, fist bump with youth, etc.). Some use the tradition of Passing the Peace. This entails people saying, "Peace be with

you" and the respondent saying back, "And also with you." Many today who visit worship services find a greeting time annoying, feeling it is contrived and insincere. Often visitors feel left out as church members seem to focus on one another during such times giving little attention to them as guests. Consider the cultural expectations and attitudes with this potential worship element. If this element is not used in the service, encourage the congregation to greet one another before and/or after the service. It is not healthy for people to go to worship and leave without talking to anyone. To encourage such an attitude is to treat worship and church like an impersonal entertainment experience.

- **Pray for one another in the service during corporate prayer.** Many Reformed churches unknowingly encourage a vertical only mentality by calling their corporate prayer the pastoral prayer. This fosters the idea that the pastor does all the work in prayer and they are simply observers. This is why it is better to call the prayer time a corporate prayer to encourage the people to actually engage with the pastor or leader who leads the prayer.
    o Encourage people to join in the prayer as they pray for one another.
    o Include praying about the needs, ministries, leaders, praises, and missionaries of church.
    o Pray for government leaders, the community, and the lost.
    o Give moments for silent prayer. Encourage attendees to pray for the salvation of people in the service, edification of fellow worshippers, blessings upon the families of the church, protection of the children, encouragement of visitors, protection of the church officers and their families, and blessings upon the ministries of the church.
    o When the pastor alone prays, he should remind congregants to unite their hearts in prayer with him.
- **In Communion, explain our covenantal unity in Christ and need for us to pray about our covenantal connection in Christ.** While fencing the table, encourage attitudes of

reconciliation, love, and forgiveness toward our neighbors. Note that the call to "discern the Lord's body" not only refers to the actual body of Jesus but also includes properly thinking about and praying for brothers and sisters in the church who join us in communion both locally and abroad.
- **Encourage reporting**. This may include reports of missionaries, reports about missionaries, and reports of ongoing ministry in the church. Note that reporting on ministry occurred in the New Testament church (Acts 14:27; 15:4; 21:19; Eph. 6:22; Col. 4:8).
- **Ask attendees to be mindful of their neighbors and their spiritual/physical needs**. This may inform their prayers, responsive readings, and ministry through singing.
- **Encourage people to respond to the gospel**. Regarding consideration of potential unbelievers in the service, the pastor should call attendees to respond to the gospel with a general call asking people to repent of their sins and believe in Christ alone. Encourage believers present to pray for God to effectually call unbelievers to himself through his Holy Spirit (John 3:3; 6:44). Ask Christians to pray for the Lord to open hearts to repent, believe, and receive Christ.
- **Confess sin**. Encourage the people to confess their sins in not loving their neighbor. Horizontal sins may include lying, stealing, coveting, gossiping, slandering, showing favoritism, hating, resentment, holding a grudge, murdering someone in our hearts, not caring about someone's salvation, apathy about the spiritual growth of our neighbor, choosing to avoid correcting someone for fear of people, not caring about others in our worship, engaging in acts of injustice, etc.
- **Perform music well to avoid distractions**. Singers and instrumentalists should practice well ahead of time giving serious consideration to making sure God is honored and attendees can understand the truths conveyed. Encourage musicians to minister with their gifts from their hearts to the people God has brought to

worship him. Remind them to lead in a way that does not draws attention to themselves.

- **Sing songs with horizontal themes.** Choose songs that call believers to love, serve, correct, teach, admonish, pray for, build up, protect, and encourage one another. Songs that deal with the communion of the saints are appropriate.

- **Encourage musical grace.** Ask God's people to learn the songs that their brothers appreciate out of love for their fellow worshippers. Jack Harris, one of my dear elders who was in his eighties, exemplified the attitude we should all have. Although a classically trained concert pianist, he once said, "Don, I don't necessarily like all the contemporary music, but I know it blesses others, so I will try to like it." He was gracious to those who had different musical preferences. Accustomed to singing traditional songs, Jack later came to appreciate and love some of the contemporary tunes he once disliked. He was horizontally concerned and was willing to regard others more highly than himself (Phil. 2:3). He grew in his walk with the Lord and set a godly example for everyone in the church.

- **Encourage worshippers to sing from their hearts to God and to biblically encourage other people who are present in corporate worship.** Remind believers that the Word calls them to minister to one another in song during worship (Col. 3:16; Eph. 5:18-21). Many people today go to worship with an entertainment mentality or a vertical-only attitude. They do not take seriously their calling to participate in singing praises to God to minister to the people who are worshiping with them. They act like spectators rather than participants during worship. They do not sing but rather resign themselves to listening to the minister, worship leader, and musicians as if they were attending a concert or movie. This sort of sinful attitude happens in both contemporary and traditional services. Educate people about this common problem. Remind them often that God expects them to participate and to minister to others in worship.

- **Encourage horizontal thinking during the offering.** During the offering time, ask those who are giving gifts to consider the horizontal dimension in light of the vertical. Inform them that their gifts to God should be given for his glory and the building of his kingdom through his church. Remind them that their gifts meet the needs of the church's ministries such as paying salaries, providing utilities to aid in the proclamation of the gospel, helping needy people in the church, providing for people outside the church, supporting local mercy ministries, funding local and foreign missions, supporting denominational ministries, funding crisis pregnancy centers, keeping up God's property, funding our local church ministries, and training people to share the gospel, etc. Often tithes and offerings are taken up without an explanation of how the gifts will be used. Some people do not think about how their gifts fund ministry to others through the church. Giving is very mysterious to many. People should prayerfully ask the Lord to use their gifts to minister to others. Christians commonly give without prayer or forethought. Worship leaders need to educate the church about the good horizontal/vertical work that believers are helping to fund and promote. Such instruction will encourage the body of Christ to give cheerfully, prayerfully, and thankfully (2 Cor. 9:6-7)

BIBLIOGRAPHY

Adams, Jay E. *A Thirst for Wholeness*. Wheaton, IL: Victor Books, 1988.

Alexander, Archibald. "Spiritual Worship." In *Practical Sermons,* xx-xx. Greenville, SC: Greenville Presbyterian Theological Seminary Press, 1997.

Alfred, Nicolas. "A Principled Approach to the Worship of God: The Vertical Principle." *thedecablog*, February 21, 2015. Accessed March 6, 2018. https://thedecablog.wordpress.com/2015/02/21/a-principled-approach-to-the-worship-of-god-the-vertical-principle/#_ftn1.

Allen, Leslie C. *The Books of Joel, Obadiah, Jonah, and Micah*. 2nd ed. Grand Rapids: Eerdmans, 1976.

Anderson, Bernhard W. *Out of the Depths: The Psalms Speak for Us Today*. Rev. ed. Philadelphia: Westminster Press, 1983.

Aniol, Scott. "Martin Luther's Worship Reforms." October 30th, 2010. Accessed July 13, 2017, http://www. http://religious affections.org/articles/articles-on-worship/martin-luthers-worship-reforms/.

Arndt, William, Frederick W. Danker , and Walter Bauer. *A Greek-English Lexicon of the New Testament and Other Early Christian Literature*. 3rd ed. Chicago: Univ. of Chicago Press, 2000.

Augustine of Hippo. *St. Augustin: On the Holy Trinity, Doctrinal Treatises, Moral Treatises*, Vol. 3, *On the Trinity*, edited by Philip Schaff, translated by Arthur West Haddan, A Select Library of the Nicene and Post-Nicene Fathers of the Christian Church, First Series. Buffalo, NY: Christian Literature Company, 1887.

Bainton, Roland H. *Here I Stand: A Life of Martin Luther*. Peabody, MA: Hendrickson Publishers, 2009.Barber, John. "Luther and Calvin on Music and Worship." *Reformed Perspective*, June 25 to July 1, 2006.

Barker, William S. *Puritan Profiles: 54 Influential Puritans at the Time When the Westminster Confession of Faith Was Written*. Fearn, Ross-shire, Scotland: Mentor, 1996.

Barrett, C K. *The First Epistle to the Corinthians.* Peabody, MA: Hendrickson, 2000.

Baxter, Richard, and William Orme. *The Practical Works of the Rev. Richard Baxter.* Vol. 5. London: James Duncan, 1830.

———. *The Reformed Pastor.* Edinburgh: The Banner of Truth Trust, 1974.

Beeke, Joel R. *The Family at Church: Listening to Sermons and Attending Prayer Meetings.* 2nd ed. Grand Rapids, MI: Reformation Heritage Books, 2008.

Berkhof, Louis. *Systematic Theology.* 4th ed. Grand Rapids, MI: Eerdmans, 1949.

Betters, Daniel A. "The Perpetual Significance of the Lord's Day." master's thesis, Reformed Theological Seminary, 2008.

Blocher, Henri. "Calvin on the Lord's Supper: Revisiting an Intriguing Diversity Part 1." *The Westminster Theological Journal* 76, no. 1 (2014): 55–93.

Boice, James Montgomery. *Ephesians: An Expositional Commentary.* Grand Rapids, MI: Baker, 2006.

———. *Foundations of the Christian Faith: A Comprehensive and Readable Theology.* Rev. ed. The Master Reference Collection. Downers Grove, IL: InterVarsity Press, 1986.

———. *Psalms 42–106: An Expositional Commentary.* Grand Rapids, MI: Baker, 2005.

———. *Whatever Happened to the Gospel of Grace? Recovering the Doctrines That Shook the World.* Wheaton, IL: Crossway, 2001.

The Book of Common Worship. Philadelphia, PA: General Division of Publication of the The Board of Christian Education of the United Presbyterian Church in the United States of America, 1946.

The Book of Psalms for Singing. 25th ed. Pittsburgh, PA: C & C Publications, 1998.

Bratcher, Robert G., and William David Reyburn. *A Translator's Handbook on the Book of Psalms.* New York: United Bible Societies, 1991.

Brown, Francis, Samuel Rolles Driver, and Charles Augustus Briggs. *Enhanced Brown-Driver-Briggs Hebrew and English Lexicon.* Oxford: Clarendon, 1977.

Bruce, F. F. *The Epistles to the Colossians, to Philemon, and to the Ephesians.* The New International Commentary on the New Testament. Grand Rapids, MI: W.B. Eerdmans, 1984.

———. *The Gospel of John.* Grand Rapids, MI: Eerdmans Pub. Co., 1994.

Bruce, Robert. *The Mystery of The Lord's Supper: Sermons on the Sacrament Preached in the Kirk of Edinburgh.* 2nd ed. Edited and translated by Thomas F. Torrance. Edinburgh: Rutherford House, 2005.

Bullock, C Hassell. *An Introduction to the Old Testament Prophetic Books.* Chicago: Moody Press, 1986.

Burke, T Patrick. "God and My Neighbor." *Worship* 41, no. 3 (March 1967): 161-73.

Calvin, Jean. *Calvin's Commentaries.* Vol. 5, *The Commentary on the Book of Psalms.* Grand Rapids, MI: Baker, 1974.

———. *Calvin's Commentaries.* Vol. 13, *The Prophet Hosea.* Grand Rapids, MI: Baker, 1974.

———. *Calvin's Commentaries.* Vol. 7, *The Prophet Isaiah.* Grand Rapids, MI: Baker, 1974.

———. *Calvin's Commentaries.* Vol. 14, *The Prophet Micah.* Grand Rapids, MI: Baker, 1974.

Calvin, John. *Calvin's New Testament Commentaries.* Edited by David W. Torrance and Thomas F. Torrance. Translated by T. H. L. Parker. 12 vols. Grand Rapids, MI: Eerdmans, 1959-72.

———. *Institutes of the Christian Religion.* 2 vol. Edited by John T. McNeill. Translated by Ford Lewis Battles. Louisville, KY: Westminster John Knox Press, 2011.

———. "The Necessity of Reforming the Church." In *Calvin: Theological Treatises.* Vol. 1. Edited and Translated by J. K. S. Reid, 183-215. Louisville, KY; London: Westminster John Knox Press, 2006.

———. *Preface to the Psalter*, 1543. From the facsimile edition of: "Les Pseaumes mis en rime francoise par Clément Marot et Théodore de Béze. Mis en musique a quatre parties par Claude Goudimel. Par les héritiers de Francois Jacqui" (1565); Published under the auspices of La Société des Concerts de la Cathédrale de Lausanne and edited, in French, by Pidoux, Pierre, and in German by Ameln, Konrad. (Baeroenreiter-

Verlag, Kassel, 1935). Accessed March 21, 2019. https://www.ccel.org/ccel/ccel/eee/files/calvinps.htm.

———. "Short Treatise on the Holy Supper of our Lord and Savior Jesus Christ." In *Calvin: Theological Treatises*. Edited and Translated by J. K. S. Reid, 142-149. Louisville, KY; London: Westminster John Knox Press, 1954.

Carson, D. A. *The Gospel according to John*. The Pillar New Testament Commentary. Leicester, England: Inter-Varsity Press, 1991.

———. *The Expositor's Bible Commentary*, Vol. 8, *Matthew*, Edited by Frank E. Gaebelein, Grand Rapids, MI: Zondervan, 1984.

———. *Showing the Spirit: A Theological Exposition of 1 Corinthians 12-14*. Grand Rapids, MI: Baker, 1987.

———. "Worship Under the Word." In *Worship by the Book*, edited by D. A. Carson, 11-63. Grand Rapids, MI: Zondervan, 2002.

Castleman, Robbie. *Parenting in the Pew: Guiding Your Children Into the Joy of Worship*. expanded ed. Downers Grove, IL: InterVarsity Press, 2002.

Chapell, Bryan. *Christ-Centered Worship: Letting the Gospel Shape Our Practice*. Grand Rapids, MI: Baker Academic, 2009.

———. *Ephesians*. Reformed Expository Commentary. Phillipsburg, NJ: P & R, 2009.

Chemnitz, Martin, and Fred Kramer. *Examination of the Council of Trent*. Part 1. St. Louis, MO: Concordia Pub. House, 1971.

Childs, Brevard S. *The Book of Exodus: A Critical, Theological Commentary*. The Old Testament Library. Philadelphia: Westminster Press, 1974.

Clowney, Edmund P. "The Final Temple." *Westminster Theological Journal* 35, no 2 (Winter 1973): 156-189.

———. *Living in Christ's Church*. Philadelphia, PA: Great Commission Publications, 1986.

———. "The Singing Savior." *Moody Monthly*, July-August, 1979.

Clark, Carl A. "Neglected Commandment." *Southwestern Journal of Theology* 3, no. 1 (October 1960): 61-73.

Cole, R A. *Exodus; an Introduction and Commentary*. Vol. 2. Tyndale Old Testament Commentaries. Downers Grove, IL: InterVarsity Press, 1973.

Concordia: The Lutheran Confessions—A Reader's Edition of the Book of Concord. Saint Louis, MO: Concordia Publishing House, 2005.

Dabney, R. L. *Systematic Theology*. 2nd ed. Houston: Banner of Truth, 1985.

Dallimore, Arnold A. *George Whitefield: God's Anointed Servant in the Great Revival of the Eighteenth Century*. Westchester, IL: Crossway, 2010.

Davids, Peter H. *The Epistle of James: A Commentary on the Greek Text*. The New International Greek Testament Commentary. Grand Rapids, MI: Eerdmans, 1982.

Davies, Horton. *The Worship of the American Puritans, 1629-1730*. Morgan, PA: Soli Deo Gloria, 1999.

———. *The Worship of the English Puritans*. Morgan, PA: Soli Deo Gloria, 1997.

Davis, John Jefferson. *Worship and the Reality of God: An Evangelical Theology of Real Presence*. Downers Grove, IL: IVP Academic, 2010.

Dawn, Marva J. "Body Building: Worship That Develops Strong Community." *Reformed Worship* 45 (September 1997): 26–29. Accessed March 21, 2019, http://search.ebscohost.com.rts.idm.oclc.org/login.aspx?direct=true&db=rfh&AN=ATLA0001029668&site=ehost-live.

———. *Reaching Out Without Dumbing Down: A Theology of Worship for This Urgent Time*. Grand Rapids, MI: W.B. Eerdmans, 1995.

———. *A Royal Waste of Time: The Splendor of Worshiping God and Being Church for the World*. Grand Rapids, MI: W.B. Eerdmans, 1999.

———. "Worship and Reconciliation." *Vision* 8, no. 1 (2007): 18–23.

De Andrado, Paba Nidhani. "Ḥesed and Sacrifice: The Prophetic Critique in Hosea." *The Catholic Biblical Quarterly* 78, no. 1 (January 2016): 47–67.

Detwiler, David F. "Church Music and Colossians 3:16." *Bibliotheca Sacra* 158, no. 631 (July 2001): 347-69.

Dever, Mark and Sinclair Ferguson, ed. *Westminster Directory of Public Worship*. Fearn, Ross-shire: Christian Heritage, 2008.

Dieter, Emily A. "Martin Luther the Worship Leader: Processes and Methods of Liturgical Reform through the Reformation."

Senior thesis, Liberty University, 2010. Accessed September 10, 2017. http://digitalcommons.liberty.edu/cgi/viewcontent.cgi?article=1117&context.

Dunn, James D G. *The Epistles to the Colossians and to Philemon: A Commentary On the Greek Text*. The New International Greek Testament Commentary. Grand Rapids, MI: William B. Eerdmans, 1996.

Ecumenical Creeds and Reformed Confessions. Grand Rapids, MI: CRC Publications, 1987.

Edwards, Brian. *Shall We Dance? Dance and Drama in Worship*. Welwyn: Evangelical, 1984.

Engelsma, David, Barry Gritters, and Charles Terpstra. *Reformed Worship*. Grandville, MI: Reformed Free Pub. Association, 2004.

Enns, Peter. *Exodus*. Grand Rapids, MI: Zondervan, 2000.

Erickson, Millard J. *The Concise Dictionary of Christian Theology*. Wheaton, IL: Crossway, 2001.

Farley, Michael A. "Reforming Reformed Worship: Theological Method and Liturgical Catholicity in American Presbyterianism, 1850-2005." PhD diss., Graduate School of Saint Louis University, 2007.

———. "What Is 'Biblical' Worship? Biblical Hermeneutics and Evangelical Theologies of Worship." *The Journal of the Evangelical Theological Society* 51, no. 3 (September 2008): 591-613.

Fee, Gordon D. *The First Epistle to the Corinthians*. Grand Rapids, MI: W.B. Eerdmans, 1987.

Ferguson, Sinclair B. *The Big Book of Questions and Answers About Jesus*. Tain: Christian Focus, 2000.

Foulkes, Francis. *The Letter of Paul to the Ephesians: An Introduction and Commentary*. 2nd ed. The Tyndale New Testament Commentaries. Leicester, England: Inter-Varsity Press, 1989.

Frame, John. *Contemporary Worship Music: A Biblical Defense*. Phillipsburg, NJ: P & R, 1997.

———. *The Doctrine of the Christian Life*. Phillipsburg, NJ: P&R, 2008.

———. "A Fresh Look at the Regulative Principle: A Broader View." *Frame-Poythress.org*. Last modified June 4, 2012. Accessed

September 16, 2016. http://frame-poythress.org/a-fresh-look-at-the-regulative-principle-a-broader-view/.

———. "Serving One Another in Worship." *Frame-Poythress.org*, May 28, 2012. Accessed March 29, 2018. https://frame-poythress.org/serving-one-another-in-worship/.

———. "Some Questions about the Regulative Principle." *The Westminster Theological Journal* 54, no. 2 (September 1992): 357-66.

———. "Worship and the Reformation Gospel." *Frame-Poythress.org*. Last modified May 30, 2012. Accessed January 4, 2017. http://frame-poythress.org/worship-and-the-reformation-gospel/.

———. *Worship in Spirit and Truth*. Phillipsburg, NJ: P & R, 1996.

France, R T. *The Gospel According to Matthew: An Introduction and Commentary*. Leicester, England: Inter-Varsity Press, 1987.

Futato, Mark D. *Interpreting the Psalms: An Exegetical Handbook*. Grand Rapids, MI: Kregel Academic & Professional, 2007.

Gaffin, Richard B. *Calvin and the Sabbath*. Fearn, Ross-shire: Mentor, 1998.

Gale, Stanley D. "God's House of Prayer—Extreme Makeover Edition." *Presbyterion* 39, no. 1 (2013): 1–8.

Garland, David E. *1 Corinthians*. Baker Exegetical Commentary on the New Testament. Grand Rapids, MI: Baker Academic, 2003.

Gerstner, John H., Douglas F. Kelly, and Philip B. Rollinson. *A Guide: The Westminster Confession of Faith*. Signal Mountain, TN: Summertown Texts, 1992.

Glodo, Mike. "Motel 6 Worship." *Refmin.net* (blog), May 29, 2015. Accessed July 6, 2018. https://refmin.net /2015/ 05/29/motel-6-worship/.

Godfrey, W. Robert. "Worship: Evangelical or Reformed?" *Lux Mundi* 22, no. 1 &2 (March/June 2003):31-32.

Gore, Jr., R. J. "Reviewing the Puritan Regulative Principle of Worship." *Presbyterion:* 20, no. 1 (1994): 41–50.

———. "Reviewing the Puritan Regulative Principle of Worship Part II." *Presbyterion* 21, no. 1 (1995): 29–47.

Hamilton, Victor P. *Handbook On the Pentateuch: Genesis, Exodus, Leviticus, Numbers, Deuteronomy*. Grand Rapids, MI: Baker, 1982.

Hart, D.G., and John R. Muether. *With Reverence and Awe: Returning to the Basics of Reformed Worship*. Phillipsburg, N.J.: P & R Publishing, 2002.

The Heidelberg Catechism with Scripture Texts. Grand Rapids, MI: CRC Publications, 1989.

Hendriksen, William, and Simon J. Kistemaker. *Exposition of Colossians and Philemon*. Vol. 6. New Testament Commentary. Grand Rapids: Baker, 2001.

———. *Exposition of Ephesians*. Vol. 7. New Testament Commentary. Grand Rapids: Baker, 2001.

———. *Exposition of the Gospel According to John*. Vol. 4. New Testament Commentary. Grand Rapids: Baker, 1954.

———. *Exposition of the Gospel According to Matthew*. Vol. 9. New Testament Commentary. Grand Rapids: Baker, 1973.

———. *Exposition of James and the Epistles of John*. Vol. 14. New Testament Commentary. Grand Rapids: Baker, 2001.

Henry, Matthew. *Matthew Henry's Commentary on the Whole Bible: Complete and Unabridged in One Volume*. Peabody: Hendrickson, 1994.

Hinkle, Mary. "Learning What Righteousness Means: Hosea 6:6 and the Ethic of Mercy in Matthew's Gospel." *Word & World* 18, no. 4 (September 1998): 355-63. Accessed September 30, 2016. *ATLA Religion Database with ATLASerials*, EBSCO*host*.

Hodge, Archibald Alexander. *The Confession of Faith*. London: Banner of Truth Trust. 1992.

Holladay, William Lee and Ludwig Kohler. *A Concise Hebrew and Aramaic Lexicon of the Old Testament*. Leiden: Brill, 2000.

Holt, Bradley P. "Common Prayer and Local/global Mission." *Word & World* 5, no. 2 (1985): 199–205.

Horton, Michael. *A Better Way: Rediscovering the Drama of God-Centered Worship*. Grand Rapids, MI.: Baker, 2003.

Hubbard, David Allan. *Joel & Amos: An Introduction and Commentary*. Vol. 22b. Tyndale Old Testament Commentaries. Downers Grove, IL: InterVarsity Press, 1989.

———. *Hosea: An Introduction and Commentary*. Vol. 22a. Tyndale Old Testament Commentaries. Downers Grove, IL: InterVarsity Press, 1989.

Hughes, R Kent. *Ephesians: The Mystery of the Body of Christ*. Preaching the Word. Wheaton, IL: Crossway, 1990.

———. *James: Faith That Works*. Preaching the Word. Wheaton, IL: Crossway, 1991.

———. *John: That You May Believe*. Wheaton, IL: Crossway, 1999.

Johnson, Terry L. *Contemporary Worship: Thinking About Its Implications for the Church*. Edinburgh: Banner of Truth Trust, 2014.

———. *Leading in Worship: A Sourcebook for Presbyterian Students and Ministers Drawing from the Biblical and Historic Forms of the Reformed Tradition*. Rev. ed. Power Springs, GA: Tolle Lege, 2013.

———. *Reformed Worship: Worship that Is According to Scripture*. Rev. ed. Jackson, MS: Reformed Academic, 2010.

———. *Serving with Calvin: Leading and Planning Service of Worship in the Reformed Church*. Welwyn Garden City, UK: EP Books, 2015.

———. *The Family Worship Book: A Resource Book for Family Devotions*. Fearn, Ross-shire, Great Britain: Christian Focus, 2005.

———. *Worshipping with Calvin: Recovering the Historic Ministry of Worship of Reformed Protestantism*. Welwyn Garden City, UK: EP Books, 2014.

Jolly, Jason L. "Diversity in Public Worship: A Biblical Understanding of the Regulative Principle." master's thesis, Reformed Theological Seminary, 2015.

Kaiser, Walter C. *Micah-Malachi*. Vol. 21. The Communicator's Commentary Series. Dallas, TX: Word, 1992.

Kauflin, Bob. *True Worshippers: Seeking What Matters to God*. Wheaton, IL: Crossway, 2015.

———. "Who Turned the Lights Out?" *WorshipMatters.com* (blog), February 26, 2015. Accessed July 6, 2018. https://worshipmatters.com/2015/02/26/who-turned-the-lights-out/.

———. *Worship Matters: Leading Others to Encounter the Greatness of God*. Wheaton, IL: Crossway, 2008

Keifert, Patrick R. "Guess Who's Coming to Worship: Worship and Evangelism." *Word & World* 9, no. 1 (1989): 46-51.

Keil, Carl Friedrich, and Franz Delitzsch. *Commentary on the Old Testament.* 10 vols. Peabody, MA: Hendrickson, 1996.

Kelly, Joe Wayne. "Seated in the Heavenlies: Integrating John Calvin's Principles of Worship in a Baptist Context." Doctor of Ministry diss., Reformed Theological Seminary, 2010.

Kidner, Derek. *The Tyndale Old Testament Commentaries.* Vol. 15, *The Proverbs: an Introduction and Commentary.* Downers Grove, IL: InterVarsity Press, 1964.

Kistemaker, Simon. *Exposition of the First Epistle to the Corinthians.* New Testament Commentary. Grand Rapids, MI: Baker, 1993.

Kline, Meredith G. "Dynastic Covenant." *The Westminster Theological Journal* 23, no. 1 (November 1960): 1-15.

Kuyper, Abraham. *Abraham Kuyper: A Centennial Reader.* Edited by Mr. James D. Bratt. Carlisle: Wm. B. Eerdmans Publishing Co., 1998.

———. *Our Worship.* Edited by John D. Witvliet and Harry Boonstra. Translated by Harry Boonstra, Henry Baron, Gerrit Sheeres, and Leonard Sweetman. Grand Rapids, MI: Eerdmans Publishing Company, 2009.

Kuyvenhoven, Andrew. *Comfort and Joy: a Study of the Heidelberg Catechism.* Grand Rapids, MI: CRC Publications, 1988.

Ladd, George Eldon. *A Theology of the New Testament.* Rev. ed. Grand Rapids, MI: Eerdmans, 1993.

Lange, Dirk G. "Martin Luther's Reform of Worship." *Oxford Research Encyclopedia of Religion.* (March 2017): 1-24. Accessed July 15, 2017. http://religion.oxfordre.com/view/10.1093/acrefore/9780199340378.001.0001/acrefore-9780199340378-e-357.

Lenski, R. C. H. *The Interpretation of the Epistle to the Hebrews and of the Epistle of James.* Columbus, OH: Lutheran Book Concern, 1938.

———. *The Interpretation of St. Matthew's Gospel.* Minneapolis: Augsburg Publishing House, 1961.

———. *The Interpretation of St. Paul's First and Second Epistle to the Corinthians.* Minneapolis: Augsburg Publishing, 1963.

Longman, Tremper, III. *How to Read the Psalms.* Downers Grove, IL; Nottingham, England: IVP Academic; InterVarsity Press, 1988.

Luther, Martin. *Luther's Works.* Vol. 40, *Church and Ministry II.* Edited by Lehmann, Helmut T., and Conrad Bergendoff. Philadelphia: Fortress Press, 1958.

———. *Luther's Works.* Vol. 53, *Liturgy and Hymns.* Edited by Ulrich S. Leupold. Philadelphia: Fortress Press, 1965.

———. "On the Babylonian Captivity of the Church." In *Three Treatises*, 2nd rev. ed. by Frederick C. Ahrens and Abdel Ross Wentz. Philadelphia: Fortress Press, 1978.

Macpherson, John. *The Westminster Confession of Faith: With Introduction and Notes Handbooks for Bible classes and private students.* 2nd ed. Edinburgh: T. & T. Clark, 1881.

Marshall, I. Howard. *The Epistles of John.* Grand Rapids, MI: Eerdmans, 1978.

Martin, Ralph P. *The Worship of God: Some Theological, Pastoral, and Practical Reflections.* Grand Rapids, MI: W.B. Eerdmans, 1982.

———. *Worship in the Early Church.* Rev. ed. Grand Rapids, MI: Eerdmans, 1974, 1975 printing.

McGrath, Alister E. *Understanding the Trinity.* Grand Rapids, MI.: Academie Books, 1988.

Miller, Samuel. *Thoughts on Public Prayer.* Harrisonburg, VA: Sprinkle, 1985.

Mohler Jr., R. Albert. "Expository Preaching: Center of Christian Worship." In *Give Praise to God: A Vision for Reforming Worship: Celebrating the Legacy of James Montgomery Boice*, edited by Phillip Graham Ryken, Ligon J Duncan, Derek W. H. Thomas, and Derek W H Thomas, 107-21. Phillipsburg, NJ: P&R, 2011.

Moo, Douglas J. *The Letter of James.* The Pillar New Testament Commentary. Grand Rapids, MI: Eerdmans, 2000.

———. *The Letters to the Colossians and to Philemon.* The Pillar New Testament Commentary. Grand Rapids, MI: William B. Eerdmans, 2008.

Moore, Peter Charles. "The Spirit of Calvin and 'Intimations' in 'Religious Worship.'" *The Reformed Theological Review* 69, no. 2 (August 2010): 88-100.

Morgenthaler, Sally. *Worship Evangelism.* Grand Rapids, MI: Zondervan, 1999.

Morris, Leon. *Expository Reflections On the Gospel of John*. Grand Rapids, MI: Baker, 1988.

———. *The First Epistle of Paul to the Corinthians: An Introduction and Commentary*. Rev. ed. Grand Rapids, MI: InterVarsity Press, 1985.

———. *The Gospel According to John: The English Text with Introduction, Exposition and Notes*. The New International Commentary on the New Testament. Grand Rapids, MI: Eerdmans, 1971.

———. *The Gospel according to Matthew*. The Pillar New Testament Commentary. Grand Rapids, MI: Eerdmans, 1992.

Motyer, J A. *Isaiah: An Introduction and Commentary*. Vol. 18. The Tyndale Old Testament Commentaries. Downers Grove, IL: InterVarsity Press, 1999.

———. *The Message of Amos: The Day of the Lion*. Leicester, England: Inter-Varsity Press, 1988.

———. *The Message of James: The Tests of Faith*. Leicester, England: Inter-Varsity Press, 1985.

Muller, Richard A., and Rowland S. Ward. *Scripture and Worship: Biblical Interpretation and the Directory for Public Worship*. Phillipsburg, NJ: P & R Publishing, 2007.

Murray, Iain Hamish. *Revival and Revivalism: The Making and Marring of American Evangelicalism 1750-1858*. Edinburgh: Banner of Truth Trust, 1994.

Newman, Barclay Moon, and Philip C. Stine. *A Handbook on the Gospel of Matthew*. UBS Handbook Series. New York: United Bible Societies, 1992.

Nolland, John. *The Gospel of Matthew: A Commentary on the Greek Text*. New International Greek Testament Commentary. Grand Rapids, MI: Eerdmans; Paternoster, 2005.

O'Brien, Peter Thomas. *The Letter to the Ephesians*. The Pillar New Testament Commentary. Grand Rapids, MI: W.B. Eerdmans, 1999.

Old, Hughes Oliphant. *Leading in Prayer: A Workbook for Ministers*. Grand Rapids, MI: Eerdmans, 1995.

———. *Worship: Reformed According to Scripture*. Rev. ed. Louisville, KY: Westminster John Knox Press, 2002.

Olson, Roger E. "Horizontal and Vertical Churches: Where's the Balance?" *patheos* (blog), July 30, 2015. Accessed March 29, 2018. http://www.patheos.com/blogs/rogereolson/2015/07/horizontal-and-vertical-churches-wheres-the-balance/.

Oswalt, John N. *The Book of Isaiah Chapters 1-39*. Grand Rapids, MI: Eerdmans, 1986-1998.

Ottenheijm, Eric. "The shared meal—a therapeutical device: the function and meaning of Hos 6:6 in Matt 9:10-13." *Novum Testamentum* 53, no. 1 (2011): 1-21.

Owens, Ron, and Jan McMurray. *Return to Worship: A God-Centered Approach*. Nashville, TN: Broadman & Holman, 1999.

Packer, J I. *A Quest for Godliness: The Puritan Vision of the Christian Life*. Wheaton, IL: Crossway, 1990.

Parrish, Archie. *A Simple Way to Pray: The Life and Wisdom of Luther for Today*. 4th ed. Marietta, GA: Serve International, Inc., 2005.

Peterson, David. *Engaging with God: A Biblical Theology of Worship*. First North American ed. Grand Rapids, MI: W.B. Eerdmans, 1993.

———. "Further Reflections on Worship in the New Testament." *The Reformed Theological Review* 44, no. 2 (May 1985): 34-41.

Peterson, Robert A. *Getting to Know John's Gospel: A Fresh Look at Its Main Ideas*. Phillipsburg, NJ: Presbyterian and Reformed, 1989.

Poole, Matthew. *Annotations Upon the Holy Bible*. 3 vols. New York: Robert Carter and Brothers, 1853.

Pratt, Richard L. *I and II Corinthians*. Vol. 7 in the Holman New Testament Commentary. Nashville, TN: Broadman & Holman, 2000.

Book of Common Worship. Louisville, KY: Westminster/John Knox Press, 1993.

Pribble, Stephen. *The Regulative Principle and Singing in Worship*. Greenville, SC: Greenville Presbyterian Theological Seminary, 1994.

Pinson, J. Matthew, ed., *Perspectives on Christian Worship: Five Views*. 1st ed. Nashville, TN: B&H Academic, 2009.

Rayburn, Robert. *O Come Let Us Worship: Corporate Worship in the Evangelical Church*. Scarsdale, New York: Westminster Publishing House, 1980.

Rayburn, Robert Gibson. "The Relevance of Worship." *Presbyterion* 13, no. 1 (1987): 1-6.

———. "Worship in the Reformed Church." *Presbyterion* 6, no. 1 (1980): 17-32.

Reyburn, William David, and Euan McG. Fry. *A Handbook on Proverbs*. UBS Handbook Series. New York: United Bible Societies, 2000.

Reymond, Robert L. *A New Systematic Theology of the Christian Faith*. Nashville: Thomas Nelson, 1998.

Richard, Guy. "Worship Class Notes." Presentation at Ligonier Academy, Sanford, FL, January 18-20, 2016.

Robertson, O Palmer. *The Christ of the Covenants*. Grand Rapids, MI: Baker, 1980.

Robertson, Don W. *The Christian Sabbath*. Coulterville, IL: New Creation Publications, 2001.

Schwartzbeck, Robert James. "The Offering of Corporate Prayers of Confession in the Worship Service." Doctor of Ministry diss., Covenant Theological Seminary, 2005.

Schweizer, Eduard.. "Service of Worship: An Exposition of 1 Corinthians 14." *Interpretation* 13, no. 4 (1959): 400-408.

Shedd, William Greenough Thayer. *Dogmatic Theology*. Edited by Alan W. Gomes. 3rd ed. Phillipsburg, NJ: P & R Publishing, 2003.

Shaw, Robert. *An Exposition of the Westminster Confession of Faith: With An Introductory Essay By WM. M. Hetherington*. 8th ed. Edinburgh: Blackie and Son, 1857.

Smith, Frank J. and David C. Lachman, eds. *Worship in the Presence of God: A Collection of Essays on the Nature, Elements, and Historic Views and Practices of Worship*. Greenville, SC: Greenville Presbyterian Theological Seminary Press, 1992.

Smith, Morton H. *The Regulative Principle of Worship: Is It Biblical?* Greenville, SC: Greenville Presbyterian Theological Seminary, 1995.

———. *Systematic Theology*, 2 Vol. Greenville, SC: Greenville Presbyterian Theological Seminary, 1994.

Sproul, R C. *A Taste of Heaven: Worship in the Light of Eternity*. Orlando, FL: Reformation Trust Publishing, 2006.

———. *How Then Shall We Worship? Biblical Principles to Guide Us Today*. Colorado Springs: David C. Cook, 2013.

———. *John*. St. Andrew's Expositional Commentary. Lake Mary, FL: Reformation Trust, 2009.

———. ed., "Music in the Church." *The Reformation Study Bible*. Nashville: Thomas Nelson, 1995.

———. ed. *The Reformation Study Bible: English Standard Version (2015 Edition)*. Orlando, FL: Reformation Trust, 2015.

———. *Truths We Confess: A Layman's Guide to the Westminster Confession of Faith*. Vol. 3. Phillipsburg, NJ: P & R Publishing, 2007.

Spykman, Gordon J. *Never on Your Own: a Course of Study On the Heidelberg Catechism and Compendium*. Rev. ed. Grand Rapids, MI: Board of Publications of the Christian Reformed Church, 1984.

Stott, John R. W. *The Letters of John: an Introduction and Commentary*. 2nd ed. Vol. 19. Leicester, England: Inter-Varsity Press, 1988.

———. *The Message of Ephesians: God's New Society*. Leicester, England: Inter-Varsity Press, 1986.

Stulac, George M. *James*. Vol. 16. Downers Grove, IL: InterVarsity Press, 1993.

Taylor, Justin. "Don't Neglect the Horizontal Dimension of Singing and Worship." *justin-taylor* (blog), The Gospel Coalition, August 26, 2011. Accessed March 6, 2018. https://www.thegospelcoalition.org/blogs/justin-taylor/dont-neglect-the-horizontal-dimension-of-singing-and-worship/.

Thiselton, Anthony C. *The First Epistle to the Corinthians: A Commentary On the Greek Text*. Grand Rapids, MI: W.B. Eerdmans, 2000.

Thompson, Bard. *Liturgies of the Western Church*. Philadelphia: Fortress Press, 1980.

Thompson, J A. *Deuteronomy: An Introduction and Commentary*. Vol. 5. London: Inter-Varsity Press, 1974.

Tozer, A. W. *The Purpose of Man: Designed to Worship*. Edited by James L. Snyder. Ventura, CA: Regal, 2009.

———. *Whatever Happened to Worship?: A Call to True Worship*. Camp Hill, PA: WingSpread, 2006.

Trueblood, Elton. *Confronting Christ*. New York: Harper and Brothers, 1960.

Ursinus, Zacharias, and G. W. Williard. *The Commentary of Dr. Zacharias Ursinus on the Heidelberg Catechism*. Cincinnati, OH: Elm Street Printing Company, 1888.

Van Dixhoorn, Chad B. *Confessing the Faith: A Reader's Guide to the Westminster Confession of Faith*. Edinburgh, Scotland: The Banner of Truth Trust, 2014.

Visscher, James. *I Belong: A Course of Study On the Heidelberg Catechism*. Teachers ed. n.p.: Premier Printing Ltd, 1998.

Waltke, Bruce K. *The Book of Proverbs*. Vol. 2, *The New International Commentary on the Old Testament*. Grand Rapids, MI: William B. Eerdmans, 2005.

———. *Obadiah, Jonah, Micah*. Downers Grove, IL: InterVarsity Press 1988.

Westminster Assembly. *The Westminster Confession of Faith: Edinburgh Edition*. Philadelphia: William S. Young, 1851.

The Westminster Confession of Faith. 2nd ed. Atlanta, GA: The Committee for Christian Education & Publication, 1986.

The Westminster Confession of Faith and Catechisms As Adopted By the Presbyterian Church in America with Proof Texts. Lawrenceville, GA: Christian Education & Publications, 2007.

Whitney, Donald. *Spiritual Disciplines of the Christian Life*. Colorado Springs: NavPress, 1977.

Wiersbe, Warren W. *Real Worship: Playground, Battleground, or Holy Ground?* 2nd ed. Grand Rapids, MI: Baker, 2000.

Williamson, G I. *The Heidelberg Catechism: A Study Guide*. Phillipsburg, NJ: P & R, 1993.

———. *The Westminster Confession of Faith: For Study Classes*. Philadelphia, PA: Presbyterian and Reformed Publishing, 1964.

Witvliet, John D. "Psalm Singing, Discerning the Body, and Projected Song Texts." *Reformed Worship*, no. 90 (December 2008): 45.

Wood, Leon J. *The Expositor's Bible Commentary: Daniel and the Minor Prophets with the New International Version of the Holy*. Vol. 7, *Hosea*. Edited by Frank E. Gaebelein. Grand Rapids, MI: Zondervan, 1992.

Woodhouse, John. *1 Samuel: Looking for a Leader*. Wheaton, IL: Crossway, 2008.

The Worship Sourcebook. 2nd ed. Grand Rapids, MI: Calvin Institute of Christian Worship, 2013.

Wright, N T. *The Epistles of Paul to the Colossians and to Philemon: An Introduction and Commentary*. Leicester, England: Inter-Varsity Press, 1986.

Youssef, Michael. *I Praise You, O God: Experiencing His Power in Your Private Worship*. Colorado Springs: Waterbrook, 2002.

Zerwick, Max, and Mary Grosvenor. *A Grammatical Analysis of the Greek New Testament*. 5th ed. Roma: Pontificio Istituto Biblico, 1996.

SCRIPTURE INDEX

Old Testament

Genesis
1:26 21
1:27 113
2:15-17 23
2:28-30 23
3:15 ....25, 256
3:17 23
9:6 113
17:7 26
Exodus
2:24 32
3:5 259
6:6-7 26
15:20 259
19:1-6 32
19:4-5 26
20:1-2 33
20:1-6 253
20:1-11 ....32, 281
20:1-17 ....31, 281
20:3 36
20:3-5 36
20:3-6 230
20:3-11 49
20:5 34
20:8-11 36
20:10 33
20:11 ....33, 34
20:12 34
20:12-17 ....34, 282
20:14 34
20:15 35
20:16 66
20:17 36
20:22 66
23:8 68

Leviticus
11:45 26
19:9-18 ....38, 111
19:15 66
19:18 .... 48, 49, 52
19:31 37
Numbers
6:24-26 245
Deuteronomy
5:6 ....,...................... 33
5:6-21 ....7, 31
5:7-10 230
5:7-15 32
5:14 33
5:16 34
5:16-21 34
5:19 35
5:21 36
6:4-9 48
6:5 ....48, 52
7:6-13 25
10:17 109
16:19 66
16:27 66
18:9-15 37
18:16-20 66
Joshua
3:16 41
Judges
7:15 10
1 Samuel
15:2 36
15:3 37
15:21 37
15:22 37
15:22-23 ....7, 36, 39,

274
15:23 37
15:24 ....37, 38
15:26 ....37, 39
16:23 127
2 Samuel
6:15 260
6:16 260
1 Kings
12:31 42
2 Kings
3:15 127
11:17 26
13:23 78
15:25 42
1 Chronicles
16:23 73
16:36 260
16:40 73
2 Chronicles
7:14 79
Nehemiah
8:6 260
9:19 78
Esther
9:22 259
Job
6:14 78
Psalms
9:1 259
9:11 259
12:5 66
22:27 259
28:2 259
33:1 259
40:1-2 ....81, 274

Scripture Index

40:3 .... 82, 83
40:5 .... 81, 82, 274
40:6 82
40:8 .... 81, 82, 274
40:9-10 ..... 81, 82, 83, 274
40:10 .... 81, 274
40:13-17 .... 81, 274
41:13 260
47:1 259
50:8 39
63:4 259
67:3 262
72:19 260
74:2 66
82:1 66
82:2-4 .... 65, 66
82:3 .... 66, 77
82:5-8 67
82:6-7 65
82:7 67
82:8 67
86:15 78
89:52 260
95:6 259
96:9 262
98:8 259
100:1 262
103:8 78
106:48 260
116:5 78
119:156 78
121:2 133
122:1 273
134:2 259
140:12 77
145:8 78
149:3 259

Proverbs
3:5-6 79
6:17 35
6:19 35
17:23 68
18:5 .... 8, 68

Isaiah
1:2-23 83
1:10 .... 70, 265
1:10-17 212
1:10-20 .... 8, 70
1:10-23 265
1:11 .... 39, 71
1:11-15 266
1:12 71
1:13 71
1:14-15 71
1:15 71
1:16-17 72
1:16-19 72
1:17 .... 70, 72, 265
1:18-19 72
1:20 72
1:21 .... 34, 265
1:21-23 .... 70, 265
1:22-23 265
29:13 .... 83, 85, 107
29:13-14 .... 8, 83
29:14 85
53:4-5 241
55:12 259
56:7 223
57:8 34

Jeremiah
6:20 39
9:2 34
17:9-10 7
22:3 77
31:31-34 27

Ezekiel
6:9 34
16:15-19 34
16:30 34
36:25-28 27
36:26-27 88

Hosea
2:2-5 34
3:1-5 34
4:1 40
6:5 42

6:6 ..... 39, 42, 44, 45, 47, 111, 287, 322, 327
6:6-8 .... 7, 39
6:7 41
6:8 42
6:8-9 42
6:10 42
6:11 43
9:1 34

Joel
2:12 259
2:28 88

Amos
2:6 74
2:6-7 .... 8, 73
2:7 74
2:26 74
5:10 74
5:11 74
5:12 74
5:13-15 73
5:21 73
5:21-24 .... 8, 73
5:22 73
5:23 73
5:24 74
5:27 .... 73, 74
8:4 111
8:4-5 75
8:5-6 .... 8, 73

Micah
2:1-2 76
2:3 76
6:6 75
6:6-8 .... 8, 75, 269
6:7 76
6:8 .... 76, 77, 78

Scripture Index

New Testament

Matthew
1:21 .... 8, 47
2:11 236
3:17 .... 19, 22
4:10 .... 10, 252
4:19 53
5:5 79
5:7 .... 50, 112
5:21-22 111
5:21-24 71
5:24 144
5:43 50
5:43-47 49
6:7 262
6:19-20 243
7:1-5 257
7:24-27 .... 238, 245
9:9 43
9:9-12 285
9:9-13 257
9:11 .... 44, 49
9:12 .... 44, 47
9:13 .. 43, 44, 47, 111
11:29 90
15:1-7 84
15:7-19 84
15:14 86
16:23 69
18:20 182
20:28 .... 249, 271
21:13 223
22:34-40 233
22:36 48
22:36-40 48, 148, 281
22:37 49
22:37-40 ..... 111, 254, 283
22:39 49
22:40 50
23:4 49
23:15 49
23:23 49
23:34-35 49
26:28 .... 26, 249
28:18-20 ... 9, 14, 213
28:19 259

Mark
3:29 158
8:33 69
10:45 249
12:30-31 8
14:24 26

Luke
1:6-10 221
1:10 221
1:11-13 222
4:8 10
16:19-31 158
18:9-14 257
22:20 .... 26, 249
22:24 213
23:34 78
24:25-27 256
24:27 90
24:36 233

John
1:14 90
1:29 .... 33, 249
1:45 256
3:3 ... 26, 90, 211, 263, 311
3:3-8 21
3:10 8
3:15 111
3:16 .... 8, 59
3:35 19
4:7-21 .... 7, 51
4:14 47
4:19-21 28
4:21-24 86
4:22 86
4:22-24 10
4:23 ...... 59, 86, 87, 89
4:23-24 .... 8, 107
4:24 .... 87, 252, 255, 257, 263
4:36 53
5:39 90
6:44 311
6:47 256
13:31-35 51
13:34 53
13:34-45 22
13:35 62
14:6 .... 90, 256
14:31 19
15:1-17 52
15:5 52
15:8-17 254
16:4 20
16:13-15 90
17:1-13 272
17:20-23 22
20:19 233
20:26 233

Acts
1:8 53
2:16-21 88
2:38 .... 8, 256
2:42 ...... 138, 139, 182
2:42-47 254
2:46 258
4:12 211
8:20 20
13:22 273
14:27 .... 259, 311
15:4 .... 259, 311
16:31 8
20:7 258
21:19 .... 259, 311

Romans
3:10-18 69
3:11 7

Scripture Index

3:22 8
3:24 8
3:25 .... 8, 77
3:26 8
3:28-30 8
5:1 26
5:8 25
5:9 25
6:15-23 33
8:18-25 11
8:26-27 22
10:9-10 259
11:36 9
12:1 .... 11, 251
12:1-3 261
12:13 59
13:7 208
16:16 139

1 Corinthians
1:2 256
1:17 58
1:17-18 101
1:23 .... 58, 256
2:2 101
2:12 211
2:14 307
9:19-23 261
9:22 216
10:11 .... 8, 91
10:12 163
10:14-17 ... 8, 91, 214, 276
10:14-22 276
10:16-17 91, 144, 163
10:17 .... 91, 183
10:23-26 260
10:31 .... 9, 57, 61, 254
10:31-11 .... 7, 11, 57
10:31-33 254
10:32 60
10:32-33 58
10:33 58
11:1 .... 58, 60
11:17-34 ...... 92, 212, 214, 278, 279
11:18 96
11:20 139
11:21-22 93
11:22-33 276
11:23 96
11:24 248
11:25 .... 26, 27
11:27-28 163
11:29 .... 61, 96
11:31 58
11:33 .... 61, 96, 142
12:4-6 59
12:12-31 277
12:22-25 97
12:26 98
12:31 61
13:1 61
13:1-3 62
13:13 62
14:1-25 294
14:5 .... 104, 290
14:6-11 207
14:17 253
14:19 253
14:20-25 297
14:22-25 214
14:23-25 230
14:24-25 .... 253, 263
14:25 .... 212, 303
14:26 .... 206, 208
14:26-40 10
14:40 .... 133, 255
15:3-4 8
16:20 139

2 Corinthians
1:2 233
2:16 252
5:20 233
6:16 .... 26, 89
9:6-7 313
10:5 9
13:12 139
13:14 238

Galatians
2:6 109
3:7 27
3:13 11
3:23-29 27
5:22 .... 62, 78
5:22-23 .... 20, 89

Ephesians
1:4-5 .... 21, 25
1:7 21
1:11 9
1:13-14 .... 21, 89
2:1 263
2:1-5 26
2:8-9 8
2:11-22 .... 27, 89
2:12-13 256
2:19 27
2:22 89
4:2 198
4:3-6 28
4:4 27
4:4-6 .... 59, 145
4:11-16 190
5:1 .... 5, 20, 21, 60, 109, 289
5:2 249
5:18-20 235
5:18-21 312
5:19 ..... 192, 206, 208, 258, 260, 289
5:20 292
5:29 105
5:32 234
6:22 .... 259, 311

Philippians
2:1-11 109
2:3 .... 215, 218, 312
4:11-13 36

Colossians
1:20 26
3:16 .... 8, 105, 183, 192, 206, 208, 260, 289, 312, 319

Scripture Index

3:16-17 291
4:8 .... 259, 311
4:16 258
1 Thessalonians
3:2 258
4:3 59
5:11 .... 190, 258
5:26 139
1 Timothy
2:1 258
4:16 105
5:17-18 258
2 Timothy
2:15 .... 254, 261
3:16 20
3:16-17 ..... 40, 89, 90, 141
4:2 258
Titus
2:14 249
3:5 .... 21, 26
Hebrews
8:6-8 27
8:10 26
9:1 .... 11, 251
9:4 11
9:28 249
10:23-26 309
10:24 160
10:24-25 ..... 206, 208, 213, 214, 254
12:22 .... 11, 257
12:28 .... 11, 251
12:28-29 257
13:20-21 258
James
1:17 36
2:1-4 253
2:1-7 212
2:1-13 .... 8, 68, 108
2:3 .... 8, 108
3:1-12 112
3:10 113
3:12 113

4:8 85
4:10 257
1 Peter
4:8-9 59
5:7 59
5:12-14 258
2 Peter
3:9 59
1 John
3:17 56
4:7-21 .... 7, 51
4:7-22 54
4:8 .... 5, 20
4:10 25
4:19-21 28
4:21 .... 50, 56
5:15 158
Revelation
4:8 262
4:10 .... 10, 252
5:9 263
5:12 256
7:19 260
19:4 260
19:16 9
21:3 27

337

VITA

Don W. Robertson, son of the late Don and Brenda Robertson, was born January 25, 1968, in Petersburg, Virginia. He attended public schools in Dinwiddie County, Virginia.

His education includes a Bachelor of Arts, with a major in Biblical Studies and a minor in Music from Covenant College in 1990. He was awarded a full year scholarship from the Bible department at Covenant College to attend Covenant Theological Seminary where he received a Master of Divinity, cum lade, in 1994. Dr. Robertson fulfilled the requirements for a Doctor of Ministry degree in 2019 from Reformed Theological Seminary in Orlando, FL.

His work experience involves three years as a supervisor and program director at Sunshine Mission in St. Louis, Missouri, where he ministered to the homeless and needy of the inner city. Since his ordination in 1995, he also has served as an ordained pastor in three churches. In the first church, he served as an evangelism and youth pastor at First Reformed Church in Thunder Bay, Ontario. Then he served as the pastor of Grandcote Reformed Presbyterian Church in Coulterville, Illinois.

Pastor Robertson has also published a book called *The Christian Sabbath* that presents a biblical case for and practice of the Lord's Day.

Currently he has served as the pastor of Faith Community Church in Pearland, Texas, since 2001. He has been happily married to Cathy Robertson since 1989 and they have a son named Micah and daughter-in-law named Alexandra. Don loves to write, compose music, play guitar, fish, and read good books. More than anything, he loves to share the Gospel of Jesus Christ.

www.ingramcontent.com/pod-product-compliance
Lightning Source LLC
Chambersburg PA
CBHW032038090426
42744CB00004B/53